A CONCISE DICTIONARY OF
ENGLISH
idioms

TEACH YOURSELF

A CONCISE DICTIONARY OF
ENGLISH
idioms

B. A. Phythian

Hodder & Stoughton
LONDON SYDNEY AUCKLAND

A CIP catalogue record for this book
is available from the British Library

ISBN 0 340 57494 1

First *Teach Yourself* edition 1993

© 1993 B. A. Phythian

Typeset by Rowland Phototypesetting Ltd,
Bury St Edmunds, Suffolk
Printed in Great Britain for the educational publishing
division of Hodder & Stoughton Ltd, Mill Road, Dunton Green,
Sevenoaks, Kent by Clays Ltd, St Ives plc

PREFACE

This dictionary aims to be a simple and practical guide to the most frequently used idiomatic expressions in English—those countless expressions which everyone uses, which frequently evade the normal rules of grammar, and which often have implications quite unconnected with the normal meanings of the words themselves.

The reader should be aware that it is frequently difficult to decide under what word an idiom should be entered. Should 'See how the land lies' be entered under 'See', 'Land' or 'Lie'? Cross-references have frequently been used, but complete cross-referring would have increased the size of this volume several times; accordingly, if an expression does not appear in the place expected, the reader is asked to look it up under another key word in the expression. Similar difficulties have occurred in deciding on the correct alphabetical order of idioms within any one entry; idioms usually consist of several words, and have more than one key word, with the result that exact alphabetising is impossible. Again the reader is requested to bear with the editor, and to be prepared to look in more than one place under an entry.

There are a number of deliberate omissions from the dictionary: foreign words or phrases, commercial and technical idioms, dialect words, and, for the most part, single words, the idiomatic variations of which can be discovered in any ordinary dictionary. Some slang expressions are included, but for a more comprehensive coverage the reader should consult the companion *Concise Dictionary of Slang*. Another dictionary in this series, *A Concise Dictionary of Phrase and Fable*, gives information about the derivation and history of many of the expressions contained in the present volume.

B. A. Phythian

1

Abbreviations

LIT Literal meaning

MET Metaphorical meaning

Old f. Old fashioned

abc
The first rudiments; the beginning; the alphabet.

abeyance
be in or *fall into abeyance* Be in a state of waiting or suspense (until some decision is made).
- *The whole matter is in abeyance until after Christmas.*

abide
abide by Remain faithful to (an agreement or decision).

about
out and about Outdoors and moving around.
up and about Out of bed and moving around.

above
above all That which is of the greatest importance.
- *Above all, be careful.*
above-board Honest and unconcealed.
- *His conduct has been entirely above-board.*
get above oneself Become conceited.

abuse
terms of abuse, or *abusive terms* Bad, uncomplimentary, or violent language.

accident
chapter of accidents Succession of mistakes.

accommodate
accommodate oneself Adjust oneself to the circumstances; accept the conditions.

accommodate with Supply with; allow the use of.

accord

of one's own accord Voluntarily; without being compelled.

with one accord Unanimously; all together.

according to 1. As agreed or arranged. In a manner consistent with.

2. As reported by. On the authority of.

- *According to the newspaper, it will rain later today.*

account

account for Explain (the cause of).

- *Did they account for the delay?*

an account to settle [LIT] A debt to pay. [MET] A grudge or a grievance to avenge.

bring (person) to account Cause (person) to explain or justify what he or she has done.

by all accounts In everyone's opinion.

call to account Summon, in order that statement of justification be made.

a good account of A satisfactory story about or impression of.

give a good account of oneself Behave in a way which brings credit to oneself.

- *The whole team gave a very good account of themselves.*

keep an account of Keep a record of.

of no account Of no value or importance.

on account As partial payment.

- *He owed £50, and sent me £10 on account.*

on account of Owing to; because of.

on my account Because of me.

on no account In no circumstances.

- *On no account walk home by yourself.*

on that account For that reason.

open an account Deposit a sum of money (e.g. in a bank) for the first time.

settle an account Pay a bill.

square accounts Take some action which will cancel out a wrong or disadvantage, and make one equal.

take account of Estimate. Include in one's calculations.

take into account Make allowance for. Consider.

- *Taking into account all the circumstances, he felt it wise to say nothing further.*

turn to (good) account Make useful.

- *She turned her illness to good account by writing letters all day.*

accountable
be accountable for or *to* Be responsible for something *or* to a person.

ace
play one's ace Use one's strongest resource.
within an ace of Within a very little distance of; very near indeed to.
- *The boy was (came) within an ace of being drowned.*

Achilles
Achilles' heel The weak or vulnerable spot in a person's character or circumstances.

acquaint
acquaint one with Make one aware of.
be acquainted with Know (person, subject etc.)

acquire
an acquired taste A liking for something unusual; a taste developed gradually.
- *I don't know whether you'll like this drink; it's rather an acquired taste.*

acquit
acquit oneself Conduct or exhibit oneself; behave; perform a part or function.

across
get (something) across Make (something) understood or clear.
put across Communicate.

act
act a part Conceal one's real emotions, etc., as an actor does.
act on or *upon* Take definite action as a result of (what one knows).
- *The police immediately acted on the information they received.*
act up Misbehave.
get in on the act Join in something successful.
in the act In the process (of doing something) (i.e. while doing it).
- *He was caught in the act of stealing the car.*
put on an act Pretend. Behave ostentatiously to gain attention.

action
go into action Start work.
out of action Not working.

Adam
not known from Adam Completely unknown and unfamiliar.

add
add up Make sense.

addition
in addition to Furthermore; as well as.

address
address oneself to Direct one's attention or energy to.

advantage
have the advantage of Be in a superior position to.
take advantage of 1. Gain through another person's ignorance or innocence.
  - *The dealer took advantage of the student's ignorance.*
  2. Act at a propitious or fortunate moment.
  - *I took advantage of the fine weather to play tennis.*
to advantage In a way that displays merit.
turn to advantage Benefit from.

affirmative
in the affirmative Yes. Opposite: *in the negative.*

after
after all In spite of everything that has been said or done.
be after 1. Intend. Want.
  - *What are you after?*
  2. Pursue.
  - *He knew the police would be after him.*

again
again and again; time and again Repeatedly.
half as much again One and a half times as much.

against
up against it In difficulties.

age
at an advanced age Very old.
age before beauty Those who are old must take precedence.
come of age Attain the age of legal responsibility.

for ages (and ages) For a very long time.

ripe or green old age Very old (but often with the implication of being healthy as well).

under age Less than the age specified by law.

agog

all agog In a state of excitement.

agree

agree to differ Agree that there must be a difference of opinion.

ahead

ahead of one's time Having ideas too advanced to be understood or put into practice in one's own day.

ahead of time Before the expected time.

aid

in aid of To help; with the object of assisting.

air

air a grievance Bring forward for discussion some hardship, grievance or other matter which should be made public.

by air In an aircraft.

in the air 1. In a state of uncertainty; unsettled.

- *We go to Lancaster on Monday, but after that all our plans are in the air.*

2. Spreading about.

- *Rumours of rebellion are in the air.*

See *Castle*.

into thin air Into nothingness. (To 'vanish into thin air' is to disappear entirely.)

take the air Go out of doors.

up in the air Undecided.

airs

give oneself airs Try to show one's (sometimes imaginary) superiority, usually to impress. Similar to *put on airs, put on side, show off*.

alarm

give the alarm Give warning, usually when some danger or disaster is discovered. Also *raise the alarm*.

false alarm Untrue report of disaster.

alert

on the alert In a state of awareness; ready for anything that may happen.

alive

alive and kicking Vigorous and active.
- *I'm glad to see that Ann is still alive and kicking.*

alive with Crowded with.
- *The streets were alive with people.*

all

all along All the time; from the beginning.
- *I suspected all along that she was unhappy.*

all and sundry Everybody.

all at once; all of a sudden Suddenly; unexpectedly.
- *All at once there was a tremendous crash.*

all for the best All for the ultimate good. (Commonly used to console someone for bad news.)

all the best A common form of farewell, an abbreviation for 'May all the best things happen to you'.

all but Very nearly.
- *The proposals are all but meaningless.*

all ends up In every way.

all for In favour of.

all in 1. Exhausted.
- *They're all in after their swim.*
2. With everything included.
- *The holiday will cost £40 all in.*

all in a day's work Part of one's responsibilities.

all in all In summary.

all one Of no importance; immaterial. Just the same.
- *It's all one to me whether you stay here or go home.*

all out Using full power.
- *The builders are going all out to finish the job before the winter.*

all over 1. Entirely covering.
- *There was ice all over the pavement.*
2. Finished.
- *The funeral was all over by the time I arrived.*

all over the place 1. Scattered untidily.
- *Collect your papers; they are all over the place.*
2. In many directions.
- *Her work takes her all over the place.*

all right 1. Certainly.

2. I agree.

3. Satisfactory.

all-round Complete. Many-sided. Hence *all-rounder*: a person with many skills, talents, etc.

all the same 1. Alike, in a general sense.

- *It's all the same to me if we go today or tomorrow.*

2. Nevertheless.

- *All the same, I'm not going.*

all there Sane.

all the time Continuously.

all set Fully prepared.

- *All set? Then let's go.*

all things to all men Able to agree with everyone (by changing one's own opinions).

all-time Record.

- *Unemployment is at an all-time low.*

all told Altogether.

all very well Possibly true (usually followed by expression of dissent).

at all In any way.

- *Did he promise anything at all?*

be all up with Be hopeless circumstances for.

damn all Nothing.

for all that Nevertheless; in spite of that.

in all In total number.

- *There are seventeen buses in all.*

get away from it all Remove oneself from one's everyday life and anxieties.

not all there Crazy.

on all fours On one's hands and knees.

one and all Everybody.

when all's said and done The conclusion, stated briefly. When all the facts are considered.

allow

allow for Take into consideration. Excuse. Leave a margin of time or space for.

- *Allow half-an-hour for the journey.*

allowance

make allowance for Similar to *allow for*.

- *We must make some allowance(s) for his inexperience.*

alone
go it alone Act independently.

along
all along see **all**.
along with In company with. In conjunction with.
  • *We need to buy chairs along with the table.*
go along with Agree, co-operate, with.

ambition
the height of ambition Strongest, most powerful desire.
  • *To be an airline-pilot was the height of her ambition.*

amends
make amends Compensate (e.g. for some injustice or wrong).
  • *This will make amends for his disappointment.*

analysis
in the final or *last analysis* After all consideration.

anchor
anchor-man Person playing vital part, especially compère in radio or tv programme.
ride at anchor Be anchored. (Sometimes, move gently with the tide while anchored.)
weigh anchor Pull up the anchor prior to sailing away.

angel
on the side of the angels Supporting what is right.

answer
answer back Retort; reply impudently.
answer or *be answerable for* Accept responsibility.
answer to Have. Use. Correspond to.
  • *A man answering to that description lives next door.*
answer to the name of Be called.
know all the answers Be alert and well-informed.

any
any amount of A great deal of.
any day In any circumstances.

anybody
anybody's guess Unpredictable.

anything
anything but Far from.

10

apart
tell apart Distinguish between.

apology
an apology for A very poor example of.

appearance
keep up appearances Maintain an outward show.
make (put in) an appearance Show oneself.
to all appearances To the eye; outwardly.

apple
apple of one's eye See under **eye**.
apple-pie order Perfectly tidy and neat.
upset the apple-cart Spoil plans.

apron
tied to one's (mother's) apron-strings [MET] In the position of a
    small child who is compelled to rely on its mother for every
    thing; humiliatingly dependent.

argue
argue something away Argue that something does not exist.
    Attempt to destroy by argument.
argue the toss Be disputatious.

arm
at arm's length [LIT] The length of one's extended arm.
    ● *She held the picture at arm's length.*
    [MET] In a state of formality and unfriendliness.
    ● *He prefers to keep his neighbours at arm's length.*
a babe in arms [LIT] A child too young to walk. [MET] An
    inexperienced or immature person.
twist one's arm Persuade one.
up in arms Angrily roused to protest or action.
with open arms With warmth and pleasure.

around
to have been around To have acquired worldly experience.

as
as it were In other words; speaking metaphorically.
    ● *He was intoxicated, as it were, by the soft air and sunshine of
    spring.*
    Similar to *so to speak* and *in a manner of speaking*.
as yet Up to this or that time.

ascendant

in the ascendant Rising in power or popularity. Increasing in influence or ability. Hence:

one's star is in the ascendant One is growing in influence, etc.

ask

ask after Make enquiries about.

ask for it Behave in a way which invites trouble. Also *ask for trouble*.

asking price Price set by the seller.

for the asking Available. To be easily acquired.

if you ask me In my opinion.

ass

make an ass of Make (person) look foolish.

astray

go astray Stray. [LIT] Wander from the right path. [MET] Depart from what is correct. Become lost.

at

at it At work.

attach

strings attached Conditions. Restrictions.

- *We can have the use of the premises with no strings attached.*

attention

call (draw) attention to Ask for consideration to be given to.

pay attention to Attend to; listen to.

attitude

attitude of mind Settled way of thinking.

strike an attitude Stand or sit in a dramatic, self-conscious position.

avail

of or *to little* or *no avail* Almost (or quite) without any result.

avenue

leave no avenue unexplored or *explore every avenue* Employ every possible source of information; make every possible enquiry.

aversion

pet aversion Special object of dislike.

away
do away with Abolish.
get away with Do with impunity.

axe
axe to grind A private and personal object to achieve (or favour to obtain). A grievance.

B

baby
holding the baby Bearing an (unwanted) responsibility.
throw away the baby with the bathwater Dispense with something essential while disposing of something unwanted.

back
at the back of one's mind In one's thoughts, but not uppermost in them.
back and forth From one place to another, then back again.
backbone [MET] Chief support. Main strength.
back down Abandon a claim.
back of beyond Very remote place.
back out of Withdraw from an agreement.
back stairs Indirect and unofficial.
backstairs gossip gossip by subordinates.
back up Give support to.
behind one's back When one is absent. Deceitfully.
break one's back Overburden one. Hence *backbreaking*: very burdensome.
break the back of Complete the most difficult or the chief part of.
  • *We shall break the back of the work by tonight.*
fed up to the back teeth Very annoyed.
go back (a) on a person; (b) on one's word (a) Betray; desert; *(b)* contradict or withdraw (a statement, etc.).
have on one's back Be harassed by.
have one's back to the wall Be in difficulties.
like the back of one's hand Intimately.

on one's back 1. Ill in bed.

    2. Harassing one.

put one's back into Use all one's efforts.

put one's back up Annoy; make hostile.

take a back seat Occupy an inconspicuous position.

turn one's back on Abandon. Ignore.

when one's back is turned When one is absent, or occupied over some other matter.

background

keep or remain in the background Remain inconspicuous and unnoticed.

- *I'm going to keep in the background during the discussion.*

backhanded

backhanded compliment Indirect, insincere compliment.

backwards

know backwards Know very well.

bacon

bring home the bacon Succeed (in doing something).

save one's bacon Enable one to escape or succeed.

- *He would have failed the examination, but his history paper saved his bacon.*

bad

a bad egg; a bad hat; a bad lot A person with a bad character.

bad debts Debts which are 'written off' as complete losses. See **write off.**

bad form Not accepted as socially correct; ill-mannered.

badly off (for) Lacking (in). Short of money.

go from bad to worse Deteriorate still more.

go bad Become stale or rotten.

not (so) bad Fairly good.

too bad Unfortunate.

with bad grace Reluctantly.

bag

bag and baggage Luggage; with all one's portable possessions.

bag of bones Very thin person or animal.

it's in the bag It is concluded successfully.

bail

bail out [LIT] Pay money as security so that a prisoner may be

released pending trial. [MET] Come to the rescue in any way.
See **bale**.

balance

in the balance Uncertain.

keep one's balance Not fall.

lose one's balance Fall from precarious position.

strike a balance Balance or weigh certain objects or facts against
one another, in order to discover their comparative value or
importance.

on balance Taking everything into consideration. Having regard
to all aspects of a matter.

bald

bald as a coot Absolutely hairless.

bale

bale or bail out 1. Remove water or other fluid from a vessel by
means of a ladle, pail, etc.

2. Escape from an aeroplane by parachute.

ball

ball of fire Very energetic person.

have a ball Have a good time.

have the ball at one's feet Have every quality and opportunity
of being successful.

have the ball in one's court Be responsible for the next move.

keep one's eye(s) on the ball Remain alert.

keep the ball rolling Continue (the conversation, proceedings,
etc.) successfully.

on the ball Alert. Efficient.

play ball Cooperate.

start the ball rolling Make a beginning.

balloon

the balloon went up Trouble began. Uproar broke out.

bananas

go bananas Become very angry.

bandwagon

jump on the bandwagon Join a movement or fashion.

bank

bank on Rely on.

bang
bang goes That is the end of.
go with a bang Pass off very successfully.

bare
bare-faced Impudent.
with one's (own) bare hands By hand. Unaided.

bargain
bargain for Anticipate; prepare for.
  ● *We didn't bargain for so many people coming to tea.*
drive a hard bargain Conclude a bargain the terms of which are
  harsh.
into the bargain In addition; moreover.
  ● *He bought the house, and the furniture into the bargain.*
make the best of a bad bargain Accept difficulty, misfortune,
  etc., cheerfully.
strike a bargain Reach a final compromise.
  ● *We argued for a long time over what I should pay, but finally
  struck a bargain.*

bark
one's bark is worse than one's bite What one threatens to do is
  worse than what one actually does. One's manner of speaking is deceptively severe.

barrel
over a barrel Helpless.
scrape the (bottom of the) barrel Use the (unsatisfactory)
  remains of one's resources.

bat
have bats in the belfry Be crazy.
not to bat an eyelid Show no sign of emotion.
off one's own bat On one's own initiative. Unaided.

bated
with bated breath In a state of anxious expectation.

battle
battle royal A general fight.
half the battle A great help.
pitched battle One in which both sides are fully engaged.

17

bay

at bay In a situation so desperate that one is compelled to turn and face one's enemies.

keep at bay Keep at a distance.

be

be-all and end-all Whole (of a matter).

be that as it may Even so.

let it be Do not disturb it.

beam

on one's beam-ends In a desperate and almost hopeless condition.

- *Tom's already spent all his pocket money, and is on his beam-ends.*

bean

full of beans In high spirits. Having plenty of energy.

spill the beans Reveal a secret.

bear

bear a charmed life Be almost incredibly fortunate in escaping disasters and accidents.

bear down upon To approach with determination or with an obvious purpose.

bear enquiry, investigation, etc. Produce a satisfactory answer to enquiries. (Frequently used in the negative.)

- *The business he has been connected with won't bear enquiry.*

bear fruit Have results.

bear-garden Scene of uproar and confusion.

bear malice or a grudge Retain bitter or angry feelings, usually as the result of a dispute or quarrel.

bear a meaning Convey a meaning.

- *That sentence doesn't bear the meaning you seem to think it does.*

bear in mind Retain in one's memory. Take note.

- *Bear in mind that the train leaves at midnight.*

bear the name of Possess the name of. Have the same name as.

- *Their son bore the name of his grandfather, and was christened Joseph.*

bear out 1. [LIT] Carry away.

- *They bore out the body.*

2. Confirm; support.

- *Her statement bears out what the police told me.*

bear up Sustain one's strength and spirits.

- *Her father's death was a terrible shock, but she is bearing up well.*

bear with Endure as sympathetically as possible.

bear witness Act as a witness. Give evidence.

bring to bear Apply. Aim.

- *The outcry in the local newspapers brought a good deal of pressure to bear on the Council.*

like a bear with a sore head In a bad temper.

lose one's bearings Lose one's way or sense of direction.

no bearing on No connection with; irrelevant.

bear a date, signature, etc. Have written upon it.

- *His latest letter bears the date April 1st.*

beard

beard the lion in his den Confront boldly one's opponent (or superior) on his own ground (e.g. in his own home or office) to discuss a matter in dispute.

beat

beat about the bush Avoid or delay a straightforward discussion; approach a subject in a roundabout way.

beat down 1. Crush opposition.

- *The rebellion was beaten down.*

2. Compel a person to reduce his price.

- *He wanted five pounds, but I beat him down.*

beat hollow Be entirely superior to.

beat off Repel.

- *The garrison beat off all the enemy attacks.*

beat someone to it Forestall someone.

beat up Strike repeatedly and severely.

dead beat Utterly exhausted.

- *After walking all day in the rain, we were dead beat.*

off the beaten track Away from main roads.

take a lot of beating Be difficult to surpass.

beauty

beauty is only skin deep One must not judge by appearances.

the beauty of it is The especially satisfying thing is.

beaver

eager beaver (Over-) zealous person.

beck

at one's beck and call In a position of being under one's domination.

bed

bed and board Accommodation and meals.

bed of roses A state of ease and luxury. (Frequently used with a negative.)

between you, me and the bedpost In confidence.

die in one's bed Die of natural causes, or peacefully.

get out of bed on the wrong side Behave in a disagreeable fashion.

have made one's bed and must lie in it Must endure consequences of one's own actions.

bee

bee in one's bonnet Obsession; some particular idea or conviction, usually slightly crazy.

make or follow a bee line Proceed in a straight line (as a bee does on its way home).

the bee's knees The very best.

beer

beer and skittles Amusement.

think no small beer of Have high opinion of.

beg

beg the question Assume that something which is a matter for dispute is in fact true. (Often loosely used to mean 'avoid the issue being discussed'.)

beg to differ Disagree.

go begging Not wanted by anyone.

beggar

beggars can't be choosers People in need must take what is offered them.

beggar description Be so extraordinary that one cannot find words in which to describe it.

behaviour

be on one's good or best behaviour Conduct oneself as correctly and properly as possible.

behind

come from behind Succeed from unpromising position.

fall behind Lag.

put behind one Forget.

belief

beyond belief Unbelievable; astounding.

to the best of my belief In my genuine opinion.

believe
believe one's ears or *eyes* Accept the truth of what one hears or sees.

bell
clear or *sound as a bell* Very clear or sound. [Not confined to what one hears.]

below
below one's breath Almost inaudible (but intended to be heard). In a mutter, so as to be heard privately, not publicly.

belt
hit below the belt Attack unfairly.
tighten one's belt Make economies.
under one's belt As part of one's experience. In one's possession.

bend
bend over backwards Do everything possible.
catch one bending Have one at a disadvantage.
round the bend Mad.

beneath
beneath contempt So despicable as not to deserve even the effort of expressing one's dislike of it.
beneath one's breath See **below**.

benefit
give one the benefit of the doubt Assume that one is right, or innocent, when it is not certain.

bent
bent upon Determined to take a certain action.
  • *Jane was bent upon walking the entire distance that same night.*

berth
give a wide berth to Avoid; keep as far from as possible.

beside
beside the mark or *point* Irrelevant; unconnected with the matter being discussed.
beside oneself In such a state of emotion that one is incapable of knowing what one is doing.

best

at best Even in the best possible circumstances.

at the best of times In the most favourable conditions.

best man The bridegroom's chief friend and assistant at a wedding.

best part Most.

do one's level best Try as hard as one can.

for the best; all for the best The best that can happen; for the ultimate good.

have the best of Win (an argument, contest, etc.).

make the best of (a bad bargain or job) Be contented with (something unsatisfactory).

past one's best Less good than one was (usually because of age).

put best foot forward Walk as quickly as possible. Exert effort.

to the best of one's ability As well as one can.

with the best As well as anyone.

bet

you bet! Certainly.

better

better half Wife (a gently ironic complimentary phrase).

better off In better circumstances.

better oneself Improve one's worldly position.

for better or worse Whatever the outcome.

get the better of Triumph over; prove stronger than.

 • *His anger got the better of him, though he was sorry later.*

know better (than) Not to be so foolish (as).

 • *He should have known better than to take the risk.*

no better than The same as.

think (all) the better of Have more favourable opinion of.

think better of Reconsider, and decide to alter one's plan (usually from prudence or fear).

 • *He was going to protest, but thought better of it.*

between

between ourselves; between you and me; between these four walls; between you, me and the bed- or gate-post Speaking privately and confidentially.

betwixt and between In the middle.

read between the lines Find information which is not stated but implied.

beyond

beyond (one's) expectation Beyond anything (one) expected.
- *The beauties of Florence were far beyond his expectation.*

beyond measure Exceedingly. Very much indeed.

beyond the pale Unacceptable.

bib

best bib and tucker Best clothes.

bid

bid fair to Appear likely to.

bid welcome, farewell To express a welcome, or a farewell greeting.

make a bid for Make an attempt to secure.

big

talk big Boast.

too big for one's boots Conceited.

bill

bill and coo Speak lovingly and intimately.

clean bill of health Assurance that one is in sound health.
- *The doctor gave her a clean bill of health.*

bird

a bird in the hand Immediate possession is worth much more than a mere promise.

an early bird An early arrival.
- *The entertainment did not begin till eight, but we were early birds and got to the hall at seven-thirty.*

bird-brained Foolish.

bird has flown Person has escaped or left.

birds of a feather Similar people (e.g. having similar views, etc.).

bird of ill omen [LIT] A bird—e.g. the raven, the owl or the crow—whose appearance is supposed to indicate the coming of bad luck. [MET] Any person who has a reputation for bringing bad news. [Old f.]

bird of passage [LIT] A bird like the swallow, starling, etc., which migrates from one country to another according to the season. [MET] A person who is constantly travelling from place to place and has no permanent home; one who remains only temporarily.

get or give the bird Receive *or* offer criticism.

kill two birds with one stone Produce two results with a single action.

like a bird Without difficulty.

a little bird told me I don't want (I refuse) to say who told me. See **view**.

birthday

in or wearing one's birthday clothes or suit Wearing no clothes at all; naked (as one is born).

bit

a bit of Rather. Some.
- *It's a bit of a nuisance.*

champing at the bit Impatient. Eager to start.

do one's bit Make one's contribution.

every bit as Just as.

not a bit (of it) Not at all.

take or have the bit between one's teeth Become (to be) uncontrollably eager (to do something, etc.).

thrilled to bits Made very happy.

bite

bite or lick the dust Be killed in battle. Be finished.
- *At the next election, I expect the Tories will bite the dust.*

bite off more than one can chew Undertake more than one can cope with.

bite one's head off Speak angrily and sharply to a person.

bite (on) the bullet Show endurance. Bravely accept something unpleasant.

bite the hand that feeds one Injure one's benefactor.

two bites at the cherry Two separate attempts to achieve a result.

what's biting him? What is worrying or annoying him?

bitten

once bitten, twice shy Once having been hurt (damaged, disappointed, swindled, etc.), one is understandably careful.

bitter

the bitter end The very end (however painful). See under **pill**.

black

black art Art or craft derived from the Devil; vile or supernatural practices.

(as) black as thunder or a thundercloud Very angry.

black and blue Discoloured with bruises.

in one's black books In disfavour; with a bad reputation.

black looks Angry (sometimes evilly threatening) appearance.

black out 1. Obliterate; obscure.

2. Become unconscious.

in black and white In writing or print.

in the black Solvent.

not so black as one is painted Not as unpleasant as people say.

two blacks don't make a white A wrong act is not justified by being provoked by another wrong act.

blank

draw a blank Fail (usually to gain a response).

blanket

wet blanket A person who by his manner or conversation extinguishes the cheerfulness and enthusiasm of others (as, literally, a wet blanket extinguishes fire).

blast

(at) full blast At full power.

bleed

my heart bleeds (for) I am very sorry (for).

blessing

blessing in disguise Something apparently unfortunate but actually fortunate.

blind

blind alley Unprofitable line of enquiry or course of action.

blind impulse An illogical, sudden or thoughtless impulse.

● *Acting on blind impulse, she turned the car to the left.*

blind leading the blind Unqualified person offering advice to someone equally unqualified.

blind side The aspect of a man's character in which he is tender-hearted or weak. Also, in sport, the unguarded part of the field.

blind spot Area where one's understanding is lacking.

none so blind No one is so difficult to persuade as a man who is determined not to listen to arguments or persuasion.

turn a blind eye to Pretend not to notice or know about.

blink

on the blink Not functioning correctly.

block
a chip off the old block One exhibiting the characteristics of his parents or ancestors.

blood
bad blood Ill-feeling; antagonism.
- *There's been bad blood between them for ages.*

one's blood being up Being excited and angry.
- *His blood was up, and a quarrel was inevitable.*

blood-and-thunder Highly sensational; melodramatic. Hence, a story, book, film, etc., having such characteristics.
See **penny dreadful**.

blood is thicker than water Relations are more closely connected than mere friends or acquaintances, and should receive better treatment.

blood-letting 1. Bloodshed.
2. Quarrel etc. having victim(s).

blood sports Sports that involve the shedding of blood, usually of animals (e.g. fox-hunting, bull-fighting, etc.).

blue-blooded Aristocratic.

first blood First success (in a contest, debate, trial of strength, etc.).

fresh or new blood New members (of an organisation, club etc.).

get blood out of a stone Find evidence of human feeling in someone who lacks it. (More generally) Attempt the impossible.

hot blood Quick temper. Anger.

in cold blood Deliberately; coolly.

in the blood Part of one's nature; born with one. Hence *runs in the blood* Is a family trait.

make one's blood boil Make one furiously angry.

one's blood runs cold One experiences fear, acute apprehension or disappointment.
- *His ruthlessness makes my blood run cold.*

out for blood Determined to win.

taste blood Be stimulated by success.

young blood New young members (of an organisation, etc.).

blot
blot one's copy book Spoil one's previously good reputation.
blot out Efface; obliterate; forget.
- *It will be many years before memories of the accident will be blotted out.*

blow

blow-by-blow description, account etc. Detailed description etc.

blow hot and cold Be inconsistent and unreliable.

blow or *hang it!* or *the expense*, etc. Disregard it.

blow the gaff Reveal a secret.

blow (let) off steam Get rid of surplus energy.

blow one's own trumpet Boast.

blow one's top Lose one's temper.

blow out 1. (Verb) Extinguish.
- *Blow out the candles.*

2. (Noun) A large and luxurious meal.
- *We had a tremendous blow-out at the hotel.*

blow over Subside. [LIT] Applied to a storm of wind, etc.
- *The storm will soon blow over.*

[MET] Applied to quarrels, disagreements, etc.
- *We have frequent quarrels, but they soon blow over.*

blow up 1. Explode.
- *The mine blew up soon after the soldiers passed.*

2. Inflate.
- *The tyre needs blowing up.*

Hence: [MET] Exaggerate.
- *Its importance has been blown up out of all proportion.*

come to blows Fight.

strike a blow for or *against* Act in support or opposition.

blue

blue-eyed boy Favourite.

blue murder An angry scene. (Also used in a number of phrases as emphasis, e.g. *shout blue murder* (=loudly), *like blue murder* (=very quickly).
- *There'll be blue murder when she hears of this.*

blue riband or *ribbon* Highest attainable honour or prize.

out of the blue Unexpectedly.

See also under **bolt**.

bluff

call a man's bluff Challenge a statement or action which one believes has nothing to support it.
- *If you think he's asking too much for the house, call his bluff by pretending you're not interested in buying.*

blush

at (the) first blush At first sight.

- *At first blush the proposals seem generous.*

spare one's blushes Not embarrass one by praise.

board

across the board For everyone. In all respects.

go by the board Be lost, forgotten or eliminated.

sweep the board Take all the available rewards or prizes.

boat

in the same boat Similarly situated.

- *It's no use grumbling—we're all in the same boat.*

miss the boat Fail to seize an opportunity.

rock the boat Endanger a cause one belongs to.

body

in a body Collectively; all together.

keep body and soul together Remain alive.

- *I'm managing to keep body and soul together.*

bog

bogged down Held back, unable to progress.

boil

boil down to Amount to.

boil over 1. [LIT] Boil so that the fluid rises above the edge of
the saucepan or kettle.

2. [MET] Become so angry that self-control is lost.

come to the boil Reach critical stage.

make one's blood boil Make one extremely angry.

bold

make bold to; make so bold as to Presume to. Dare to. (Used
ironically, usually.)

bolster

bolster up Add to (e.g. one's confidence, a statement, etc.) in
order to strengthen.

- *The Government bolstered up its position by imprisoning all its
outspoken opponents.*

bolt

a bolt from the blue A complete surprise. A sudden and entirely
unexpected disaster.

bolt upright Absolutely straight and perpendicular.

bomb

go like a bomb 1. Move very quickly.

2. Be a great success.

make a bomb Make a lot of money.

bone

a bone to pick A matter for reproof or blame.

bone of contention The subject of argument or dispute.

bone-dry Quite dry.

bone idle Utterly idle.

feel in one's bones Be quite sure.

● *The train will be full; I can feel it in my bones.*

make no bones about Not attempt to disguise.

● *I'm disappointed, I'll make no bones about it.*

near the bone Indelicate.

See also under **finger**.

book

bring to book Bring to justice; punish.

closed book Something one does not understand.

go by the book Adhere strictly to rules

in my book As I see matters.

in one's good (or bad or black) books Liked and appreciated (or the reverse).

read someone like a book Understand person's character, motives, etc., fully.

suit one's book Agree with one's plans.

● *That arrangement will suit my book very well indeed.*

take a leaf out of a person's book Follow his example. Imitate him.

● *I think I'll take a leaf out of his book and go to bed early.*

throw the book at Make all possible accusations against.

boot

put the boot in Take decisive, usually harsh, action.

the boot's on the other foot (or leg) The advantage (power, responsibility, truth, etc.) now lies on the opposite side to where it formerly did.

born

born before one's time Possessing ideas and theories that belong to a later period in history.

in all one's born days In all one's life. (Used to emphasise.)

● *I've never been so surprised in all my born days.*

born with a silver spoon in one's mouth Born into a wealthy family.

not born yesterday Not without experience.

not know that one is born Not realise how fortunate one really is.

borne

borne in upon one Impressed upon one's mind.

- *It was borne in upon her that they would never meet again.*

borrow

borrowed plumes Anything worn or assumed to which one is not entitled.

borrowed time Unexpected prolongation of time, especially of life.

bosom

bosom friend Intimate friend.

both

having something both ways Choose two contradicting or alternative lines of action, etc., for one's own benefit, when only one is available.

- *If you don't give up smoking, you won't be able to afford a holiday: you can't have it both ways.*

bother

cannot be bothered Will not take trouble.

bottle

bottle-neck A passage which becomes suddenly narrow, like the neck of a bottle, through which objects are compelled to move slowly; hence [MET] anything which causes a delay.

bottle up Suppress.

- *He bottled up his anger and said nothing.*

hit the bottle Begin to drink alcohol excessively.

on the bottle Drinking alcohol to excess.

bottom

at the bottom of Really responsible for.

bet one's bottom dollar Stake everything one possesses.

bottom falls out Collapse takes place.

bottomless pit Hell.

from the bottom of one's heart Genuinely. Most sincerely.

get to the bottom of Find the truth, cause, meaning of.

knock the bottom out of Show to be of no value.

touch bottom [LIT] Reach the bottom of the sea.

- *The boat's keel touched bottom.*

[MET] Reach the lowest depths (e.g. of misery, etc.).
See **rock-bottom**.

bound

beyond the bounds of Outside the limits of.

I'll be bound I am certain.

- *He'll be late again tomorrow, I'll be bound.*

out of bounds Beyond the official boundary or limit.

- *All the hotels in the town have been placed out of bounds to the troops.*

within bounds 1. Within the official boundary or limit.

    2. Within reasonable limitations and restraint.

- *She could never keep her temper within bounds.*

within reasonable bounds Within restraint.

within the bounds of possibility Just possible.

- *It is, of course, within the bounds of possibility that the shipwrecked crew may have reached some desert island.*

bow

bow out Withdraw from a situation.

bow to the inevitable Accept what is unavoidable.

shot across the bows Warning.

two strings or another string to one's bow More resources than one. An alternative, a second plan in case the first should fail.

bowl

bowl along Go fast and smoothly.

bowled over 1. [LIT] Overturned; knocked down.

- *The nun was bowled over in the rush to the train.*

    2. [MET] Overcome (usually with surprise, joy).

- *When I heard the news I was completely bowled over.*

box

box on the ears Blow on the side of the head.

boy

boys will be boys Immature behaviour must be tolerated.

jobs for the boys Favours for one's friends.

brain

brain wave Sudden good idea, plan; inspiration.

brainchild Original idea or invention.

brains trust A group of experts, meeting publicly to discuss and answer questions, problems, etc.

cudgel or rack one's brains See **cudgel**.

have something on the brain Be totally preoccupied with something.

make one's brain reel Stagger one mentally. Applied to an almost incredible statement or fact.

pick a person's brains Question a person (sometimes informally or tactfully) to extract information, advice, etc., from him.

See under **Crack, Hare, Scatter.**

brake

put the brake(s) on [LIT and MET.] Cause to slow down.

branch

branch out Develop (into or away from) (as branches grow from trees). Become independent.

- *The chip-shop is branching out into a café as well.*
- *He's left the firm, to branch out on his own.*

brand

brand-new Absolutely new.

brass

bold as brass Extremely or excessively self-assured.

get down to brass tacks Deal with the basic realities.

have the brass neck to Be so impudent as to.

brazen

brazen out Defiantly defend, or deny.

breach

breach of the peace (*strictly speaking*, **the Queen's peace**) Any action which breaches or breaks the law and may lead to violence and disturbance.

heal the breach Bring a serious or prolonged quarrel to an end.

step into the breach Deputise.

- *The organist fell ill, but his assistant stepped into the breach at the last moment.*

bread

bread and butter Routine daily work.

bread-winner The person whose earnings support the family.

know which side his bread is buttered on Know where his interest, advantage, etc., lies.

on the breadline Having just enough to live on.

want one's bread buttered on both sides Want undue benefits.

break

break away Free, or detach oneself, by a definite effort.

- *I broke away from the association ten years ago.*

break the bank Exhaust the bank's resources.

break a blow or *fall* Mitigate its effect.

break cover Come out of hiding.

break down 1. Smash by force.

- *We shall have to break down the door to get in.*

2. Cause to diminish and finally disappear.

- *It took a long time to break down his shyness.*

3. Collapse under great pain or emotion.

- *When she heard he was dead, she broke down completely.*

break even Show neither profit nor loss.

break from or *forth* Escape from. Sound from.

- *Cheers broke from the crowd when the teams appeared.*

break a habit Cease to be subject to a habit.

break new ground Begin something new or different.

break of day Dawn.

break one's heart Cause profound distress.

- *It will break his heart to retire.*

break the ice Break an uncomfortable silence; put an end to formality or stiffness.

break in 1. Enter a building by force.

2. Interrupt.

- *I could tell this story better if so many people didn't break in.*

3. Train someone, usually an animal, in obedience.

- *I've spent nearly six months breaking in my pony.*

break in on Interrupt.

break a journey Interrupt it by stopping at some point on the way, and resuming the journey later.

- *We are breaking our journey at Chester for one night.*

break loose Escape.

- *The dog broke loose from its chain.*

Similar to **break away**.

breakneck speed (Dangerously) fast pace.

break one's neck Be in a considerable hurry.

- *I broke my neck to arrive in time.*

break the news Pass on information. (Usually, startling or bad news, as tactfully and gently as possible.)

break off End (suddenly, or temporarily).

- *We were discussing our plans, but had to break off when the telephone rang.*

33

break out 1. [LIT] Force one's way out.
- *He broke out of prison, but was caught again later.*

2. [MET] Begin.
- *A roar of cheering broke out.*

break ranks Leave one's position (usually in disorder).

break the record Surpass all previous performances.

break the thread Interrupt a story, a line of thought, etc.

break through (Verb) Penetrate (the surroundings or impediment, etc.).
- *The sun broke through the clouds.*
- *The crowd broke through the lines of police.*

break-through (Noun) Successful development.

break up [LIT] Break into small pieces. [MET] End, dismiss, destroy, depart.

break with Have no further connection with.

break one's word, or promise Fail to do what one has undertaken to do.

make the break Similar to *break away (from)*.

the weather breaks The weather changes. Hence *a break in the weather:* a change.

breast

make a clean breast (of) Confess all.

breath

a breath of (fresh) air [LIT]
- *Let's go into the garden for a breath of air.*

[MET] Someone or something invigorating, refreshing, delightful.
- *The new typist is a real breath of fresh air.*

catch one's breath Stop breathing for a moment (because of surprise, sudden emotion, etc.).

get one's breath back Recover from exertion.

hold one's breath Stop breathing (out of fear etc.).

in the same breath At the same time; simultaneously. (Usually in connection with two contradictory statements.)

keep one's breath to cool one's porridge Not speak.

out (short) of breath Unable to breathe (because of exertion, illness, etc.).

take away one's breath Leave one breathless through intense astonishment, delight, etc. Thus *breathtaking* Astonishing.
- *Your offer is so generous that it takes my breath away.*

under or below one's breath Very softly; almost in a whisper.

See under **save, waste.**

breathe

breathe again Recover (from fear, inconvenience, etc.).
- *The floods subsided, and the villagers breathed again.*

breathe down one's neck Supervise closely.

breathe (e.g. *revenge, curses, blessings,* etc.) Murmur; utter in low intense tones, or passionately.

breathing-space Pause (for recovery or relaxation from effort).

not to breathe a syllable or word Remain absolutely silent; keep secret.

See **fire and brimstone.**

bred

born and bred Born and brought up.

brick

beat or *bang one's head against a brick wall* Have no success (in trying to get something done, etc.) because of resistance.

brick up Fill up an opening in a building, etc., with bricks.
- *There was once a window there, but it has been bricked up for centuries.*

drop a brick Make a tactless mistake.

make bricks without straw Make something without having the necessary materials.

bridge

cross a bridge when one comes to it Deal with a difficulty when it occurs, not anticipate it.

brief

in brief In short. Concisely.

hold no brief for Refrain from arguing in favour of.

bright

bright and early Very early.

bright idea Clever idea.

bright lights Places of entertainment. Town where these may be found.

bright spark Quick-witted person.

look on the bright side Find reason for hope (in a situation).

brim

to the brim [LIT] To the edge of any vessel made to contain fluid. [MET] To completion. Also *brim-full.*
- *She was filled to the brim with happiness.*

bring

bring about; bring to pass Cause to happen.

bring-and-buy sale Sale, usually for charity, at which people donate items for sale.

bring to bear Apply (influence, etc.). Concentrate one's efforts with some special object.

bring to book Detect someone in a mistake; bring a wrongdoer to punishment.

bring or *call into being* Cause to exist.

bring into play Cause to operate.

bring into the world Give birth to.

bring to a close End; conclude.

bring down 1. Cause a penalty to fall on.
- *He'll bring trouble down on himself.*
2. Lower.
- *Prices are being brought down.*
3. Cause to end.
- *This controversy could bring down the Government.*

bring forth Produce; display.

bring forward Introduce; initiate.

bring to a head Cause to reach a climax or crisis.

bring home to one Cause one to realise, to feel, to understand. Convince one.

bring in Introduce. Produce (as income or profit). Deliver (verdict).

bring off Succeed.

bring to mind Recall.

bring into play Cause to operate.

bring up the rear Follow at the end.
- *Policemen on horseback brought up the rear.*

bring on 1. Cause.
- *The heat brings on my headaches.*
2. Cause to appear.
- *Bring on the dancing girls!*
3. Advance progress of.
- *Pruning will bring on the roses.*

bring oneself to Persuade oneself to.
- *He couldn't bring himself to apologise.*

bring out 1. Exhibit clearly.
- *Hardship sometimes brings out the best in people.*
2. Publish.
- *The new edition of the dictionary will be brought out next year.*

bring round 1. Bring from a short distance.

    2. Restore to consciousness. Also *bring to.*

- *We threw water over the woman to bring her round.*

    3. Persuade (to a point of view).

- *The strikers are taking a long time to be brought round to accepting the management's offer.*

bring to Restore to consciousness.

bring to one's senses Make one realise that one must behave more sensibly.

bring up 1. Refer to some matter requiring discussion (also *bring forward*).

- *Please bring up the matter at our next meeting.*

    2. Care for and educate.

- *He was very well brought up.*

bring word Convey information.

bristle

bristle with Be (unpleasantly) full of.

- *The whole plan bristles with difficulties.*

Bristol

(all) shipshape and Bristol fashion In good order.

broad

it's as broad as it's long Either alternative will lead to the same result.

broadly speaking Speaking generally; stated in simple terms.

broad-minded Tolerant.

broken

broken accents Imperfect or hesitating speech.

broken English Inaccurate and imperfect English.

broken-hearted Crushed with grief.

broken reed An ally or support who has proved useless or unworthy.

See under **break**.

broom

new broom Newly appointed person eager to improve matters.

brow

lowbrow Having to do with popular, undemanding forms of art, literature, music, etc.

highbrow Having to do with highly developed, intellectual tastes in the arts.

knit one's brows Frown (usually in thought).

brown

browned off Bored. Annoyed.

in a brown study In a reverie. Apparently thinking deeply; sometimes hardly thinking at all.

brush

a brush A light, not serious, encounter.

- *He's out of sorts because he's just had a brush with a traffic-warden.*

brush aside Ignore. Dismiss.

get or give the brush-off Receive or give rebuff.

brush up Renew one's memory of. Revise.

- *You can brush up your French by watching the TV programme.*

brute

brute force Physical force or strength.

- *The police had to use brute force to take her to the station.*

buckle

buckle (down) to Get to work vigorously. Set about.

- *We shall have to buckle to if we are to catch that train.*

bud

nip in the bud Prevent at an early stage.

build

build up (Verb) 1. Gradually build or increase.
2. Praise.

build-up (Noun) Advance publicity creating anticipation.

bull

bull-at-a-gate Forceful.

bull in a china shop Clumsy wrecker.

take the bull by the horns Tackle problem boldly.

buoy

buoy up Support; encourage.

burn

burn one's bridges or boats Make a change of plan impossible; make certain that the decision is final.

burn the candle at both ends Fail to conserve one's energy. Work hard or for long hours, or live very energetically, usually with consequent exhaustion.

burn one's fingers Suffer because of rashness, meddling or financial speculation.

money burns a hole in one's pocket One is very eager to spend money.

one's ears are burning One is being talked about while not present.

burst

burst into laughter or tears or out laughing Suddenly erupt into laughter or tears.

bury

bury the hatchet Forget past quarrels, and become friends. See *pipe of peace* and *bygones be bygones.*

bury one's head in the sand Obstinately refuse to accept or face facts.

bus

busman's holiday Holiday spent doing what one normally does for a living.

miss the bus Miss an opportunity.

business

get down to business Begin seriously.

go out of business Cease to trade; discontinue one's usual work.

have no business Have no right.

like nobody's business In a remarkable way.

make it one's business to Assume personal responsibility for. Undertake to.

 • *I'll make it my business to call on him.*

mean business Intend to take definite (and sometimes unpleasant) action.

 • *There's a bull in the field, and I'm afraid he means business.*

mind one's own business Refrain from interfering.

the business end The part that does the work.

butt

butt in Interrupt. Intervene. Interfere.

butter

butter someone up Flatter someone.

look as if butter wouldn't melt in one's mouth Appear demure, innocent.

fine words butter no parsnips The truth can not be hidden or changed by mere words.

butterflies
have butterflies (in one's stomach) Feel nervous.

buttonhole
Intercept and speak privately to. Detain a reluctant listener.

buy
buy off Pay to be rid of (usually person). Bribe.
buy out Pay person(s) to give up business, prosperity, etc.
buy up Purchase large quantities or whole of.
a good buy A bargain.

by
by and by Soon; in the near future.
by and large In general terms; comparing the advantages and
　disadvantages. On the whole.
　● *By and large, the bus service is getting worse.*
by himself, herself 1. Unaided.
　● *The baby can now walk by himself.*
　2. Alone.
　● *I spent all the afternoon by myself.*
by the by Incidentally.
by the way See under **way**.

bygones
let bygones be bygones Let past quarrels or disagreements be
　ignored or forgotten. See *bury the hatchet*.

byword
become or be a byword Become (be) notorious, proverbial.

C

Cain
raise Cain Make a great fuss.

cake
cakes and ale A very enjoyable experience. Merry-making.
have one's cake and eat it Obtain two contradictory advantages
from the same thing or by the same means. Similar to *have
it both ways.*
like hot cakes Very quickly.
piece of cake Something very easy.
slice of the cake Share of the benefit.

calculate
calculated to Likely to; tending to.
- *His conduct is calculated to offend people.*
calculate upon Expect; estimate.
- *We calculate upon a hundred people attending.*

call
call away Summon.
call to the bar Admit as a barrister.
call down Invoke.
call for 1. Demand.
- *The present emergency calls for special measures to be taken.*
2. Arrive to take away or accompany.
- *We will call for you on our way to the concert.*
call a halt End. Order to end.
- *The referee called a halt to the bout in the fourth round.*
call in Recall something that has been issued, e.g. coins or
stamps.

call into question Express doubt about. Dispute.
call to mind Recall; remember.
- *I can't call to mind where I've met you.*

call names Abuse.
- *She called him every name she could think of.*

call off 1. Order to cease. Cancel.
- *The search was called off at nightfall.*

2. Change one's mind, and abandon plans previously made.
- *We were going to give a party, but had to call it off.*

call on 1. Visit.

2. Request.

call one's bluff Challenge one's attempt to deceive.
call out 1. Raise one's voice; shout.
- *Call out the name of the winner.*

2. Summon to keep public law and order.
- *Rioting began, and troops were called out.*

call over Read through a list of names aloud, in order to ascertain who are present. Also *call the roll.*

call the shots Be in control.
call a spade See **spade**.
call a thing one's own Have normal benefits of possession.
call to account See **account**.
call the tune Give the orders. Be in a position of superiority.
call up Summon.
close call Narrow escape.
no call to No need to.
- *There's no call to be alarmed.*

on call Ready when wanted.
pay a call Make a visit.

camel
break the camel's back Go too far. See *last straw* under **straw**.

camp
camp-follower Hanger-on.

can
can of worms Very complicated matter.
carry the can Take the blame.

candle
burn the candle at both ends See **burn**.
not fit to hold a candle to Not fit even to assist; not good enough even to be compared with.

(game) not worth the candle (Matter) not justifying the trouble, cost etc.

cap

put on one's thinking-cap Give a problem some thought.

a feather in one's cap See **feather**.

cap in hand Humbly. Hence *go cap in hand*: solicit meekly; ask a favour.

if the cap fits (wear it) If something (e.g. remark, statement) is appropriate or true (take note of it).

set one's cap at Attempt. Also applied to a woman who is making a determined effort to persuade a man to marry her.

take (send, pass) the cap round Make a collection of money by circulating some container among people.

to cap To go one better (e.g. *to cap a joke*: to tell a better one). Outdo.

capital

make capital out of Turn to good account.

captain

captain of industry Industrial magnate.

cards

cards are stacked Odds are.

get one's cards Be dismissed from one's employment.

have card(s) up one's sleeve Have plan in reserve.

house of cards Unstable plan or operation.

on the cards Possible; likely to happen.

• *It's on the cards that I may go to Australia.*

play one's cards close to one's chest Act secretively.

play one's cards right or *well* Act or plan, negotiate, etc. sensibly.

put one's cards on the table Be absolutely candid, and conceal nothing.

care

have a care! Be careful.

take care Be careful.

take care to Be sure to.

take care of Protect.

career

chequered career One including many changes; successes and failures.

carpet

on the carpet Summoned before a superior to be reprimanded.
red carpet, roll out the Treat with great respect.
sweep under the carpet Conceal. Ignore.

carrot

carrot and stick Incentive and punishment.
hold out a carrot Offer an inducement.

carry

carry all before one Be overwhelmingly successful.
carry (along) with Persuade.
carry away 1. Transport.
   2. Deprive of self-control.
carry coals to Newcastle Do something superfluous.
carry conviction Be very persuasive.
   ● *His arguments don't carry much conviction.*
carry the day Reach final success; win.
   ● *Their greater skill eventually carried the day.*
carry off 1. Take away by force.
   ● *The invaders carried off many hostages.*
   2. Conduct oneself successfully (in a difficult situation).
   ● *He carried off the interview very well.*
carry on 1. Continue (e.g. one's work or recreation.)
   2. Grieve.
   3. Behave irregularly and badly.
carry one's point Succeed in convincing one's opponent.
carry out Put into practice.
carry over Postpone.
carry through Complete. Bring safely out of difficulties.
carry weight Exert influence.

cart

put the cart before the horse Make two statements in reverse order
  of their importance; put the second and less important thing
  first; place the effect before the cause.

case

as the case may be Whichever of several things may happen.
   ● *Suppose your son becomes an artist, or a poet, as the case may be?*
a case in point See under **point**.
in any case Whatever may occur.
in case Lest. In the event that.
   ●*Close the window in case it rains while we're away*

in case of In the event of. Also *just in case.*

in that case If that is true or should happen. That being so.

in the case of As regards. In the matter of.

is or is not the case Is true *or* false.

make out a case for Argue in favour of.

cash

cash down Immediate payment.

hard cash Currency (not cheques etc.).

cash in on Benefit from.

cash on the nail Money (not cheques or any other substitute).

cast

cast about Seek for.

- *I've been casting about for some village in which I can spend a quiet holiday.*

cast adrift Abandoned.

cast aside Reject as worthless.

cast aspersions on Comment unfavourably upon; decry. See *run down.*

cast away Wrecked.

cast a clout Discard one's winter clothing.

cast down Depressed; unhappy.

cast an eye over Look at, usually quite casually. Similar to *cast a glance at.*

cast or throw light upon Reveal; exhibit.

- *Pepys' diary casts a light on life in England in the seventeenth century.*

cast or throw in one's lot Decide to share the life, the good and bad fortunes, of another person or society.

cast the net Search widely.

cast off (Verb) 1. Unfasten the mooring ropes, chains, etc., preparatory to sailing.

2. Repudiate. Throw away.

cast-off (Noun) Unwanted. Used up.

cast out Expel.

cast pearls See under **pearl.**

cast a shadow over Have a dispiriting influence on.

cast a spell over Bewitch; control by magic.

casting vote A vote given by the chairman of a meeting when the number of votes for and against any proposal is equal. It is the casting vote that then decides the matter.

the die is cast An irrevocable decision has been taken.

castle

castle in the air A dream building; a mere vision of happiness which has no basis in fact.

castle in Spain The French version *(Château d'Espagne)* of the above.

an Englishman's home is his castle One's home is private, and may not be entered by force.

cat

a cat may look at a king! Whatever may be their (social) positions, one person is as good as another.

cat-call Expression of disapproval (usually whistling) at theatre, etc.

cat-and-dog life A life of continual quarrelling and fighting. Also *fight like cat and dog.*

cat-and-mouse game Cautious manoeuvring, bargaining, negotiation, etc.

cat-nap Brief sleep.

curiosity killed the cat Do not be inquisitive.

enough to make a cat laugh Very funny.

let the cat out of the bag Allow a secret to escape unintentionally.

like a cat on hot bricks Restless. Fidgety. Uneasy.

like something the cat brought in Bedraggled.

not a cat in hell's chance No chance at all.

not room to swing a cat Confined space.

put the cat among the pigeons Create a sensation, uproar, contention, by doing something, e.g. by taking some initiative in a given situation.

rain cats and dogs Rain very heavily.

which way the cat jumps What events indicate as a probability. Similar to *which way the wind blows* (under **wind.**)

cat's paw One who is used merely for the convenience of a cleverer or stronger person.

cat's pyjamas or whiskers Something very good.

play cat and mouse with Amuse oneself with, by not revealing one's intentions.

catch

catch-all Designed to include every contingency.

catch cold Become ill with a common cold.

catch fire (catch light; catch alight) Ignite; burn.

- *The spilt oil caught fire, and the house was burnt down.*

catch a glimpse of See momentarily.

catch hold of Take a hold on. Take hold of.

catch someone napping [LIT] Discover someone asleep. [MET] Obtain an advantage through discovering someone being careless or ignorant.

catch out Find out; expose. Discover someone making a mistake.

catch penny Cheap, or superficially attractive, because purely commercial.

catch-phrase Phrase in common use.

catch a person's eye See under eye.

catch sight of See for a moment.

catch up 1. Snatch up; seize suddenly.

● *He caught up his briefcase and dashed out.*

2. Become level with.

● *He ran so fast that he soon caught up with me (or caught me up).*

catchword Slogan.

you will not catch me doing that I will never do that.

caught

be caught bending or napping or out Be put at a disadvantage by someone else's greater alertness.

cause

good cause Organisation, event, etc. deserving support (e.g. charity).

lost cause Undertaking that has no hope of success.

caution

throw caution to the winds Behave rashly.

caviare

caviare to the general Something good which is beyond the appreciation or understanding of the general public.

centre

centre of attraction Person or thing attracting principal attention.

ceremony

stand on ceremony Insist on formal behaviour.

with no further (without) ceremony Promptly. Informally.

chain

chain reaction A result which, in turn, produces an effect which, in turn, produces a similar result, and so on.

chain store One of a number of precisely similar stores, controlled by the same company, and selling goods of the same type and price.

chair

take the chair Occupy the chair, i.e. the seat of the chairman. Preside over a meeting as chairman.

chalk

by a long chalk; by long chalks By a great deal; thoroughly.
  - *The boy will win the race by a long chalk.*

as different as chalk from cheese Totally different.
  - *The music of Strauss is as different from Bach's as chalk from cheese.*

chalk up Score.

chance

an eye to the main chance See under **eye**.

chance one's arm Take a risk.

fat chance No chance.

game of chance Game depending on luck, not skill.

on the off chance In the hope.

sporting or fighting chance A chance, though not a great one.
  - *There's still a sporting chance that the horse will win.*

stand a good or fair chance of Be very (quite) likely to.
  - *We stand a good chance of being late.*

take a chance or take chances Run a risk.

taking no chances Taking no risks.
  - *He has two bolts on every door, and an extra one on the window; he's taking no chance of burglars getting in.*

the chances are The probability is.
  - *The chances are that there will be a strike.*

the chances are against it or even It is unlikely *or* reasonably likely.

change

change hands Change owners.
  - *That shop has changed hands only once in a hundred years.*

change of air Different climate or environment.

get no change out of Fail to receive satisfaction from.
  - *I complained to the manufacturers, but I didn't get any change out of them.*

change one's tune Change one's attitude, manner, language, etc.

ring the changes Do something in a variety of ways.

small change Coins of small value.
- *I had to give the conductor a five pound note; I had no small change.*

chapter
chapter of accidents A series of accidents or misfortunes.

chapter and verse Exact authority for a statement; details by which the truth of a statement can be checked.

character
in character In harmony with a person's known habits or temperament. Opposite: *out of character.*

charge
charge with 1. Formally accuse of some crime.
   2. Entrust with.

charged with 1. Filled, loaded with.
   2. Entrusted with.

in charge of Responsible for.

charity
charity begins at home Kindness is due first to one's kith and kin. One should look after one's own interests, and those of one's relatives and friends, before showing kindness to strangers.

cold as charity Very cold. Unsympathetic.

charm
have a charmed life Appear to have magical powers enabling one to succeed, escape, etc.

work like a charm Work very well.

cheap
cheap as dirt; dirt cheap Extremely cheap; a bargain.

on the cheap Cheaply.

check
check out Pay one's bill and leave.

keep in check Restrain.

cheek
cheek by jowl Close together, very near.

have a cheek Be impertinent.

have the cheek to Have the impertinence, effrontery, to.

turn the other cheek Fail to retaliate.

cheer
cheer up Recover your cheerfulness!

cheese
cheesed off Bored and dissatisfied.
cheese-paring Parsimony.

cherry
two bites at the cherry A second attempt or opportunity.

chest
get something off one's chest Say something (usually something one has been intending to say for some time).
play something or one's cards close to one's chest Act secretively.

chestnut
old chestnut Very familiar device, anecdote, rumour, etc.
pull chestnuts out of the fire 1. Do someone's dirty work for him.
2. Salvage some success from disaster.

chicken
chicken-hearted Cowardly; easily terrified.
count one's chickens before they are hatched Make definite plans about profits or advantages before it is certain that you will obtain them.

child
child's play Very simple task.

chill
cast a chill over Have a depressing influence on.
 • *If he comes, he'll only cast a chill over the proceedings.*
catch a chill Develop a cold.
take the chill off Warm slightly.

chime
chime in Add in support of something already said.
chime in with Harmonise with.
 • *Those blue curtains will chime in with the carpet.*

chin
keep one's chin up Stay cheerful.
take on the chin Receive blow courageously.

chip

chip off the old block See under **block.**

have a chip on one's shoulder Be touchy or bitter.

when the chips are down When it comes to the point.

choice

Hobson's choice No choice at all; the acceptance of what one is offered.

spoiled for choice Presented with many choices.

take one's choice Decide between several possibilities.

chop

chop and change Frequently alter one's decisions or methods. Be inconsistent, vacillating, variable.

get the chop 1. Be dismissed from employment.

2. Be discontinued.

chord

strike a chord Bring back to one's memory.

touch a chord or the right chord Appeal to emotions.

chorus

chorus of approval General approval.

chuck

chuck away Waste. Lose. Throw away carelessly

chuck out Expel. Throw out.

chuck up Stop; abandon (in disgust).

circle

come full circle End at starting-point.

go round in circles Make no progress.

run round in (small) circles Be very busy.

vicious circle Actions and consequences which make each other worse and worse.

circumstance

extenuating circumstances Excuses; causes which make forgiveness possible.

in (under) the circumstances In the present condition or state of affairs; after consideration of what has happened.

circumstantial

circumstantial evidence Evidence which gives no direct proof. Known facts which are hard to explain unless one accepts that they *appear* to constitute proof.

claim
stake a claim Claim.

clamp
clamp down on Be stricter about.

clap
clap eyes on Catch sight of. See. (Usually used in negative.)
- *I haven't clapped eyes on him for some weeks.*

clap-trap Worthless, valueless talk, generally used in an attempt to become popular or appear learned.

clappers
like the clappers Very quickly.

Clapham
the man on the Clapham omnibus Ordinary people.

class
in a class of its own Unequalled.

clean
clean bill of health [LIT] An official document certifying that a ship has left port with no case of infectious illness on board. [MET] Indication that there is no risk of infection, or, alternatively, that no illness, infectious or otherwise, exists.

clean down Rub until clean.

clean out Empty.

clean sheet No record of wrong-doing.

clean slate Freedom from commitments. Freedom from blame.

clean up Make (person or thing) clean.

come clean Confess.

make a clean breast of See **breast**.

make a clean sweep of See under **sweep, heel.**

one's hands are clean One is innocent.

cleaners
take to the cleaners 1. Take one's money.
2. Criticise severely.

clear
clear away 1. Remove.
- *I'll clear away all this rubbish.*
2. (*With get*) Escape completely.
- *The burglars got clear away.*

clear conscience Feeling that one is innocent.

clear as crystal Obvious; absolutely plain. Also
crystal clear.

clear-cut Clearly defined.

clear the decks for action Prepare. Get ready.

clear as mud Not clear at all.

clear of Free from.
- *The river is clear of weeds, and delightful to swim in.*

clear off Go away; depart.

clear out 1. Make clean; remove impurities, etc.
   2. Similar to *clear off.*

clear the air Remove misunderstandings, quarrels, ambiguities,
etc., which are impeding progress towards the successful outcome of a particular matter.

clear up 1. Make plain and clear.
- *I am trying to clear up any misunderstanding.*
   2. Make tidy by removing or rearranging.
- *You'll have to clear up the things on the table before we have tea.*
   3. Become fine.
- *The weather has cleared up.*

clear the way Remove obstructions [LIT or MET].
- *This new law will clear the way for many educational
improvements.*

clearing-house Office for the exchange of information.

steer clear of Avoid.

the coast is clear No one is about to see or interfere.

cleft

in a cleft stick In a state of uncertainty. In a dilemma.

cliff

cliff-hanger Event, story, etc. with thrillingly uncertain outcome. Also *cliff-hanging.*

climb

climb down Withdraw from decision, position, etc., previously
taken.

clinch

clinch (an argument, a dispute, the matter, etc.) Settle finally and
completely; conclude.

clip

clip the wings of [LIT] Cut the wing-feathers of a bird so that it is unable to fly at any height. [MET] Limit the powers or authority of a person.

clipped speech Words uttered in short, staccato tones, with the final consonants sharply stressed.

cloak

cloak-and-dagger Surreptitious.

clock

against the clock Under pressure of time.

as regular as clockwork Very regular(ly).

beat the clock Finish before a stated time.

like clockwork Without a hitch.

put the clock back Return to previous (outmoded) ways.

round the clock All day long.

watch the clock Be anxious to finish working-day on time. Hence *clock-watcher* Person who does this.

close

at close quarters Near to.

behind closed doors Privately; secretly.

a closed book Something unknown.

close call or shave Lucky escape.

close down Shut permanently.

close in upon Approach and surround.

close on Almost.

close one's eyes to Ignore.

close ranks Refuse to allow division within an organisation, body, etc.

close season Period of time during which sporting events, etc., do not take place.

close with Grapple with; grasp violently.

close up 1. Move closer together.

2. Fill. Block.

3. Same as *close down.*

closed shop See under **shop.**

cloud

cloud-cuckoo-land An ideal realm.

every cloud has a silver lining Every misfortune has its consolations.

in the clouds Day-dreaming, with one's thoughts elsewhere.

on cloud nine Extremely happy.

under a cloud Regarded with disfavour and distrust; with an injured reputation.

with one's head in the clouds Unrealistic.

clover

in clover In a condition of luxury; very well off.

club

club together Join, combine together (usually to share payment).

clue

be clued up Be well informed.

not have a clue Not know or understand.

clutch

clutch at a straw or straws Eagerly seize any help, support, solution, etc., however flimsy it may be.

coach

drive a coach and four or horses through Easily evade or make ineffective.

coals

carry coals to Newcastle Do something superfluous.

haul over the coals Find fault; blame for some error.

coast

the coast is clear There is no enemy in view; no probability of interference.

coat

cut one's coat according to one's cloth Limit oneself (or one's expenses) to the resources (or money) available.

trail one's coat Seek to pick a quarrel.

cobweb

blow away the cobwebs Revive oneself, usually by going into the open air.

cock

cock-a-hoop Triumphant. Exultant. Boastful.

a cock-and-bull story A fantastic and unbelievable story.

cock-eyed Having a squint. Crooked, not straight or level. Irregular.

cock a snook at Express contempt for. Make a contemptuous

gesture at. (Strictly speaking, placing thumb to nose with fingers outspread.)

cock sure Aggressively sure and certain. Very self-confident. Also *cocky.*

cock of the walk The chief; the dominant person.

go off at half cock Succeed only partially, disappointingly. Proceed half-heartedly, with sense of anti-climax.

knock into a cocked hat Make to appear insignificant.

live like fighting cocks Live on the best and richest food.

cockles

warm the cockles of one's heart Make one's body glow, as with wine. Be deeply moving, delightful. Be emotionally affecting.

coffin

a nail in one's coffin A mistake contributing to one's downfall.

coin

coin money Produce riches very rapidly.

pay back in his own coin Retaliate or retort by the same method as that used against one. Similar to *give tit for tat.*

other side of the coin Opposite aspect of a matter.

to coin a phrase Invent new expression. [Usually ironic apology for using cliché or stating the obvious.]

cold

cold comfort Very slight satisfaction (the phrase is generally used ironically).

get cold feet Lose courage.

give the cold shoulder to Avoid. Shun. Adopt an aloof manner towards.

in cold blood Deliberately. With premeditation.

knock cold Render unconscious.

leave one cold Fail to impress one.

left out in the cold Ignored.

pour or throw cold water on Discourage. Behave very unenthusiastically towards (an idea, proposal, etc.). See also **war.**

collar

hot under the collar Angry. Embarrassed.

colour

colour-blind Unable to distinguish colours correctly, though otherwise possessing normal sight.

give or lend colour to Support; help to prove.

in one's true colours As one really is (as distinct from what is pretended, or supposed).

lend colour Make more believable.

nail one's colours to the mast Adopt a position from which one does not intend to budge.

off-colour Slightly ill.

see the colour of one's money See proof that one has money.

under false colours Falsely; pretending to be what one is not.

with flying colours Triumphantly.

column

dodge the column Avoid duty.

come

come about Occur; happen.

come across 1. [LIT] Cross.
- *He came across the road to speak to me.*

2. [MET] Find casually, discover.
- *Yesterday, when tidying my desk, I came across some old letters.*

3. Project.
- *On television he comes across very unsympathetically.*

come along Make haste.

come to an arrangement Agree; mutually arrange.

come away Leave. Become detached.

come back (Verb) Return. Recur to memory.

come-back (Noun) A return from obscurity to the prominence and success of the past.
- *He's far too old to stage a come-back to professional football.*

come to blows Proceed to fight.

come by Acquire.

come a cropper Fail.

come down Reduce. Fall. Decide. Lose status.

come down on Rebuke. Punish. Also *come down (on one) like a ton of bricks.* See under **ton.**

come in useful Become useful.

come into Inherit.

come into one's own Be seen to one's best advantage.

come into existence Exist; be born; function.
- *The regulations came into existence on June 1st.*

come forward Present oneself.

come to grief Suffer disaster.

come in for Receive; inherit. Encounter.
- *He came in for a good deal of praise for his action.*

come into force Begin to operate.

come in handy Prove to be useful.

come of Become; result from.

- *I don't know what will come of all these developments.*

come off [LIT] Be removable.

- *I can't make the lid come off the saucepan.*

[MET] Reach a successful result.

- *The comedian did his best to amuse us, but it didn't quite come off.*

come off it! Don't be silly!

come off well, badly, etc. End with credit, discredit, etc.

- *For over an hour he was examined in court by the lawyer, and came off well.*

come on 1. Hasten! Move more quickly! Also *come along.*

2. Begin.

- *It came on to rain soon after midnight.*

come out with Utter.

come over 1. Affect, overpower, master, with emotion or illness.

- *I don't know what came over me.*

2. Sound. Project. Make an impression. Perform.

- *His speech on the radio came over very well.*

3. Similar to *come round* (2).

come right Prove itself to be correct.

- *I can't make this sum come right.*

come round 1. Recover (from a faint).

- *We splashed water on her face, and she soon came round.*

2. Visit someone not far away.

- *Come round and see us when you've time.*

3. Modify one's own account or accept another person's view.

- *I discussed the subject for an hour before he came round to my opinion.*

come to (oneself) Identical with *come round* (1).

come to grief Encounter disaster.

come to light Be revealed.

- *No further information has come to light.*

come to nothing Have no results.

come to pass Happen.

come to rest Stop moving.

come to terms Reach a formal agreement.

- *We expect to come to terms about the house very soon.*

come true Actually happen.

come under 1. Be classed among.

2. Be subordinate to.

come upon Encounter. Similar to *come across* (2).

come up to Reach the level of [LIT and MET].

- *The water came up to the top of the bath.*
- *This picture does not come up to the one you showed me yesterday.*

come up to scratch See under **scratch.**

come up with 1. Draw level with.

- *We came up with the travellers at the top of the hill.*

2. Produce. Devise. Suggest.

- *Can you come up with a better way of doing it?*

come what may Whatever may happen in the future.

coming man Person of growing importance.

easy come, easy go What is gained without difficulty may be lost without pain.

have it coming to one Deserve it.

how come? How did that happen?

if it comes to that In that case.

it comes or amounts to this Summarising the situation; stated briefly.

comfort

creature comforts Things which give physical comfort (e.g. food, clothes).

command

at one's command At one's service; available; capable of being used.

commission

out of commission Not working.

common

by common consent By general agreement.

common ground Basis for agreement.

common knowledge Something generally known.

common or garden Ordinary.

common origin An origin in common. The same beginning.

common parlance Plain, ordinary speech.

in common Shared; possessed by each (or all).

in common with Together with.

short commons Not much food.

company

be good company Be a pleasant companion. Hence *in good company.*

in bad company With people of poor reputation.
in company with Together with.
in good company With (counted among) people of merit.
keep person company Be companion to person.
part company Separate; part.

compare
compare notes Discuss impressions and opinions.

comparison
comparisons are odious Any comparison between two persons or things is almost certain to lead to dissatisfaction and trouble.
in comparison with When compared to.

compliment
complimentary tickets Free tickets, given as a compliment to the receiver's position and importance.
compliments of the season Traditional Christmas and New Year greetings.
fish for compliments Speak deprecatingly of oneself in the hope of being contradicted.
give or pay a compliment Express praise politely.
give or send one's compliments Transmit an expression of formal greetings.
return the compliment Repay a pleasant, speech or a kindly action by another.

concern
as far as I am concerned In my opinion.

concert
in concert Unitedly; all together.

conclusion
arrive at or come to the conclusion 1. Perceive; realise after considering all the facts.
  * *I think you'll arrive at the conclusion that it is suitable for the job.*
  2. End.
  * *The debate came to a conclusion soon after midnight.*
foregone conclusion An end so obvious that one is justified in assuming it.
jump to a conclusion Assume rashly and without justification.
try conclusions Test by opposing; fight against.

condition
on condition that If. Provided that.
out of condition In a poor state (e.g. of health, fitness, etc.).

conduct
line of conduct Behaviour.

confidence
confidence trick Swindle based on persuading someone to
entrust money, etc., to one as a sign of confidence in his
honesty.
in strict confidence Absolutely privately.
take person into one's confidence Give person some confidential
information.

confusion
confusion worse confounded Disorder and confusion made even
worse than before.

conjecture
hazard a conjecture Guess.

conjunction
in conjunction with Added to; together with.
- *What you've told me, in conjunction with what I already know,
fills me with confidence.*

conjure
to conjure with Of great importance.

connection
in connection with Relating to. Referring to. Regarding. About.
in that connection As far as that matter is concerned.
miss the connection Miss a train, boat (etc.) which one's present
mode of transport is intended to arrive in time for.
- *My train arrived late at Crewe, and I missed the connection to
Manchester.*

conscience
conscience money Money paid to settle one's conscience.
have on one's conscience Feel guilty about. Also *have a conscience about.*
in all conscience In any imaginable set of circumstances.

consequence
of no consequence Totally unimportant.
- *Don't apologise for breaking the cup—it's of no consequence.*

take the consequences Accept the results (usually of one's own behaviour, actions, etc.).

consideration
in consideration of In return for.
take into consideration Make allowance for.
under consideration Being considered.

construction
put a false construction on Misinterpret; assume wrongly.

contact
come in contact with Meet; encounter.

contempt
bring into contempt Cause to be despised.
fall into contempt Become despised.
hold in contempt Regard with contempt or scorn.

contradiction
contradiction in terms A statement which contradicts itself.

contrary
on the contrary The reverse; the opposite.
  • *I haven't finished. On the contrary, I've only just started.*
contrary to expectation The reverse of what was expected.
  • *Contrary to expectation, he was not present.*
to the contrary To contradict. The opposite.
  • *Unless I hear to the contrary, I'll expect you to arrive on Sunday.*

convenience
at your convenience When, where, etc. it suits you.
at your earliest convenience As soon as you can.
make a convenience of Use for one's own purpose, irrespective of feelings of others.

convert
convert into Change into.
preach to the converted Attempt to persuade people who need no persuasion.

conviction
carry conviction Convince; compel belief in.
  • *His excuse doesn't carry much conviction.*

cook
cook the books Falsify statements (usually financial ones).

cook one's goose Create problems for one.
cook up Prepare. Concoct.
too many cooks spoil the broth One organiser is enough.
what's cooking? What's happening?

cool

cool as a cucumber Completely calm and unexcited.
cool customer (card, hand) A calmly audacious person.
cool down [LIT] Become less heated. [MET] Become calmer.
cool one's heels Wait. Be kept waiting (often as punishment, etc.).
lose one's cool Lose one's temper.
play it cool Deal with it calmly.

copy
copy-cat Imitator.

core
to the core Throughout.

corner
cut corners Do something too rapidly or carelessly.
in a (tight) corner In a difficult position, awkward situation.
just around the corner Very close.
turn the corner Be improving.

correct
speak under correction May be wrong.
stand corrected Accept correction.

cost
at all costs Whatever may be involved; whatever efforts or sacrifice may be needed.
count the cost Consider the risks before acting.

counsel
keep one's own counsel Remain discreetly silent; say nothing of one's own plans.

count
count on Rely on: be sure of.
count one's blessings Be grateful for what one has.
count one's chickens See under **chicken**.
does not count Is immaterial; does not make any difference.
  • *Personal friendship does not seem to count in politics.*

countenance

keep one's countenance Refrain from laughing. Maintain one's composure. Similar to *keep a straight face* (under **face**).

counter

go or *run counter to* Be opposite to. Also *act counter to*: behave contrary to.
- *It is a philosophy which runs entirely counter to everything I believe in.*

courage

Dutch courage Temporary courage created by drinking.

have the courage of one's convictions Be brave enough to speak and act as one really believes.

take one's courage in both hands Nerve oneself (to do something difficult).

summon or *pluck up courage* Succeed in showing bravery in spite of fears.

course

adopt a course Take a certain definite and considered action.

change course Change direction.

in due course Eventually; ultimately; at the appropriate time.

in the course of During.

embark on or *continue a course* Begin a connected series of actions or words.

a matter of course The normal or expected procedure.

run or *take its course* Complete its natural development.

stay the course Have strength to continue to the end.

court

ball is in one's court It is one's turn to act.

hold court Preside (usually over hangers-on, admirers etc.).

Coventry

send to Coventry Disregard completely; refuse to associate with.

cover

cover-up Improper concealment of error (or crime).

cover up for Conceal mistakes of.

from cover to cover From beginning to end (of a book, document, etc.).

take cover Shelter.

under cover 1. [LIT] (a) Sheltered.
- *We were under cover when the rain fell.*

(b) Covered by a wrapping or envelope.

- *I am sending you a parcel under separate cover.*

2. [MET] Concealed by a pretence.

- *Under cover of friendship, he betrayed their trust.*

cow

till the cows come home For an indefinite period; for ever.

- *If we wait for him, we shall wait till the cows come home.*

crack

crack-brained Crazy. Similar to **hare-brained, scatter-brained.**

crack of dawn, at the Very early in the morning.

crack of doom The Day of Judgement, the last day. Commonly used to indicate an infinitely future period.

- *This shed is built to last till the crack of doom.*

crack down on Take firm action to stop.

crackpot Eccentric (person).

crack the whip Show one's authority. Demand more effort (as of man driving a horse).

fair crack of the whip Enough opportunity.

not all it's cracked up to be Not as good as it is said to be.

wisecrack Joke.

creature

creature comforts The material things which make life comfortable—good food, warm clothing, etc.

credit

a credit to A source of honour to or for.

get the credit for Receive due praise for.

give credit to Give praise where it should be given. Believe. Also ***credit where credit is due.***

redound to one's credit; reflect credit upon Be worthy of praise or honour.

creeps

give one the creeps Cause one to shudder with nervous fear. (Generally used less literally to express dislike.)

make one's flesh creep Make one feel as if things were crawling over one's skin (as result of repugnance, fear, etc.).

crest

crestfallen Dejected.

on the crest of a wave Enjoying success.

crocodile
crocodile tears Hypocritical show of regret.

crop
crop up Appear unexpectedly (above the surface) [LIT] and [MET].
- *Weeds always crop up in our flower-bed.*
- *I never expected that this problem would crop up again.*

cross
cross one's mind Occur to one.

(talk) at cross purposes (Discuss) from incompatible points of view, owing to a misunderstanding.

cross or pass the Rubicon Take any irrevocable step.

cross as two sticks In an extremely bad temper.

cross swords See **sword.**

get or have one's wires crossed Misunderstand.

keep one's fingers crossed or cross one's fingers Hope for good luck.

paths do not cross Ways of life do not cause people to meet each other.

crow
crow's feet The small wrinkles which age, ill-health or trouble cause to form at the corners of one's eyes.

as the crow flies In a straight line, regardless of obstructions.
- *The villages are ten miles apart as the crow flies, but nearly fifteen miles by road.*

crow over Boast about one's triumph over.

crown
to crown it all As a final misfortune.

cruise
cruising speed An economic travelling speed, less than full speed.

crumb
crumb of comfort A tiny amount of comfort.

crunch
when the crunch comes or when it comes to the crunch When the decisive moment arrives.

cry
cry for the moon Ask for the impossible.

cry off Refuse, or cease, to share in or co-operate.

cry one's eyes or *heart out* Weep bitterly.

cry out for Stand in obvious need of.

cry over spilt milk Express regrets too late, or when nothing is to be gained by expressing them.

cry stinking fish Speak unfavourably about one's own profession, trade, family, endeavours, etc.

cry wolf Cause excitement or anxiety by spreading false news.

crying need Urgent need.

a far cry A long way. Very different.

● *Farm eggs are a far cry from the ones we get in the local shops.*

in full cry Noisily pursuing.

crystal

crystal ball Means of foretelling the future.

crystal clear Extremely clear.

cuckoo

cuckoo in the nest Unwanted intruder.

cud

chew the cud Reflect.

cudgel

cudgel or rack one's brains [LIT] Beat one's brains (a 'cudgel' is a stick) to compel them to work. [MET] Try to compel one's brains to function, and to understand or remember. Think hard.

● *I've cudgelled my brains, but I can't recollect where I put it.*

take up the cudgels Vigorously defend or support a cause.

cue

take one's cue from Follow example or advice of.

cuff

off the cuff Without prior thought, planning, preparation, etc.

● *I won't prepare a speech: I'll talk off the cuff.*

cup

one's cup (of happiness) is filled One's happiness is absolutely complete.

● *With his family around him and no fears for the future, his cup was filled.*

cup that cheers Tea.

in one's cups In the process of getting drunk. Intoxicated.

not one's cup of tea Not something that interests or suits one.

cupboard

cupboard love Affection shown only in the hope of obtaining something in return.

curl

curl up Experience embarrassment.
enough to make one's hair curl Frightening.

currency

acquire or *obtain* or *gain currency* Circulate; become publicly discussed.

curry

curry favour Attempt by flattery, bribery, etc., to become popular.

curtain

curtain raiser Event preceding a more important one.
curtains for The end of.
ring down the curtain Bring to an end.

customer

ugly (awkward, tough, etc.) customer A difficult or dangerous person to deal with.

cut

a cut above Better than.
cut across Transcend.
cut back on Reduce. Also *cut-back.* Reduction.
  - *Production at the factory has been cut back because of the strike.*
cut both ways Has a second and compensating effect. Has an effect on both sides (of an argument, etc.).
  - *Her refusal to live with him cuts both ways—he won't be responsible for maintaining her.*
cut a dash, a figure Exhibit oneself as a smart or fashionable person.
cut dead Ignore (person).
cut down 1. [LIT]
  - *He cut down a tree.*
  2. [MET] Reduce.
  - *He has cut down his expenses since he changed his job.*
cut down to size Reduce (person's) sense of self-importance.
cut and dried Already arranged or prepared.
  - *His plans for leaving were all cut and dried.*

cut fine Allow little margin for accident, etc.
- *You may catch the train, but you are cutting it rather fine.*

cut in 1. Interrupt.
- *Simon cut in with an interesting suggestion.*

2. Admit.
- *Shall we cut them in on the plans?*

3. (Of a car, pedestrian, etc.) Obstruct, or neatly obstruct, by placing oneself in front of another after overtaking.
- *The taxi cut in very sharply, and I had to brake.*

cut the (Gordian) knot Take a quick and drastic method of ending a difficulty.

cut of one's jib The face and general appearance.

cut one's coat See **coat**.

cut one's losses Abandon any further attempts to continue a business or enterprise which has not been profitable, and limit one's losses to those already incurred.

cut off 1. Sever; cut.
- *She is going to have all her hair cut off.*

2. Separate. Also (of telephone) disconnect.
- *That remote village will entirely cut her off from her friends.*

cut off one's nose to spite one's face Behave spitefully, damaging oneself.

cut off with a shilling Bequeath nothing, or practically nothing, to a person.

cut one's teeth on Gain early experience from.

cut out 1. [LIT] Cut round, as with a pair of scissors.

2. [MET] Supplant.

3. Designed for, suitable for.
- *I don't think you're cut out to be a soldier.*

Also *cut it out!* Stop doing or saying that!

cut-price At a reduced rate.

cut or *wounded to the quick* Hurt intensely.

cut and thrust Rapid exchange.
- *A barrister needs to be quick-witted to survive the cut-and-thrust of the court-room.*

cut short End abruptly.
- *The preacher cut short his sermon when the church caught fire.*

cut-throat Ruthless.

cut up 1. [LIT] Cut into small pieces.

2. [MET] Distressed, unhappy.
- *She was terribly cut up when she heard the news.*

cut up rough Become violently angry.
not cut out for Not suitable for.
short cut See **short.**

D

dab
a dab hand An expert.

daggers
at daggers drawn In a state of open and bitter hostility.
look daggers Look at fiercely and angrily.

damn
damn with faint praise Praise in so formal and limited a manner that it is an obvious cloak to adverse criticism or dislike.
(I'll be) damned if I know I don't know (emphatic).
do one's damnedest Do one's very best.
not give a damn Not care in the slightest.
not worth a damn Worthless.

damp
a damp squib A squib is a small firework which sends out showers of sparks and finally explodes. If, however, it is not dry, it will do neither. Hence, anything which has failed is said to have 'gone off like a damp squib'.
damp down Suppress.
put the damper on Prevent by repression.

dance
dance attendance Attend obsequiously to every whim or requirement of a person.
lead person a dance Cause person inconvenience over a time.

Darby
Darby and Joan An aged and devoted husband and wife.

dare

dare-devil A daring and reckless person.

I dare say It is probable.

dark

a dark horse A person whose qualities are not well known.

in the dark In ignorance.

keep it dark Keep it secret.

leap or *shot in the dark* Rash action, taken without being able to see the consequences.

dash

dash off 1. Hurry away.

- *He dashed off for help.*

2. Write in great haste.

- *He dashed off a note to his wife.*

dash one's hopes Abruptly destroy one's hopes.

date

out of date Obsolete; belonging to an earlier period.

up to date Recent. Fashionable. Current.

daunted

nothing daunted Not discouraged.

Davy Jones

Davy Jones' locker The sea-bed.

dawn

dawn on Become perceptible to.

day

all day or *night long* Continuously; throughout the day (or night).

all in a day's work Part of one's usual routine.

any day At any time or in any circumstances.

at the end of the day In the final reckoning.

broad daylight Full and complete daylight.

- *The house was robbed in broad daylight.*

call it a day Consider work on any particular job ended for the day or for the present time.

carry the day See **carry.**

dark days Days of trouble and distress.

daydream A reverie or flight of the imagination. Also used as a verb.

day in, day out All day and every day.

daylight robbery Exorbitantly expensive.

days or *hours are numbered* The end (e.g. death) is inevitable, and is approaching.

- *The revolution became less vigorous; it was plain that its days were numbered.*

days of old or *of yore* A long time ago; the remote past.

- *In days of yore people believed in dragons.*

day off Day spent away from work.

days to come The future.

every dog has his day Every person has some good fortune at some time or other.

fallen on evil days In misfortune.

happy as the day is long Very happy

have a field day Enjoy unusual success.

have had one's day Be past one's best or be no longer useful.

the livelong day All day; the whole of the time. [Old f.]

make one's day Make one happy.

name the day Literally, the day which a girl nominates as her wedding-day. (But frequently used in the sense of 'consent to marry', no exact date being specified.)

not one's day An unsuccessful time.

the good old days The past, when things were better.

the old or *olden days* The past.

one of these (fine) days Soon.

a rainy day An emergency, a period of misfortune for which money, etc., has been reserved.

see better days Be happier and more prosperous (almost always used in the past tense).

that will be the day That is unlikely to happen.

those were the days Those were good times.

dead

This word is commonly used in the sense of 'absolute' and 'absolutely', e.g. **dead centre, dead level, dead straight, dead certain, dead sure.**

dead as a doornail (Emphatically) dead. Also **dead as mutton.**

dead as the dodo Obsolete.

dead end Having no way out.

dead hand Stultifying influence.

dead heat Event in which two competitors finish at exactly the same time.

dead letter A law or regulation which exists but is never enforced.

(waiting for a) dead man's shoes (Waiting for) an advantage that may be obtained when someone dies, or retires, or is promoted, etc.

(in) dead(ly) earnest Extremely seriously.
- *He spoke quickly, in low tones, and in deadly earnest.*

dead of night The darkest, most silent time of night.

dead to the world Utterly exhausted; sleeping deeply; or unconscious for any other cause.

dead wood Useless thing or person.

over my dead body Exaggerated expression meaning 'overruling my strongest wishes'.
- *If that dog comes into the house again, it will be over my dead body.*

wouldn't be seen dead in Would under no circumstances wear or go to.

deaf

deaf as a post Unable to hear.

fall on deaf ears Be ignored.

turn a deaf ear Ignore.

deal

a raw deal Unfair or unduly harsh treatment.

a square deal An honest bargain.

it's a deal I agree.

death

at death's door On the verge of dying; desperately, almost hopelessly, ill.

be the death of Cause death to.

death-trap Dangerous thing or place.

do to death Overdo.

in at the death Arriving in time to see the climax.

jaws of death Extreme danger; risk of death.
- *The firemen rescued the child from the jaws of death.*

like grim death With all one's strength.

pale as death As pale as though already dead.

sick or tickled to death Extremely disgruntled or amused.
   (The phrase *to death* is added to many other verbs to intensify them).

a death-warrant [LIT] A legal warrant authorising execution. [MET] State of being in serious difficulties, on the verge of extinction.

- *The defeat at Culloden was the death-warrant of the hopes of the Jacobites.*

Also **death-blow.**

to the death Till one combatant is killed.

deep

go off the deep end Become very angry.

in deep water(s) Into complex matters. In difficulties.

still waters run deep What appears quiet (e.g. a person) may have hidden emotions, etc.

throw in at the deep end Require (person) to do something without preparation, training, etc.

default

by default As a result of failure to act or appear.

degree

to a degree To a certain extent.

deliver

deliver the goods Keep one's promise to do something.

delusion

delusions of grandeur Belief that one is important, or capable of becoming more powerful.

demean

demean oneself Lower one's dignity.

- *I would not demean myself by apologising.*

demon

a demon for Very committed to.

depend

depend upon Rely upon; have faith in.

- *You may depend upon our goods; they are of the best quality.*

depend upon it Be certain; have no doubt.

that depends That can only happen in certain conditions.

depth

out of or **beyond one's depth** Literally, one's 'depth' is the depth of water beyond which one's feet no longer touch the bottom, so that one must either swim or drown. Used as an idiom, 'out of one's depth' indicates a subject beyond one's knowledge or understanding.

deserve

richly deserve 'Richly' here means thoroughly, completely.

design

by design Deliberately.

have designs on Have (usually harmful or unpopular) plans for.

desire

leave a lot to be desired Have faults, deficiencies, weaknesses, etc.

despair

yield or give away to despair Give up hope.

devil

between the devil and the deep (blue) sea Between two equally dangerous or unpleasant alternatives.

devil-may-care A reckless person.

devil's advocate One who makes unpopular suggestions without seriously believing them, i.e. simply to ensure that all sides of a case have been considered.

devil take the hindmost The outcome does not matter.

give the devil his due Admit good, even in someone of whom one disapproves.

hold a candle to the devil (From fear or caution) assist someone of whom one disapproves.

needs must when the devil drives If something must be done, then it must be done.

play the very devil with Create disorder in.

  • *Too much garlic plays the very devil with my digestion.*

talk of the devil Applied (usually jocularly) to someone who has been a topic of conversation and who then unexpectedly arrives.

diamond

rough diamond Worthy person with roughness of manner, speech, dress, etc.

dice

dice are loaded against one One's chances of success are poor.

dice with death Take a risk.

die

be dying for Long for.

be dying of Be vexed by.

die away Become more and more faint, until the sound cannot be heard at all.

die down Subside; become calm after violence.

die hard Be slow to diminish.

die in harness Die while still at one's work.

die laughing Laugh so much that one is completely exhausted.

never say die Do not surrender.

the die is cast An irrevocable decision has been taken.

difference

make all the difference Be very significant.

split the difference Halve the amount in dispute.

- *You ask twelve pounds; I offer eight. Will you split the difference and accept ten?*

sink one's differences End a quarrel.

dig

dig one's heels or toes, feet in Be stubborn.

dignity

stand on one's dignity Require that one is treated with respect.

dilemma

on the horns of a dilemma In a position where a choice has to be made between alternatives that are unpleasant in either case; in a difficult position.

dim

take a dim view of Feel dissatisfaction for.

dint

by dint of By means of.

dip

dip into (one's pocket etc.) Spend from.

dirt

dirt cheap Very inexpensive.

do someone's dirty work Do someone's unpleasant task for him.

do the dirty on Play an unpleasant trick on.

discount

at a discount Not required, or not fully appreciated. (Also [LIT] At a reduced price.)

- *Books about the war are at a discount just now.*

discretion
See **valour.**

discussion
open a discussion Begin a discussion.

distance
keep one's distance Refrain from becoming familiar or intimate.

ditch
dull as ditch-water Extremely dull.

divine
divine right A right supposedly received direct from God, applied chiefly to the right of sovereigns to occupy their thrones regardless of their suitability, or of their subjects' wishes, but also applied to other situations.
- *He behaves as if he has a divine right to be unpleasant.*

do
1. Be sufficient or suitable.
- *A small loaf will do for the family's breakfast.*
2. Exert oneself.
- *I'll do all I can.*
3. Visit a theatre, etc., as part of a plan.
- *We did two concerts and the Royal Academy last week.*

do or *make away with* Dispose of, usually by destroying. Abolish.
do or die Not be deterred.
do out of Prevent (usually dishonestly) from getting.
do to death Kill; murder. Also [MET] Repeat so frequently that all interest is 'killed'.
- *The whole subject has been done to death in the newspapers.*

do up Repair.
do with Need.
doing Happening.
done Completely cooked.
- *The pudding is done.*

done in Exhausted.
have done with Cease to have any connection with.
have to do with Have dealings, relationship with.
- *I refuse to have anything to do with that matter.*

I could do with I should like. I ought.
it isn't done It is socially forbidden; taboo.

nothing doing No chance of success.
take some doing Be difficult to do.

doctor
just what the doctor ordered Exactly what is needed.

dog
a dog's chance No chance at all.
a dog's life A very unpleasant existence.
dog-days (Traditionally July 3rd to August 4th.) The hottest weeks of the summer.
dog doesn't eat dog See *honour among thieves.*
dog-eared Applied to pages which, by constant handling, have become bent or curled at the corners.
dog in the manger A person so selfish that he will not allow people to enjoy something he himself cannot enjoy. Also adjective: *A dog-in-the-manger attitude.*
dog-tired Very tired.
every dog has his day No one is always unlucky.
give a dog a bad name When one has acquired a bad reputation, it is difficult to lose.
go to the dogs Be ruined.
hair of the dog that bit you A drink taken to cure the effects of too much drinking.
help a lame dog over a stile Help someone who is in need of assistance, usually financial.
in the doghouse In disgrace.
like a dog with two tails Very happy.
not a dog's chance No chance at all.
rain cats and dogs Rain very heavily.
under-dog One who is in a helpless or inferior position, who has no power to assert his wishes or authority.

doldrums
in the doldrums Depressed and miserable.

donkey
donkey's years A very long time.
talk the hind-legs off a donkey Talk incessantly.

door
behind closed doors In secret.
close the door to Exclude.
foot in the door Chance of success.

leave the door open to Leave available the possibility of.

show a person the door [LIT] Escort him to the door. [MET] Order him to leave.

dot

dot the i's and cross the t's Put the final details to a piece of work.

on the dot Exactly. Precisely. Promptly.

the year dot Very long ago.

double

at the double or *in double quick time* Very quickly.

double back Turn and go back.

double-crossing Tricking or betraying people who believed they were dealing with trustworthy friends.

double-dealing Trickery and deceit.

double-edged Possessing a double significance. Sarcastic. Ironical.

double-quick Extremely quickly. At the double.

● *I dashed to the door, double-quick, but was too late to catch him.*

double-talk Ambiguous statement, deliberately intended to be evasive.

double time Twice the normal amount of wages.

● *We earn time and a half on Saturday afternoons, and double time on Sundays.*

doubt

beyond a doubt; without doubt With absolute certainty.

doubting Thomas Disbelieving person.

in doubt Uncertain; hesitant.

● *When in doubt, do what your conscience advises.*

shadow of doubt Very slight uncertainty. (Frequently in the negative to indicate complete certainty.)

● *The judge said he had no shadow of doubt of the prisoner's guilt.*

down

be down on Disapprove of.

do down Vilify. Cheat. Overcome.

down-and-out Destitute person. Tramp.

down-hearted Dejected.

down on one's luck Temporarily unfortunate.

down in the mouth Depressed-looking; miserable. Similar to *in the doldrums* and *in the dumps.*

down and out In a state of complete destitution.

down-to-earth Straightforward.
have a down on Disapprove of.

dozen
baker's dozen Thirteen.
dozens of Lots of.
talk nineteen to the dozen Talk incessantly.

drag
drag one's feet Display reluctance.
drag in Introduce, usually unnecessarily.
drag on Continue in tedious way.
drag out Lengthen.
drag up or in Talk about some subject which it is not tactful or necessary to discuss.

drain
down the drain Wasted.
   • *Paying that much would be money down the drain.*

draught
feel a draught Experience difficult conditions.

draw
draw a blank Have no success.
   • *The police searched all day, but drew a complete blank.*
draw aside 1. [LIT] Draw, as one draws a curtain.
   2. [MET] Separate a person from others.
   • *After the meeting, he drew me aside to discuss the situation.*
draw away Withdraw from; shrink from. Leave.
draw back Withdraw from an undertaking.
draw to an end Reach the end; finish.
draw (person's) fire Weaken person's attack by deflecting it.
draw in 1. Shrink; become shorter. (Applied especially to the period between summer and winter, when the hours of daylight decrease.)
   • *After September the days seem to draw in very quickly.*
   2. Move to the side of the road, or stop entirely.
   See *draw up* (3).
draw the line at Stop short of.
draw near Approach; come near.
draw off Cause to flow away.
   • *We must draw off the water from the tank.*
draw out 1. Remove money from a bank or company.

- *I drew out a hundred pounds last week.*
2. Encourage to talk.
- *The boy was very shy, but we succeeded in drawing him out about his hobbies.*

draw rein Pull at a horse's rein to compel it to stop.

draw up 1. Arrange in correct order (applicable both to people and to legal documents).
- *He drew up an agreement.*
- *The troops will be drawn up on the parade ground.*
2. Raise; pull up.
- *The people used to draw up water from the well.*
3. Stop; halt.
- *The taxi drew up at the station entrance.*

draw game or draw Term applied to any match or competition which ends in both sides being absolutely equal. Similar to *dead heat.*

go back to the drawing-board Begin again (usually to make plans).

dream
like a dream Exactly as one would wish.

drib
in dribs and drabs In small quantities.

drink
drink like a fish Drink (alcohol) heavily.

drive
drive away, off 1. Depart, in a vehicle.
- *I must drive away in five minutes.*
2. Compel someone or something to leave quickly.
- *These flies are a nuisance; please drive them away.*

drive a bargain Arrive at an agreement, usually after forceful negotiation.

drive home 1. [LIT] Hammer a nail, etc., as far as it can go.
2. [MET] Emphasise.
- *The message was driven home by frequent repetition in the course of his speech.*

driving or getting at Implying; hinting.
in the driver's seat In charge.

drop
at the drop of a hat Very readily.

drop 1. Cease to be friends with (a person).

2. Abandon, cease to discuss (a subject).

- *I don't wish to discuss the matter further, so let's drop it.*

drop behind Be overtaken.

drop by or in Call casually and informally.

- *Drop in for tea whenever you're passing.*

drop a hint See under **hint.**

drop a line Send a short letter.

drop in the ocean or bucket A small and inadequate matter compared with the whole subject.

drop off Fall asleep.

drop on 1. Select for questioning, etc.

2. Blame.

drop out Absent oneself; cease to compete.

a drop too much An intoxicating amount of drink.

fit to drop Very tired.

duck

dead duck Matter unlikely to continue.

make a duck or duck's egg (cricket only) Be dismissed without scoring.

make ducks and drakes 1. Send small flat stones skimming horizontally over the surface of the sea, a pond, etc.

2. Scatter one's fortune in extravagant living.

sitting duck Person or thing vulnerable to attack, criticism, etc.

take to something like a duck to water Become used to something very readily.

See **ugly.**

due

give person or the devil his due Be fair to person, however little he or she may deserve it.

dull

dull the edge of Make less enjoyable, interesting, significant, etc.

dumps

(down) in the dumps Thoroughly depressed. Similar to *in the doldrums; down in the mouth.*

duration

for the duration For a very long time.

duress

under duress Compelled by moral or physical force.

- *He confessed, under duress, to several crimes.*

dust
bite the dust Come to an end.
throw dust in the eyes Hoodwink; mislead and confuse.
shake the dust from one's feet Leave.

Dutch
double Dutch Gibberish.
Dutch courage Courage induced by drinking.
go Dutch Pay for oneself (in restaurant, etc.).
talk to one like a Dutch uncle Advise in a firm but friendly manner.

duty
in duty bound Compelled by a sense of duty.

dye
dyed in the wool Permanently ingrained.

E

ear

about one's ears Around one.

    ● *All his hopes fell about his ears.*

all ears Listening attentively.

    ● *When they came in, they were all ears.*

box a person's ears Administer a sharp slap on the side of the head.

    ● *If you don't go to bed at once I'll box your ears.*

(play) by ear 1. Without any technical knowledge, merely by a natural appreciation of the sounds.

    ● *She plays the piano entirely by ear.*

    2. Without preparation.

    ● *I haven't decided what to say when he comes; I'll play it by ear.*

come to or reach one's ears Be heard or known.

an ear for A natural appreciation for.

earshot Hearing distance.

ear-splitting Deafening; distressingly loud and shrill.

ears burning A sign that one is being talked about. (Used jocularly.)

fall on deaf ears Not be heard or listened to.

a flea in the ear Truths, usually unpleasant.

    ● *A salesman came to the door, but I sent him away with a flea in his ear.*

give one's ears Make almost any sacrifice to obtain.

    ● *I'd give my ears to visit Venice this spring.*

have or keep one's ear to the ground Be aware of what is likely to happen.

have the ear of Be in a position to advise someone.

- *If you want to get anything done about it, you'll have to find someone who has the ear of the manager.*

head over ears Completely.

in at one ear and out at the other Without being appreciated or remembered.

- *Everything we try to teach the boy goes in at one ear and out at the other.*

prick up one's ears Listen with sudden attention to something heard unexpectedly.

set by the ears Make quarrel.

throw out on one's ear Eject forcibly.

turn a deaf ear Refuse to listen.

up to the ears Deeply immersed.

wet behind the ears Inexperienced.

early

early bird Person who arrives or gets out of bed early.

early days Too early.

keep early hours Go to bed early.

earth

bring down to earth (with a bump) Make (person) face reality.

come down to earth Return to reality.

cost the earth Cost a lot of money.

go to earth Disappear from the places in which one is usually seen.

on earth Emphatic addition to many expressions.

run to earth Find after search.

earnest

in earnest; in dead or good earnest Serious; the reverse of joking.

ease

ease out Remove (person) gradually (from post, etc.).

put or set at ease Make unembarrassed and socially happy by friendliness.

- *He has a knack of putting visitors at their ease.*

ill at ease Uncomfortable. Anxious.

easy

easy on the eye (Person) enjoyable to look at.

I'm easy I don't mind.

in easy circumstances Financially comfortable; rich enough to be able to live without worrying.

in Easy Street Enjoying wealth or comfort.

easy money 1. One from whom money is easily obtained.

    2. Money which is easily earned.

go easy on 1. Not use or do to excess.

- *I'm over-weight; I'll have to go easy on fatty food.*

    2. Not make difficulties for (a person).

take it easy Relax.

eat

eat away Penetrate and use up.

- *The sea had eaten away much of the shore.*

eat one's cake See under **cake**.

eat humble pie Behave meekly, apologetically.

eat into Similar to *eat away.*

eat one's hat Be very surprised.

eat one's head off Eat very large quantities.

eat one's heart out Pine. Grieve continuously.

eat out of house and home Eat so much that one would have to sell one's house to pay for food. (Often used jokingly of hungry children.)

eat out of one's hand Do as one asks.

eat one's words Completely and ignominiously withdraw a statement.

edge

edge away Move gradually away (as a boat moves very slowly from the edge of the shore).

edge out Same as *ease out.*

have an edge on one's appetite Be hungry.

have the edge over Have a slight advantage over.

on edge In a state of nervous tension.

- *We were all on edge to know the news.*

rough edge of one's tongue A reprimand.

set one's teeth on edge Cause feelings of revulsion and general discomfort, usually at unpleasant sound, but also because of embarrassing speech or action.

take the edge off Reduce the effect of.

edgeways See **word.**

educate

educated guess Guess based on knowledge, experience, information etc.

effect

bring (carry) into effect Put into operation.
for effect In order to create a particular impression.
give effect to Make operative.
in effect Stated briefly and in other words.
take effect Operate; function.
to that effect With that meaning, result, etc.
with effect from Beginning at.

egg

As sure as eggs is eggs Stated with absolute certainty.
   • *As sure as eggs is eggs it will rain tomorrow.*
a duck's egg (cricket) See under **duck.**
don't teach your grandmother to suck eggs Don't offer advice to
   people who are more experienced than you are.
get egg on one's face Be made to look ridiculous.
put all one's eggs in one basket Invest all one's resources, financial or otherwise, in a single enterprise.

elbow

elbow one's way Push forward by thrusting with one's elbows.
   Frequently used metaphorically:
   • *They're trying to elbow their way into the tennis club committee.*
elbow-grease Physical effort using hand and arm.
elbow-room Space in which to move.
   • *We're moving to an office in which we shall have more
     elbow-room.*
out at elbows (Of garment) Worn out.
up to the elbows Very busy.

element

in one's element In a congenial atmosphere and surroundings.
out of one's element In an uncongenial atmosphere or surroundings. Similar to *a fish out of water.*

elephant

white elephant Troublesome, unwanted and unused thing.

eleven

the eleventh hour The latest possible time before it is too late.

embargo

lay or place an embargo on An embargo is a legal prohibition.
   The phrase is also loosely applied to any definite impediment.

embark
embark on Begin.

empty
empty-handed Bringing or taking nothing.
empty-headed Stupid.
on an empty stomach Not having eaten for some time.

end
at a loose end Unoccupied.
  • *Give me a ring if you're at a loose end tonight.*
at an end Finished.
at one's wits' end Mentally desperate, and unable to find a solution. Also used jocularly (as an exaggeration) to mean simply 'in a state of confusion', or 'unable to think clearly'.
come to a sticky end End in failure.
end of the road Point beyond which no progress is possible.
end on With the end of one thing next to the end of another.
end up Finish by.
to the bitter end To the extreme end, whatever may happen.
  • *I intend to see this matter through to the bitter end.*
ends of the earth [LIT] The most distant parts of the world. [MET] A considerable distance.
the end of one's tether The limit of one's endurance or patience.
  • *We had been walking all day, and were at the end of our tether.*
the end of the road or *line* Conclusion of a matter.
in the end Finally.
make (both) ends meet Make one's income enough for one's expenses. (More frequently used in the negative.)
  • *I cannot make ends meet on my salary.*
no end of Very much.
on end Continuously.
  • *The rain has been falling for days on end.*
put an end to Finish; terminate. (Applied to something which has already existed for some time.)
  • *The King decided to put an end to the barons' quarrels.*
tie up the loose ends Arrange the final details.
to no end or *purpose* Without effect or result.
  • *The priest tried to put the fire out, but to no end.*

enemy
be one's own worst enemy Bring about one's own misfortunes.

English

murder the Queen's English 'Queen's English', or 'standard English', is the English language as spoken by educated people. To 'murder' it is to use it incorrectly or to speak it with a very bad accent.

enough

enough and to spare Ample; more than is needed.

- *Ten metres of carpet will be enough and to spare.*

enough to wake the dead Very loud, noisy.

- *The racket at the party was enough to wake the dead.*

oddly enough Unexpectedly; surprisingly. ('Enough' here is equivalent to 'in the circumstances', 'considering the conditions', etc.) Similarly, *curiously, strangely, remarkably enough,* etc.

- *We met by chance in Egypt, and a year later, oddly enough, in New York.*

sure enough As was to be expected.

enquiry

in the course of enquiry While enquiries were being made; during an investigation.

- *In the course of an enquiry, it was discovered that he had never been in the Army.*

searching enquiry Close, thorough and detailed enquiry.

- *The Government promise a searching enquiry into the whole matter.*

enter

enter into 1. Comprehend; understand.

- *We can enter into your feelings of relief.*

2. Occupy oneself with.

- *We cannot enter into details at present.*
- *The two old men entered into (or upon) a long discussion.*

enter into an agreement Agree; undertake.

- *The firm will enter into an agreement to supply five thousand pairs of shoes.*

enter a protest Complain. Register a protest.

enter up Make an entry.

- *Please enter up these figures in the account book.*

enter upon Begin.

- *We are entering upon a new epoch in the history of civilisation.*

entry
make an entry 1. Record in a book.
2. Enter formally or ceremoniously.

envy
be the envy of Be envied by.

err
err on the right side or on the side of Risk possible error by attempting to avoid a more serious one.

error
clerical error Slip of the pen.

escutcheon
blot on one's escutcheon Damage to one's reputation.

essence
of the essence Of the utmost importance.

esteem
hold in (high) esteem, honour, etc. Regard as deserving.

estimate
form an estimate Judge in a general way.
rough estimate A rough calculation; an approximation.

eternity
for an eternity For a very long time.

even
even so In spite of, even after the circumstances have been considered.
be or get even with Be revenged upon; pay back an injury.
   ● *He beat me, but I'll be even with him next time we play.*
have an even chance Be equally likely to succeed or fail.
on an even keel 1. [LIT] Well balanced.
2. [MET] Smooth.
   ● *Their relationship has been stormy, but it now seems to be on an even keel.*
there is an even chance It is as likely as not.

event
at all events Nevertheless; yet.
Similar to *at any rate*.
course of events A succession of events; a number of events that followed.

● *The course of events made it necessary for him to go to America.*

in any event Whatever may happen.

● *I hope to go tomorrow; in any event I shall go before Saturday.*

Similar to *in any case; in any circumstances; happen what may.*

in the event As things turned out.

in the event of If a specified event should take place.

● *In the event of fire, ring the alarm-bell.*

be wise after the event State what should have been done to avert a disaster when it has already occurred.

ever

Widely used as a form of emphasis.

● *Did you ever hear such nonsense. Come as quick as ever you can. Whatever will he do next?*

ever such a A very.

for ever and a day [LIT] Always; eternally. [MET] For a long time.

● *We won't reach agreement if we sit here for ever and a day.*

for ever and ever Similar to *for ever and a day.*

every

every now and again. Every now and then. Every so often. From time to time.

every other 1. [LIT] Every alternate.

2. [MET] (Applied only to the singular.)

● *1. Every other man carried a lighted torch.*

● *2. She asks questions every other minute.*

evil

put off the evil hour or *day* Postpone.

example

make an example of Inflict punishment on an individual who has done wrong as a warning to others who might behave in the same way.

set an example to Behave in a way that should be copied by.

exception

take exception to Object. Feel offended by.

● *I take exception to your statement that I am bad tempered.*

the exception that proves the rule An action which draws one's attention to the fact that most people (as a rule) behave very differently, and that the action in question is an exception to the rule.

excess
in excess of More than.

exchange
exchange is no robbery Unfair exchange is better than robbery. (Jocular excuse for unfair exchange.)

excuse
excuse oneself Apologise for leaving (or not attending).

execution
put into execution Do something already planned or arranged. Similar to *carry out.*
- *They wanted to go abroad, but realised that it would be some months before they could put their plan into execution.*

exercise
exercise power Exert power or influence.
- *The Queen cannot exercise political power, though she frequently offers advice.*
object of the exercise Purpose of what is happening or planned.

exhibition
make an exhibition of oneself Act so as to appear foolish.

expect
expect me when you see me I cannot say when I shall be back.

expense
at one's expense 1. [LIT] Causing financial expense to one.
  2. [MET] Causing inconvenience, embarrassment, discredit, etc., to one.
at the expense of In a way that causes damage to.
go to the expense of Spend money on.
put one to expense Make one spend money.

explain
explain away Remove uncertainty by persuasive and reasonable explanations.
- *I didn't believe her at first, but she managed to explain away my doubts.*

extent

to a certain or ***considerable*** or ***large extent*** To a limited (considerable, large) degree; partially.

extreme

go to extremes Take an extreme course of action.

go to the other extreme Do the exact opposite.

eye

all my eye Nonsense.

apple of one's eye Loved and prized intensely.
  - *Her son was the apple of her eye.*

a black eye The result of being struck so violently in the face that the flesh surrounding the eye is bruised and blackened.

cast an eye over Glance at.

catch someone's eye Meet the gaze of a person for a brief time.
  - *The schoolboy caught the teacher's eye, and stopped talking.*

easy on the eye Pleasant to look at.

eye-opener Something surprisingly informative or revealing.

an eye for Ability to appreciate (visual).
  - *He has always had an eye for a bargain.*

See also ***an ear for; a taste for.***

an eye for an eye Revenge. Retaliation.

to eye To glance at, usually with suspicion.

have a good eye for Be clever at assessing or choosing.

have an eye to the main chance Be alert for opportunities of personal profit.

have one's eyes about one Be observant and alert.

in the eyes of Regarded by.
  - *In the eyes of our grandparents, Picasso's paintings would have seemed absurd.*

keep an eye on Watch; devote some attention to.

eye of the law See under **law.**

keep one's eyes peeled or ***skinned*** Watch intently.

make (sheep's) eyes at Ogle. Look amorously, provocatively or seductively.

in one's mind's eye Mentally; as a mental vision.
  - *In my mind's eye I can still see my old home.*

one in the eye for An unpleasant shock for.

run an or ***the eye over*** Glance over; survey quickly.
  - *Do you mind running your eye over these accounts.*

see eye to eye Regard in the same way; agree.
  - *I hope we shall see eye to eye in this matter.*

see with half an eye Realise easily, and at once.

than meets the eye Than is apparent.

up to the eyes or *eyebrows, in* Immersed; completely occupied with.

with an eye to With a definite object in one's mind.

- *I bought the barn with an eye to converting it into a cottage.*

with one's eyes open Fully aware of the circumstances.

with one's eyes shut 1. Carelessly.

- *He must have gone into the business with his eyes shut.*

2. Very easily.

- *I could do it with my eyes shut.*

with the naked eye Without the assistance of a telescope, etc.

F

face

at face value As (it) seems to be.

face; face up to Accept and meet a situation without flinching.

face about Turn in the opposite direction.

face down Overcome (person) by boldness.

face to face Directly opposite; confronting one another.

- *The brothers came face to face in a crowd.*

(one's) face fell (One) showed disappointment.

face the music Accept the unfortunate consequences.

- *We were in the wrong, so we'll have to face the music.*

face it out Meet a situation. Show effrontery.

- *He knew he was in the wrong, but was determined to face it out.*

face value Nominal or superficial value.

- *The face value of the stamp was a penny, but it was worth fifty pounds.*

fly in the face of Commit an act which is obviously rash, foolish or provocative.

have a long face or a face like a fiddle Look miserable. See also **pull.**

have the face or the nerve to Have the effrontery or impertinence to.

- *I'm surprised that you have the face to ask again.*

keep a straight face Remain serious.

Similar to *keep one's countenance.*

let's face it Let us be quite clear about it.

look one in the face (Dare to) meet one without shame.

lose face Be humiliated. Lose some of one's credit or reputation, etc.

make a face or *faces* Twist and contort one's features, usually in contempt or dislike, or to make someone laugh.

on the face of it As it appears; judging from what has been stated.

- *On the face of it, you have been very badly treated.*

put a good or *brave* or *bold face upon it* Behave cheerfully, and as though there was nothing wrong.

put a new face on Alter.

- *Moon-landings have put a new face on our scientific knowledge.*

save face Avoid shame.

set one's face against Oppose.

show one's face Appear.

to one's face Openly, when one is present.

fact

fact of life Reality that cannot be ignored.

facts and figures All the relevant details.

in fact Stated exactly or briefly.

- *He will not come; in fact, I think he never intended to.*

fag

fag-end The latter, the final remaining part. [LIT] The rough end of a piece of cloth.

- *We spent the fag-end of our holiday on the river.*

fail

words fail me I cannot express what I feel.

failing

failing that If that does not happen.

faint

not to have the faintest Not to know.

fair

all's fair in love and war In any competition, the competitors must fend for themselves (*or* have equal conditions).

fair copy A neat copy, unspoilt by corrections.

fair deal A transaction which is fair and just to both sides.

fair enough I agree.

fair game A suitable object of amusement and ridicule.

(by) fair means or foul (In) any way possible.

fair play Correct and courteous treatment between opponents; justice according to accepted rule.

fair's fair We must act fairly. Also *fair do's.*

fair and square Just; openly honest.
- *The terms of the contract are absolutely fair and square.*

fair-to-middling Moderately well.

in a fair way to Likely to; behaving so that a certain event is probable.

fair-weather friend One who is a friend only during prosperity, and who ceases to be one when trouble comes.

faith

bad faith Treachery; dishonesty.
- *It was an act of bad faith to betray his friend.*

breach of faith A dishonourable action; a broken promise, given or implied.
- *It was a breach of faith to reveal the information I gave you.*

in (all) good faith Honestly believing. With honest intention.
- *Even though he was wrong, he acted in good faith.*

pin one's faith on Place one's entire faith in; believe in.

put one's faith in Trust. Believe.

shake one's faith Make one doubtful of one's previous beliefs.
- *What you tell me shakes my faith in human nature.*

shatter one's faith Destroy one's belief completely.

fall

fall about Be helpless (with laughter).

fall apart, asunder Break up in separate pieces.

fall into arrears Fail to pay a sum due at regular intervals.

fall astern Go more slowly, till instead of being level one is behind.

fall away 1. Diminish; dwindle.
- *Trade always falls away during the summer.*

2. Separate from; desert.

fall back 1. Retire; retreat.
- *The crowd fell back to let the ambulances through.*

2. Make use of in an emergency.
- *One can always fall back upon condensed milk.*

fall or *drop behind* 1. Be passed by; be overtaken.

2. Similar to *fall into arrears.*

fall between two stools Attempt to combine two plans, and succeed with neither.

fall down on Fail.

fall flat 1. [LIT] Be prostrate.
- *The man staggered, and fell flat on the floor.*

2. [MET] Fail to amuse or interest; end in an anti-climax.

- *What was meant to be a funny story fell completely flat.*

fall for 1. Fall in love with.

2. Be deceived by.

fall foul of [LIT] Collide with; crash into. [MET] Quarrel with. Be in a state of dispute with.

- *He has a knack of falling foul of everyone he meets.*

fall into a habit Form or acquire a habit.

fall into place [LIT and MET] Take up the proper and logical place or position.

- *When he told me his story, all the facts I had known before fell into place.*

fall in with Encounter. Meet and accompany. Agree with. Coincide with.

- *It would be very convenient if you could fall in with my plans.*

fall on Seize eagerly.

fall on evil days Be in misfortune.

fall on one's feet Be successful as the result of good fortune or luck.

fall off Deteriorate.

fall out Disagree; quarrel.

- *If we talk politics we are bound to fall out.*

fall over oneself Be very eager (to help, etc.)

fall short Be less than, or below.

- *My income falls short of my expenditure by five hundred pounds.*

fall through Collapse; fail to happen.

fall to one's lot Happen to one.

- *It will probably fall to my lot to die a bachelor.*

fall to pieces Break up completely.

fall under Be classed among.

fall upon Attack.

- *The wolf fell upon the lamb and devoured it.*

fall upon a person's neck Embrace.

fall within Be included in.

false

false step Mistake.

strike a false note Cause awkwardness.

under false pretences Dishonestly.

fan

fan the flame Increase excitement, tension, pressure etc.

fancy

catch the fancy of Please. Attract.

- *It caught my fancy and I bought it without thinking.*

fancy free Not in love. Hence, carefree.

fancy oneself 1. Be conceited.

2. Think oneself expert at.

fancy price High cost.

flight of fancy or *imagination* Something visualised which is entirely imaginary; unconnected with actual events.

take a fancy to Be attracted by.

- *On second thoughts, I've rather taken a fancy to the idea.*

take one's fancy Please.

tickle one's fancy Amuse; divert. Attract.

- *Do you see anything in the shop which tickles your fancy?*

far

as far as in one lies As much as one is capable.

far and away; by far To a much greater extent or degree.

- *I was far and away happier before I changed jobs.*

far and near Everywhere.

far and wide; far and near Many places, both near and distant.

- *People came from far and wide to hear him.*

a far cry A remote connection only; distant or slightly connected.

far be it from me An apologetic phrase for interfering or criticising.

far-fetched Exaggerated and over-elaborate.

far-flung Widely extended.

far from Almost the opposite of.

- *The answer is far from easy.*

far gone In a dangerously critical condition.

- *I'm afraid he is so far gone that there is no hope.*

in so far To the extent or degree.

- *I am able to help you, in so far that I can arrange an appointment.*

go far Succeed.

go too far Go beyond what is acceptable.

so far as one can As much as one can.

so far so good Progress has been satisfactory.

farm

farm out Delegate. Sub-contract.

fashion

after a fashion In an amateurish and ineffective way.

- *He cooked the dinner after a fashion.*

fast

play fast and loose Act irresponsibly, and without regard to one's duties.

pull a fast one Act craftily.

pull a fast one on somebody Deceive somebody.

fasten

fasten on 1. [LIT] Attach.

- *I can't fasten this lid on.*

2. [MET] Pick out for a particular purpose, or as the person responsible.

- *Someone must have broken the plate, but why fasten on me?*

fat

a fat lot of Very little.

chew the fat 1. Have a chat.

2. Grumble.

fat in the fire [LIT] The splutter and flames made when fat splashes from a frying-pan into the fire. [MET] General excitement, anger, etc., when a sensational piece of news is made known.

the fat of the land The best and most expensive (food, etc.) obtainable.

fate

as sure as fate Very certain.

fate worse than death Serious consequences.

the irony of fate An ironic coincidence. An event, frequently tragic, which defies or defeats what has been intended.

fault

at fault Wrong; inaccurate.

find fault with Grumble at; complain.

to a fault Excessively.

favour

curry favour Try to ingratiate oneself.

find favour Receive approval.

fear

for fear of To avoid the risk of.

never fear There is no need to worry.

no fear Not likely.

put the fear of death or God into Frighten severely.

without fear or favour Impartially.

in high favour Extremely popular.

feather
birds of a feather People of a particular type.
feather-bed Make matters comfortable for.
feather-brained Foolish. Forgetful.
a feather in one's cap An honour; something to be proud of.
feather one's nest Gradually acquire extra money, honestly or
     otherwise.
feathered friends Birds in general.
show the white feather Behave like a coward.
you could have knocked me down with a feather I was
     astonished.

feel
feel at home Feel comfortable.
feel for Feel pity for; sympathise with.
feel like Would like.
feel up to Be ready for.

feeler
put or throw out feelers or a feeler Find out by surreptitious or
     gentle question or hint.
   ● *Why not put out a few feelers to see what the rest of the staff
     think?*

feeling
fellow-feeling The sympathy and understanding felt for a suf-
     ferer by one who has been through similar trials.
good feeling Spirit of co-operation, helpfulness, friendship, etc.
ill feeling Animosity.

feet
have feet of clay Have a fundamental weakness.
put one's feet up Have a rest.

fell
at one fell swoop In one blow. At a stroke.

fellow
hail-fellow-well-met Friendly.

fellowship
the hand of fellowship The right hand of a friend, clasped as a
     sign of goodwill and peace.

fence
fence with a question Give a non-committal answer to avoid the question.
mend fences Restore harmony.
sit on the fence Refrain from giving one's support to either side; remain entirely neutral (usually from motives of cowardice or discretion).

fetch
fetch up Come to rest.
wrong or right side of the fence In these and similar expressions, 'fence' means 'dispute'.

fettle
in fine fettle In good condition (applied to person or animal). In good spirits.

few
every few days Once in every group of a few days.
few and far between Rare, scarce.
a good few A reasonable number.

fiddle
fit as a fiddle In excellent health.
play second fiddle Take subordinate role.

field
take the field Enter a playing-field to begin a competition.

fifty
fifty-fifty Equal shares. Halves.
● *The proceeds of the event will be split fifty-fifty between two charities.*

fight
fight it out Continue dispute until conclusion is reached.
fight shy of Avoid, keep away from.
fight to a standstill Fight until both sides are too exhausted to make any further effort.
put up a fight Offer resistance.

fighting
fighting chance Reasonable chance.
fighting fit In good health.

figure

cut a figure Become prominent (often for being conspicuously well dressed). Make an impression.

figure of fun Ridiculous; absurd.

figures of speech Literary forms such as the metaphor, simile, hyperbole, allegory, etc.

file

in Indian file; in single file Singly, one behind another.

fill

fill the bill Suffice.
- *I haven't any gin; would whisky fill the bill?*

fill an office Occupy a position or post.

fill in for Replace (absent person).

fill (person) in Inform.

fill out Enlarge. Become more plump.

fill up or *in documents* Add details which are required.
- *If you require a passport, will you please fill up this form.*

drink (take) one's fill Take enough to satisfy, all that one is capable of taking.
- *We took our fill of the sunshine and fresh air.*

filthy

filthy lucre Money. Wealth. [Old f.]

final

final touch The last detail; that which completes the work.

find

find oneself in Supply oneself with.

all found Everything provided.
- *We are paying fifty pounds a week, all found.*

find guilty The legal phrase used when an accused person has been tried, and it has been 'found' that he committed the crime.

find one's feet Obtain and develop the use of one's abilities.
- *After a year in the job, I'm beginning to find my feet.*

find in one's heart Be firm enough. Be inclined.
- *I couldn't find it in my heart to refuse her request.*

must take us as you find us Must accept us as we are.

fine

cut fine Leave little room for error.

in fine Stated exactly or briefly.

fine distinction A difference perceptible only with difficulty.

not to put too fine a point on it Generally speaking.

one of these fine days Some day (used in prophesying).

- *I'll do something about it one of these fine days.*

with a fine-tooth comb Very carefully, with minute attention to detail.

- *I've been through my bank-statement with a fine-tooth comb.*

finger

fingers are all thumbs Fingers are clumsy, awkward. Also *all fingers and thumbs*: clumsy.

burn one's fingers Suffer as a result of some action.

- *If you buy that business, I think you'll burn your fingers.*

have a finger in the pie Be concerned with, or mixed up with some affair.

keep one's fingers crossed Hope for a good result. Hope for good luck.

lift or stir a finger Make the smallest effort.

point the finger at Identify.

pull one's finger out Make an effort.

put one's finger on Locate. Identify.

at one's finger-tips Immediately available. (Applied to information, knowledge, etc.)

slip through one's fingers Escape.

twist person round one's (little) finger Dominate person.

work one's fingers to the bone Work very hard (usually, with one's hands).

fire

(breathe) fire and brimstone (Utter) angry threats.

fire away Begin.

go through fire and water Face all dangers.

no smoke without fire Every rumour has an origin.

play with fire Take risks.

set the Thames on fire Do something noteworthy.

strike fire Arouse enthusiasm.

take fire [LIT] Become ignited. [MET] Become excited, indignant or enthusiastic.

through fire and water Through any kind of suffering or discomfort.

under fire [LIT] Being shot at. [MET] Being criticised.

first

at the first blush or *glance* Superficially; before examining closely.

first class Top quality. Best available.

first things first A proper order of priorities.

from first to last From beginning to end; all the time.

in the first place Firstly.

fish

a fish out of water One out of one's natural element or surroundings.

- *During my first weeks in the new job, I felt like a fish out of water.*

fish in troubled waters Interest oneself in affairs that are likely to lead to trouble and danger.

neither fish nor fowl See under **flesh.**

other fish to fry Other business to occupy the time.

- *I can't discuss the matter any longer—I've other fish to fry.*

pretty kettle of fish A thoroughly unsatisfactory state of affairs; general upheaval and excitement; a mixture of muddle and trouble.

fist

iron fist Severity. Usually *iron fist in velvet glove* Severity (of action) disguised as gentleness.

fit

In a suitable condition to work, in good health. (Also *fighting fit.*)

fit in with Co-ordinate with.

- *Your visit tomorrow will fit in with my cousin's arrival.*

fit to wake the dead Very loud.

fit up or *out* Prepare an expedition, etc.

have or *throw a fit* Become very angry.

in or *by fits and starts* Irregularly, spasmodically; in a series of spurts.

- *He does his work in fits and starts.*

not fit to hold a candle to Unworthy to be compared with.

see fit Think to be appropriate. Also *think fit.*

fix

fix up with Provide.

in a fix In difficulty.

flag

keep the flag flying Continue fighting. Show defiance.

put the flag out Celebrate.

show the flag Make people take note.

show or *hoist* or *wave the white flag* Surrender.

flake

flake out Collapse from exhaustion.

flame

add fuel to or *fan the flames* Add fresh causes for anger.

an old flame A sweetheart in past days.

flare

flare up 1. As a verb: give way to a sudden burst of anger.
  2. As a noun: a violent quarrel.

flash

flash in the pan A brief display producing no useful result.
  ● *That brilliant poem he wrote when young was a mere flash in the pan; he has produced nothing since.*

in a flash, quick as a flash Very quickly indeed.

flat

flat denial, contradiction, etc. Flat (adjective) (or flatly, adverb) is here in the sense of 'complete' and 'absolute'.
  ● *He flatly denied that he had stolen the coat.*

flat as a flounder or *pancake* Completely flat. See *fall flat.*

flat out With maximum effort or speed.

that's flat Let there be no doubt about that.

flea

sent off with a flea in one's ear Dismissed, after receiving a sharp rebuke.
  ● *If anyone wakes me up, he'll get a flea in his ear.*

flesh

neither flesh or fish, fowl nor good red herring With no definite qualities; not worth classifying.
  ● *He is extremely vague about his profession; he seems to be neither fish, fowl nor good red herring.*

flesh-pots (of Egypt) The good things of life, rich food, etc.

make one's flesh creep Horrify; shock; frighten with some ghastly story or sight.

more than flesh and blood can stand Utterly intolerable.

one's own flesh and blood Near relation. Close family.

flight
in the top flight Of the best quality.
take flight Retreat; flee away rapidly.

fling
have one's fling Indulge freely in one's pleasures.

float
float a company Organise a public company and issue shares in it.
float an idea Make a tentative suggestion.

flog
flog a dead horse Waste one's energy. Work very hard for little or no result. Persevere with a doomed endeavour.

flood
flood tide Highest degree of success, misery, etc.

floor
from the floor From a place in the audience, not the platform, at a meeting.
take the floor Begin to speak or dance.
wipe the floor with Defeat. Overwhelm with rebuke.

flown
the bird has flown The person wanted has escaped.

flowing
flowing with milk and honey Filled with all good things to eat and drink. [Old f.]

flutter
cause a flutter Cause excitement, as when a flock of birds is disturbed. (Similarly *flutter the dovecotes*: cause excitement in a society or community.)

fly
fly a kite Do something tentatively (in words or deeds) to test people's reactions to an idea or plan.
fly at Attack violently, physically or verbally.
fly-by-night Unreliable person. Similar to **here today and gone tomorrow**.
fly in the ointment The flaw, inconvenience or impediment in an arrangement.
fly on the wall Unseen observer or listener.

fly or *go off at a tangent* Abruptly abandon one subject for another.

fly off the handle Become angry.

let fly Throw. Discharge a missile. Use strong, violent or abusive language.

- *I managed to keep calm for a long time, but finally I just had to let fly at them.*

like flies In large numbers.

make the fur fly Create a violent quarrel or disturbance, as animals make the fur fly when fighting.

there are no flies on (person) (Person) is efficient, aware, clever, etc.

foam

foam with rage [LIT] To foam at the mouth, as mad dogs do. [MET] Indicate a state of extreme and ungovernable anger.

fob

fob off Persuade someone to accept a substitute.

- *I asked for butter, and will not be fobbed off with margarine.*

follow

follow one's bent Follow one's inclination; act in accordance with one's abilities and desires.

follow the dictates of one's heart Obey one's inward desires and feelings.

follow one's own devices Amuse or divert oneself as one wishes. Similar to *go one's own way.*

follow suit Behave similarly; do the same thing.

- *The conductor missed a beat, and the orchestra followed suit.*

follow up Continue a process already begun.

- *The horse kicked furiously and followed this up by trying to bite me.*

follow up (noun and adjective.) Continuation.

- *When the survey is complete, we shall keep a follow-up check on the people we questioned.*

fool

does not suffer fools gladly Is intolerant of people not thought to be of the required standard.

fool on, play the fool Act stupidly.

a fool's errand A useless journey.

fool's paradise An entirely false conception; a state of happiness unjustified by the actual facts.

fool-proof So simple and strong that even a fool cannot use it wrongly or break it.

fools rush in (where angels fear to tread) It is unwise to be over-hasty.

make a fool of Cause someone to appear ridiculous or contemptible. Similar to *take a rise out of.*

nobody's fool A sensible person.

foot

drag one's feet Show reluctance.

fall on one's feet Enjoy good luck.

feet foremost or first An elaborate evasion of 'dead'.

- *I shan't leave this house until I'm carried out feet foremost.*

foot the bill Pay whatever charge is involved.

- *If the Government grants higher pensions, the people themselves will have to foot the bill.*

get off on the wrong foot Begin by making a mistake.

have foot in both camps Belong to two (sometimes opposing) sides.

have one's feet on the ground Be reliable and level-headed.

keep one's feet Remain standing.

miss one's footing Slip; stumble.

not put a foot wrong Do or act correctly.

obtain or gain a footing Obtain a status or position ('footing' is constantly used in this sense).

on a firm footing On a sound and stable basis.

- *Since its reorganisation, the business is on a much firmer footing.*

on a friendly footing On friendly terms; friends with.

- *I like to be on a friendly footing with my neighbours.*

one foot in the grave So old or diseased that life is nearly finished.

on foot Walking or running.

put one's foot down Take firm and determined action.

- *When the girl wanted to stay out until past midnight, her father put his foot down.*

put one's best foot forward Proceed as quickly as possible.

- *We shall have to put our best foot forward if we are to reach London tonight.*

put one's feet up Rest.

put one's foot in it Make a blunder; a *faux pas*. Similar to *drop a brick.*

set foot on Step on to.
* *My father has never set foot on foreign soil.*

set on foot Initiate; begin any process or action.

set on his or her feet Help a person to regain a lost position or lost health.

stand on one's own (two) feet Be independent.

under one's feet Obstructing one.

force

by force of circumstances Compelled by events.

come into force Operate; function.
* *The new laws come into force next month.*

force one's hand Compel one to show his intentions, or to take definite action.

force of habit Custom.

force one's way Enter or make one's way by using force.

force the pace Hurry so as to cause others to hurry.

join forces Become associated with, or partners with.
* *The two explorers joined forces, and continued their journey together.*

foreign

foreign soil A foreign country.

foreign substance or body Any improper and injurious substance—dust, dirt, etc.

forfeit

forfeit the good opinion of Lose the good opinion of a person by bad or foolish conduct.

forlorn

forlorn hope Hope that is very unlikely to be fulfilled. A final effort.
* *I'll try again, but I think it's a forlorn hope.*

form

good form The correct convention.

in good form In good spirits. (Of person) working well.

matter of form Routine.

off form Not in good health or spirits. Not playing well.

on form In good condition.

top form Performing well.

fortune

make a fortune Become very wealthy.

small fortune Large sum of money.

forty
forty winks A slight, brief sleep.
the roaring forties Applied to latitude 40 degrees south, where strong winds blow throughout the year.

foul
foul play Unfair, unsporting; frequently applied to criminal action.
- *The sailor was never seen again; the police suspected foul play.*

found
ill-founded Without justification.
well-founded Justified.

fountain
fountain-head Starting-place; source.

four
four-square [LIT] Facing squarely in four directions. [MET] Facing the world firmly and without fear.
on all fours 1. On one's hands and knees.
2. In agreement with each other.

fraught
fraught with Laden with; bearing.
- *The whole matter is fraught with difficulty.*

fray
thick of the fray Where the fighting is fiercest.

free
free and easy Unconventional; not arranged according to any formal plan.
free hand (two words) Complete freedom of action.
- *I have been given a free hand in arranging the concert.*
free-hand (one word, or with hyphen) Applied to drawing in which no mechanical help from instruments is employed.
free-handed or free Generous.
free fight or free for all A general and indiscriminate dispute in which anyone may join.
- *Someone in the audience threw a cabbage at the speaker, and the meeting ended in a free fight.*

free-lance Self-employed person, or one who works for a number of organisations, instead of being regularly employed by one employer only.

free translation or *rendering* A translation which is not literal, but which conveys the general meaning and effect.

make free with Take liberties with.

Scot free [LIT] Tax free. [MET] Without any punishment or penalty.

set free Release.

French
take French leave Leave without permission.

fresh
fresh as a daisy Brisk. Active. Not tired.
fresh as (new) paint Entirely fresh and unspoilt.

friend
bosom friend a specially close and intimate friend.
friend at court someone with private influence.
make friends (plural only) Form friendships; become friendly.

frog
have a frog in one's throat Be hoarse.

fry
out of the frying pan (into the fire) Out of one difficulty into another equally or more serious.
small fry Unimportant people or things.

full
full well Very well (adverb only.)
  • *He knew full well.*
in the fullness of time Eventually.

fun
for the fun of it Without serious purpose.
fun and games Exciting happenings.
make fun of or *poke fun at* Ridicule.

funeral
that's your (etc.) funeral That is your problem.

fur
make the fur fly Create a disturbance.

fuss

make a fuss Complain.

make a fuss of (someone) Give (genuinely or apparently genuinely) affectionate attention to (someone).

G

gallery
play to the gallery Appeal to popular taste.

game
fair game A legitimate target.
mug's game Activity suited only to fools.
play the game Behave fairly.
two can play at that game Another's behaviour or misbehaviour may be copied in a way he may regret.
the game's up Further effort is useless. Similar to *all up.*

garden
everything in the garden's lovely All is in order.

gasp
at one's last gasp Exhausted.

gate
gate-crashing Entering uninvited.
gate-crasher One who so enters.

gauntlet
running the gauntlet [LIT] Driven between a row of persons each provided with sticks, ropes, etc., with which to strike the offender. [MET] Subjected to criticism or attack from an organised body of people.
- *He ran the gauntlet of criticism from every doctor in the country when he published his book.*

throw or *fling down the gauntlet* Applied to any act of defiance or challenge.
take up the gauntlet Accept the challenge.

- *After the speech of the Leader of the Opposition, the Prime Minister took up the gauntlet on behalf of the Government.*

get

get at Contact; reach.

getting at Implying, hinting, inadequately communicating.

- *He spoke so vaguely that I couldn't understand what he was getting at.*

get away Escape. Also *get away!* I don't believe that!

get away with Succeed in what one is trying to do.

get away with murder Succeed by dint of effrontery, or luck.

get away with you Jocular term of dismissal or refusal.

get cracking or *going* Make a beginning, a start.

- *It's past seven—we must get going.*

get hold of Grasp [LIT] and [MET].

- *I'll explain, and you'll soon get hold of the idea.*

get into Put on (clothes).

get off to Begin with.

- *The performance got off to a rather shaky start.*

get on 1. [LIT] Mount; climb on to.

- *The boy was too small to get on his pony without help.*

2. [MET] Agree; be friends with.

- *I hope Jack and his cousin will get on with each other.*

Similar to *hit it off.*

3. [MET] Progress satisfactorily.

- *Jane works so hard at her job that she is certain to get on.*

4. Continue.

- *I'll get on with cleaning the car.*

get on with you! Expression of disbelief.

get out of Escape from.

get out of hand Become out of control.

get over 1. Recover from.

- *He soon got over the shock.*

2. Overcome by persuasion, etc.

- *He got over her objections to the marriage.*

get rid of Dispose of something not desired or needed.

- *We're going to get rid of our old car.*

get round Persuade (person) by cajolery.

get up 1. Arrange. Begin.

2. Rise from one's bed.

get oneself up Dress smartly or strikingly.

get well soon I hope you soon recover from your illness.

get wind of Hear rumours of.

get the wind up Become apprehensive.

tell someone where to get off Reprimand someone.

ghost

ghost of a chance The slightest, the least chance.

give up the ghost Cease to hope or function.

gift

don't look a gift-horse in the mouth Do not spurn a present.

gift of the gab Ability to talk well or persuasively.

gilt

take the gilt off the gingerbread Take away the charm or advantage (sometimes the artificial attractiveness).

● *The fact that I've got to return to the office in the middle of my holiday takes the gilt off the gingerbread.*

gilt-edged investments Investments—mortgages, debentures, etc.—in which there is no risk of losing one's capital.

gird

gird up one's loins Prepare for an ordeal or combat.

give

give a brass farthing or a damn Care in the slightest. (Usually used in negative.)

● *I don't give a damn what the price is.*

give and take Willingness to compromise.

give a person or thing the go-by Ignore; treat as non-existent.

● *I shall give the whole scheme the go-by.*

give as good as one gets Retaliate sufficiently.

give away 1. Distribute.

2. Give for nothing.

3. Reveal a secret or expose a person.

give oneself away Unintentionally reveal one's intentions or emotions.

give ear Listen.

give ground Yield.

give in Surrender.

give notice Make an announcement (often formally, or in writing, etc.) of one's intention. ('Notice' often = statement of intention to quit job.)

● *Half of the cleaning-staff have given their notice.*

give off Emit.

give out 1. Issue; distribute (information, verbally or in print).

2. Be finished, all used.

- *You can't have a hot bath—the water has given out.*

give or *yield place to* Be replaced or superseded by someone or something else.

- *In the nineteenth century gas gave place to electric light.*

give rise to Cause; create.

- *The Ambassador's disappearance is giving rise to concern.*

give the game away Reveal a secret.

give up 1. Abandon.

- *I shall give up smoking.*

2. Surrender; cease to fight.

give it up Cease to attempt.

- *The puzzle is too difficult; I shall give it up.*

give oneself up Surrender to authority.

give or take Within the limits of.

- *I weigh twelve stone, give or take a few pounds.*

give way 1. Yield.

2. Break; collapse.

glance

glance at Look at swiftly.

glance over Read swiftly.

glass

people who live in glass houses Abbreviation of proverb *People who live in glass houses should not throw stones*. Those who are vulnerable to criticism should not themselves criticise.

globe

globe-trotter One who travels extensively.

glory

glory in Take great pride in.

gloss

gloss over Try to minimise by ignoring or excusing.

- *The lawyer tried to gloss over his client's bad record by saying that his parents neglected him.*

glove

fit like a glove Fit exactly.

with kid gloves Gently.

- *The whole matter needs handling with kid gloves.*

with the gloves off With great seriousness. Also *the gloves are*

off The argument (controversy, battle, etc.) is in earnest.
See **velvet**.

glutton

a glutton for punishment, work, etc. A person who is eager for
  punishment, work, etc.

go

go after Follow.

go ahead 1. [LIT] Go in front, or before.
  - *You go ahead and tell him that we're coming.*
  2. [MET] Proceed at once.
  - *If you think you can solve the problem, go ahead.*

go a long way towards Has an important effect in.

go along with Agree with.

go back on Reverse a previous promise or pledge.
  - *He said he would help us, and then went back on his promise.*

go-between One who acts as a link between two people or
  groups of people; a negotiator.

go-by See under **give**.

go by the board Be ignored. Be finished with.
  - *Caution went by the board as the match neared its conclusion.*

go down with Suffer from.
  - *He's gone down with chicken-pox.*

go far Succeed.

go fifty-fifty Receive fifty per cent each; share equally.
  - *We'll go fifty-fifty with the profits.*

go for 1. Attack.
  2. Be attracted by.

go for nothing Be without value; have no effect.
  - *All the efforts we have made will go for nothing.*

go-better Ambitious person.

go halves Same as **go fifty-fifty**.

go in for Undertake seriously, as a profession or hobby.
  - *I hear he's gone in for gardening.*

going strong Persisting vigorously.
  - *My grandfather is ninety and still going strong.*

go off 1. Succeed.
  - *I thought her speech went off well.*
  2. Explode.
  - *The terrorists' bomb went off in the High Street.*
  3. Deteriorate.
  - *The pianist's playing is rapidly going off.*

go on 1. An expression which may mean, according to circumstances, an injunction to hurry (*Go on—we shall never get there!*); an expression of disbelief (*You saw a ghost? Go on!*); a request for further information (*Please go on with the story*).

2. Use as guidance.

- *We have no information to go on.*

3. Continue.

- *If we can't find a hotel, we shall have to go on.*

go on the stage Become an actor.

go one better Improve upon; prove more skilful, etc.

go out of one's way Incur extra trouble.

- *This hotel-keeper goes out of his way to make his guests happy.*

go over Revise.

go over the ground Examine the facts, survey.

- *It is a difficult problem, and I should like to go over the ground again.*

go round Visit informally.

go through fire and water make any sacrifice; endure any sufferings.

go through with Continue to the end.

- *He has begun to study for a degree, but I don't think he'll go through with it.*

go together Match.

go to sea Become a sailor.

go to the country Hold a general election.

go to war Declare or wage war.

go under 1. Succumb. Fail.

- *If a supermarket opens here, the small grocers will go under.*

2. Be known by.

- *On the stage, she goes under a different name.*

go without Be without; lack.

- *I'm afraid you'll have to go without milk in your tea.*

go without saying Be obvious; self-evident.

have a go Make an attempt.

how are things going? What progress is being made?

make a go of Make a success of.

on the go Busy.

word go Beginning.

- *He was in trouble from the word go.*

goat

sort out the sheep from the goats Distinguish worthy people from unworthy ones.

god
God's truth The absolute truth.
in the lap of the gods Not subject to human control.

going
get going Begin.
going concern Business, etc. already working.
going to happen, occur, etc. 'Going to' here is used in the sense
  'will'.
(make) heavy going Difficult to make progress with.
  ● *This book is rather heavy going.*
to be going on with To serve for the time being.
while the going is good While the circumstances are favourable.

golden
golden boy Young man of great talent and promise.
golden mean The ideal 'middle course'; that which pleases most
  people because most moderate.
golden rule The recommended way, because it has been well
  tried.
  ● *The golden rule for frying sausages is to do it slowly.*

good
as good as Equal to. Practically.
  ● *This coat is as good as new.*
be so good as to Will you please.
do good Show kindness or helpfulness.
for good or for good and all Permanently; always.
good-for-nothing Wastrel.
good for nothing Valueless. Useless.
good wine needs no bush Things of good quality need no adver-
  tisement.
have a good time Enjoy oneself.
in good time 1. Not late.
  2. *all in good time* Wait for the proper time.
make good 1. Repair. See under **make**.
  2. Reclaim the past, see under **make**.
not good enough Unsatisfactory.
good riddance (to) I am glad to see the end (of that).
a good Samaritan One who helps a needy person.
on good terms On friendly conditions; in a friendly way.
  ● *We parted on good terms.*
put in a good word for Speak in support of.

take in good part Not be offended by.
a good turn A kindness; a friendly action.
to the good 1. Profit.
    2. General advantage.
up to no good Committing mischief.
a good while A long time.

goodness
See under **wish.**

goods
 deliver the goods Do as one has promised.

goose
all his geese are swans He thinks all his plans, etc. are better
    than they are.
cook one's goose Give one his deserts.
goose-flesh A cold and roughened condition of the skin, resem-
    bling that of a plucked goose, caused by cold or fear. People
    are said to 'go all goose-flesh' when they are terrified.
kill the goose that lays the golden egg Do away with that which
    brings good fortune.
say 'boo' to a goose Show courage. (*Note*—This idiom is always
    used in the negative.)
what is sauce for the goose is sauce for the gander One must
    accept even-handed dealing.

got
have got to Must.
    ● *I have got to finish this sewing before I go out.*

grab
how does that grab you? How do you like that?
up for grabs Available to be acquired.

grace
airs and graces Ostentatious behaviour.
fall from grace Lose good repute.
with a good grace Cheerfully; without protesting.
with a bad grace The reverse.

grade
make the grade Succeed in some specified object.

grain
against the grain Against one's inclination or wishes.

grape
sour grapes Pretending to dislike what one wants but cannot obtain.

grasp
grasp the nettle Deal with difficulty boldly.

grass
grass is always greener (on the other side of the fence) One's position is always less favourable than other people's.
not let the grass grow under one's feet Act swiftly.
grass widow A woman whose husband is away for a prolonged period.
put out to grass Retired.

grate
grate on the ear Sound harsh and unpleasant.

grave
dig one's own grave Cause one's own downfall.
have one foot in the grave Be old, infirm.
turn in one's grave Expression used of something which the deceased person referred to would have very strongly resented.
  • *That production is enough to make Shakespeare turn in his grave.*

grease
grease a man's palm Bribe him.

Greek
all Greek to me Incomprehensible. Unintelligible.

green
green-eyed monster Jealousy.
green fingers Skill in making plants, flowers, etc. grow.
green light Permission to begin.
green room The general reception room of a theatre.

grey
grey area Situation lacking clear-cut distinctions.
grey matter Brains.

grief
come to grief Meet with misfortune.

grievance
air a grievance See under **air**.

grim
hold on like grim death Cling firmly.

grin
grin and bear it Endure as well as one can.

grind
keep one's nose to the grindstone Work without stopping.

grip
come (get) to grips with Try to deal with (in a businesslike or vigorous fashion).
lose one's grip Lose control.

grist
all's grist that comes to the mill Everything that is received can be used.

groove
run (be) in a groove or rut Function in the same limited and narrow way, or by the same methods.

ground
break new ground Explore new subject.
cut the ground from under one's feet Anticipate and/or negate one's plans, arguments, etc., by having unexpected information, skill, etc.
down to the ground See **suit**.
gain ground Advance; progress.
get off the ground Make a successful start.
ground swell of opinion Increasing support.
have one's or both feet on the ground Be realistic, practical, etc.
stand one's ground Keep to one's position.

grow
growing pains Difficulties associated with early development of business, plan, etc.
grown up Adult.
grow on one Gradually impress its charm and personality.
  • *You may not like Bath at first, but you'll find it grows on you.*
grow out of 1. [LIT] Become too big for, as child *grows out of his clothes*.
    2. [MET] Become too mature for, as person *grows out of childish ways*.

grudge

bear a grudge Retain resentful feelings because of a previous dispute.

grundy

Mrs Grundy A severely conventional person.

guard

catch off one's guard Take advantage of someone temporarily distracted or forgetful.

old guard Elderly and conservative people in an organisation, etc.

on one's guard Alert; prepared.

guess

anybody's guess An uncertain thing.

gun

blow great guns Blow tremendous winds; a gale.

● *It was blowing great guns when the ship left harbour.*

go great guns Make excellent progress.

stick to one's guns Firmly maintain one's standpoint.

the big guns Important people.

habit

creature of habit Person who acts predictably.

from force of habit Because one's behaviour is normally governed by one's habits.

get out of the habit of Stop doing regularly.

hackles

make one's hackles rise Make one angry.

hail

hail from Come from.

hail-fellow-well-met Person on familiar and friendly terms with everybody one meets. (Also adjective.)

hair

get in one's hair Annoy one.

hair standing on end Indicative of extreme terror and astonishment. Also used more jocularly.

hair-raising Frightening. Very surprising.

splitting hairs Arguing or disagreeing over extremely trivial matters. (Also *hair-splitting*.)

(Not) turn a hair Show (no) signs of fear of embarrassment.

hair's breadth A minute distance, e.g., a hair's-breadth escape is a very narrow escape, an event which only just missed disaster.

halcyon

halcyon days A time of happiness and prosperity.

half

at half cock Imperfectly. Usually *go off at half cock* Take place in a desultory way.

by half Expression of exaggeration, e.g. *too clever by half; too cheeky by half.*

by halves Incompletely.

go halves Share equally.

half-and-half Divided into two equal parts or portions.

half-hearted Without energy or enthusiasm.

halfway house Half the distance.

no half measures No compromise.

the half of it The remaining and more important part.

hallmark

|LIT| The official marking (after testing) of all gold and silver goods with the 'hall' or standard mark as a guarantee of purity. [MET] A sign of good quality (in conduct, manners, ability, taste, etc.).

ham

ham-fisted Clumsy.

hammer

hammer and tongs With much noise and/or vigour and enthusiasm

- *He may have no skill as a golfer, but he certainly goes at it hammer and tongs.*

hammer away at Work hard at.

hammer out Arrive at a decision or solution by examining and discussing every detail of the subject.

- *We spent all day hammering out our plans for the holiday.*

hammering Punishment. Defeat.

under the hammer By public auction.

hand

all hands to the pumps Assistance from everyone available.

- *They'll need all hands to the pumps if the business is to be saved.*

(at) first hand Directly; straight from the person concerned. See **second.**

- *I heard the story of the match first hand from the captain.*

at hand; close at hand Near; available.

at the hands of Under the control or direction of.

by hand 1. By messenger.

2. By the use of manual labour.

high-handed Insolent. Overbearing. Supercilious.

change hands Pass from the ownership of one person to that of another.

clean hands Innocently; honestly; without fraud.

do a hand's turn Do the slightest piece of work.

from hand to mouth (Live) in poverty.

get one's hands on 1. Catch (culprit).

    2. Obtain.

hand down Pass on.

hand in glove In partnership; intimately associated.

hand in hand [LIT] Clasped hands. [MET] In close association.

hand it to someone Congratulate or admire someone.

hand to hand One person to another.

hand to mouth From day to day, without any provision for the future. Also *hand-to-mouth* (adjective).

hand over Surrender; give to someone else. Similar to *turn over*.

hand over hand or *fist* Rapidly.

    ● *He's overtaking us, hand over fist.*

hands off Leave (it) alone.

have a hand in Take a part or share in.

have one's hands full Be completely occupied, very busy.

    ● *We shall have our hands full when the visitors arrive.*

have on one's hands Be responsible for; have to dispose of.

    ● *When the house is sold I shall have the furniture on my hands.*

high-handed Presumptuous. Arrogant.

hold one's hand 1. [LIT]

    2. [MET] Act as guide to one (person).

in good hands Well cared for.

in hand or *well in hand* 1. Under one's control.

    ● *There was a little rioting, but the police soon had the situation well in hand.*

    2. In one's possession.

    ● *When all our debts are paid, we shall have over £100 in hand.*

in the hands of Being dealt with by.

    ● *The contract is in the hands of my solicitor.*

keep in hand Retain; keep under control.

keep one's hand in Keep practising.

lay hands on Find.

lend a hand Help.

    ● *All the packing has to be done; perhaps you'll lend a hand?*

lift or *raise one's hand against* Strike; attack; threaten to hit.

live from hand to mouth Have a precarious existence.

off-hand See under **off.**

off one's hands No longer as one's responsibility.

an old hand A person with considerable experience.

- *Let me help—I'm an old hand at chopping wood.*

on all hands; on every hand Universally.

on hand Same as *at hand.*

on one's hands As one's responsibility.

- *I've a lot of work on my hands at the moment.*

on the one hand Said to introduce the first part of a contrasting expression.

on the other hand Otherwise; alternatively.

- *We may leave London; on the other hand, we may remain.*

Similar to *on the contrary.*

out of hand Uncontrollable; beyond restraint.

- *The crowd became so excited that it was soon completely out of hand.*

out of one's hands No longer in one's control.

show one's hand Reveal one's real intentions

- *If he asks you to name a price, don't show all your hand at once.*

sleight of hand See under **sleight.**

stay one's hand Refrain from action.

take a hand Share; play a part in.

- *The State ought to take a hand in building new houses.*

Similar to *have a hand.*

take in hand Take immediate charge of; assume responsibility for.

the upper or whip hand The chief power; the real control.

throw in one's hand Abandon any further effort.

- *I'm so disgusted with the whole thing that I'm going to throw in my hand.*

try one's hand at Attempt; test one's powers.

- *Have you ever tried your hand at cooking?*

win hands down Win easily.

handle

deal with; direct.

- *I think the plumber is the best man to handle this.*

a handle to one's name A title.

hang

get the hang of Understand.

hang about or around Loiter.

129

hang back Hesitate to proceed; show reluctance to agree or assist.

hangdog Untrustworthy. (Sometimes used as noun, meaning 'a suspicious-looking person'.)

hang fire Fail to produce results when expected. Wait.

hang in the balance Be undecided.

- *The future of this school hangs in the balance until the Council next meets.*

hang heavy Pass slowly. (Usually applied to time.)

hang it Expression of irritation or dismissal.

hang by a thread Be in an extremely delicate and precarious state.

- *The negotiations are hanging by a thread.*

hang in the balance Be uncertain.

hang on Wait.

hang one's head Show shame.

hang out Live. Spend one's time.

hang together Collaborate closely; support one another. Be a unified whole.

- *The plan needs more details if it is to hang together.*

hang upon Depend upon.

I'll be hanged Expression of annoyance or astonishment. Also *hang it all!* See under **blow.**

- *I'll be hanged if I'll pay that much for a pair of shoes.*

thereby hangs a tale There are consequences to that.

happen

happen what may Whatever may occur. [Old f.]

happy

happy-go-lucky Careless; gaily reckless; relying on good luck for help out of difficulties.

happy medium Compromise that suits both parties.

hard

be hard on 1. Punish, criticise.

    2. Be unfair to.

go hard with Involve punishment or suffering for.

hard and fast Strict. Rigidly organised.

- *In view of the weather, we'd better not make any hard and fast arrangements.*

hard as nails Uncompromising.

hard at it Working hard.

hard bargain One without concessions.

hard-bitten Tough. Stubborn.

hard-boiled 1. [LIT] (Of food) boiled so that it is hard.

2. [MET] (Of person) rough; uncompromising; made unyielding by experience.

hard by Near. [Old f.]

hard cash Real money, not cheques, promises, etc.

hard core Stubborn minority (within a group).

hard done by Treated harshly.

hard drinker One who drinks beer, wine, etc., frequently and in large quantities.

hard-earned Earned with difficulty.

hard facts Indisputable ones.

● *We have to face the hard fact that we can't afford it.*

hard-featured Severe-looking; grim.

hard-headed Tough. Practical, not sentimental.

hard-hearted Unfeeling. Unsympathetic.

hard-hitting Vigorous.

hard lines or luck Harsh; undeservedly severe. Also *hard-luck story* Tale of misfortune.

hard nut to crack Difficult person, problem, situation, etc., to deal with.

hard of hearing Unable to hear well.

hard pressed 1. Busy.

2. Closely pursued.

hard put to it In difficulty.

hard times Difficult circumstances to bear.

hard up With insufficient money.

take a hard line (on) Take firm action (against).

hare

hare-brained (= scatter-brained) Foolish and irresponsible.

mad as a March hare See under **mad.**

hark

hark back Revert (e.g. to topic previously mentioned).

harm

out of harm's way In a safe position.

harness

in harness Actively engaged in regular work.

harp

harp on; harp on the same string or subject, etc. Talk about the same subject until the listener becomes bored or irritated.

hash

make a hash of Make a muddle of.

- *Colin made rather a hash of trying to lay the carpet.*

settle one's hash Deal with one, once and for all.

hat

at the drop of a hat Swiftly.

eat one's hat Expression used to add emphasis.

- *If the train arrives on time, I'll eat my hat.*

hats off to Let us acclaim, welcome, etc.

keep something under one's hat Keep something secret.

old hat Out of fashion. Dated.

perform the hat-trick In cricket, a bowler is said to do this when he dismisses three consecutive batsmen in three consecutive balls. Loosely used in connection with any similar triple success.

take off one's hat to [MET] Express unusual approval of some action of another's.

- *I don't expect him to succeed, but I'll take my hat off to him if he does.*

take or *send* or *pass the hat round* Ask for contribution.

throw one's hat in the ring Put oneself forward as contestant.

wear two hats Act in two capacities.

have

have anything or *nothing to do with* Be (not) concerned or connected with.

- *He's the kindest person I've ever had anything to do with.*
- *If I were you, I'd have nothing to do with that laundry.*

have done Finish; stop.

- *Have you done with the washing-up?*

have it in for Dislike.

have it in oneself Be capable of.

have it out 1. Have extracted.

- *I'll have this tooth out tomorrow.*

2. Discuss a subject (usually a dispute) openly and frankly.

- *I am going to have the whole thing out with the garage.*

have on 1. Wear.

- *Are you sure you had gloves on when you arrived?*

2. Deceive. Trick.

- *If he said he was a first-class snooker-player, he was having you on.*
3. Be busy with.
- *Have you anything on this evening?*

have what it takes Have the required qualities.

hay

make hay of Ruin; render confused and muddled.

make hay while the sun shines Take advantage of a good opportunity, or a specially suitable occasion.

hazard

hazard an opinion (or guess) Risk expressing an opinion or view.

head

above one's head Beyond one's comprehension.

come or enter into one's head Occur to one.

come to a head Reach a crisis.

count heads Count people (present, etc.).

give person his head Allow person to act freely.

go to one's head Excite; intoxicate; make irresponsible.

hang one's head See under **hang**.

have a (good) head for heights Not be troubled by giddiness, etc. when standing at a high point.

have a (good) head on one's shoulders Possess intelligence and common sense.

have one's head Go one's own way without any interference.
- *He's the sort of man who works best if you let him have his head.*

have one's head screwed on the right way Be intelligent and shrewd.

head and shoulders above Far above or superior to.
- *He's head and shoulders above the rest of the candidates.*

head off 1. Intercept; prevent escaping. Divert.
2. *Laugh, eat, etc. one's head off* Laugh, eat, heartily. See under **bite**.

head on Directly; frontally.
- *The two cars collided head on.*

head-over-ears (in love, debt, etc.). Utterly and completely.

head-over-heels Turned upside down; complete inversion.

heads I win, tails you lose An arrangement which ends in the challenger remaining the winner, whatever happens; a hopelessly unfair agreement.

heads will roll People will be dismissed.

hold one's head up or *high* Show pride or defiance.

keep one's head Remain calm.

keep one's head above water Live within one's income; avoid bankruptcy. Just manage to avoid difficulty.

keep one's head down Behave unobtrusively; act so as not to be conspicuous.

let person have his/her head Allow person to act freely without interference.

lose one's head Momentarily lose self-control; behave wildly and senselessly.

make head nor tail of Understand; comprehend. (Always used in the negative.)

- *I cannot make head nor tail of the argument.*

need one's head examined Be foolish.

off one's head Mentally weak; unbalanced; mad; so excited as to be entirely irresponsible.

off the top of one's head Without thought.

old head on young shoulders Wisdom or experience unexpected in so young a person.

on one's own head One's own personal responsibility. (The phrase is generally used as a warning.)

- *If you insist, it will be on your own head.*

standing on one's head Very easily.

- *She can repair car-engines standing on her head.*

put into one's head Suggest.

put or *lay our heads together* Consult together; discuss.

- *If they would only put their heads together, I'm sure they could reach an agreement.*

take it into one's head Take a sudden and unexpected action.

- *The boy took it into his head to play truant.*

turn one's head or *brain* Render one vain, self-conscious, irresponsible, etc.

two heads are better than one It is an advantage to have a second person's opinion; collaboration is valuable.

over one's head 1. Beyond one's comprehension.

- *Most of his speech went over my head.*

2. In preference to one having a prior claim.

- *He was appointed manager over his boss's head.*

headway
make headway Progress; go forward.

hear
hear from Receive message from.

hear of 1. Be told about.

2. *will not hear of* Refuse to consider.

hear tell of Be told about.

hearing

a fair hearing Opportunity to state one's case while being listened to impartially.

hard of hearing Partially, but not completely, deaf.

lose one's hearing Become completely deaf.

out of hearing Too far away to be heard.

heart

after one's own heart Such as one could like and appreciate. In accordance with one's tastes.

at heart As one's concern.

break one's heart Cause one extreme distress or disappointment.

by heart Firmly in one's memory.

change of heart Change of feelings.

do one's heart good Make one happy and pleased.

● *It did my heart good to see the children's delight.*

find it in one's heart Be firm or hard-hearted enough (usually used in the negative).

from the bottom of one's heart Most sincerely.

have a heart of gold Be very good-natured.

have at heart Be personally concerned or interested in.

● *Her parents naturally have the girl's happiness at heart.*

have one's heart in one's mouth Be in a state of extreme nervousness.

have the heart to See **find it in one's heart.**

heart and soul With all one's force.

heart in the right place In spite of imperfections, possessing good and sensible ideas. Well-meaning.

● *He's rather unapproachable, but his heart is in the right place.*

heart is not in it Interest is not really devoted to it.

heart's content Complete satisfaction; as much or as long as one desires.

● *We can swim in the river to our heart's content.*

heart goes out to Feelings of sympathy are with.

heart of the matter The essence, or most vital part, of something.

heart-rending Extremely distressing.

heart stands still One experiences momentary fear.

135

heart-strings Deepest feelings or affections.
heart-throb Sexually attractive person.
heart-to-heart Frank and intimate.
heart-warming Causing feelings of pleasure.
in good heart In good spirits.
know (off) by heart Know, literally and every word.
learn (off) by heart Memorise.
lose heart Become too depressed to continue.
lose one's heart to Fall in love with; be charmed.
one's heart bleeds One feels very sorry.
one's heart sinks One feels depressed.
set one's heart upon Desire intensely.
take heart Be encouraged.

- *We may take heart from the fact that the illness isn't getting any worse.*

take to heart See **take**.
wear one's heart on one's sleeve Exhibit one's intentions for all to see; be completely frank.
win the heart of Gain the affection of.

heat
in the heat of the moment During a brief time of confusion, anxiety, excitement, panic, etc.
take the heat out of Make less emotional.

heaven
Used in numerous mild exclamations such as *good heavens, heavens above, for heaven's sake.* Also emphatic phrase *in heaven's name.*

- *What in heaven's name does he think he's doing?*

heaven forbid I hope that does not happen.
heaven only knows I do not know.
move heaven and earth Act vigorously (to achieve something).
seventh heaven A state of great happiness and contentment.
the heavens opened It rained very heavily.

heavy
make heavy weather of find great difficulties in.

- *You seem to be making heavy weather of that job.*

hedge
hedge one's bets Do something to protect oneself.

heel
See **Achilles' heel**.

clean pair of heels Superior speed.

come to heel Obey humbly and completely, as a dog comes obediently to the heels of his master.

(left to) cool one's heels Be kept waiting, usually by a superior.

dig one's heels in Be stubborn.

down-at-heel Shabby and untidy, like one whose shoe-heels are worn down.

kick one's heels Waste time.

- *I had to kick my heels for an hour before he would see me.*

Similar to *cool one's heels* and *twiddle one's thumbs.*

on the heels of Immediately behind, or very soon afterwards.

show a clean pair of heels Run away from and escape.

take to one's heels Run away.

- *The boy broke the window and took to his heels.*

turn on one's heel Turn sharply away.

- *She turned on her heel, and disappeared in the crowd.*

hell

for the hell of it For no good reason.

give (person) hell Treat (person) harshly.

what the hell! What does it matter?

helm

at the helm In control.

take the helm Take charge.

help

help oneself to Select and take away without formality or waiting to ask permission.

- *The guests helped themselves to the refreshments at the buffet.*

helter skelter

Hurriedly and in confusion.

- *They dashed helter-skelter out of the room.*

hem

hem in Restrain; restrict.

hen

hen-pecked Constantly faulted, nagged, scolded, etc., by one's wife.

here

here and there Scattered; distributed. In various places.

- *They looked down upon fields and woods, with a farmhouse here and there.*

here, there and everywhere In very many places.

here today and gone tomorrow Merely temporary; staying for a short time in any place.

neither here nor there Immaterial to a matter, etc.

hero

hero's welcome Welcome with acclamation (as for hero returning from war).

Herod

out-Herod Herod To be excessively wicked.

hide

hide one's light under a bushel Conceal one's merits because of modesty.

on a hiding to nothing Doomed to failure.

high

high and dry Stranded.

high and low Everywhere.

high and mighty Arrogant.

highbrow Of cultured tastes.

highdays, holidays and bonfire nights An old-f. facetious phrase applied to celebrations in general.

high-falutin' High-flown; absurdly elaborate and fantastic (generally applied to speech).

high-flown Extravagant.

high-flier Ambitious person with the ability to succeed.

high-handed See under **hand.**

high horse See **horse.**

high life Life of luxury.

highlight Most prominent part.

highly (probable, etc.) To a great extent.

high-minded Serious in moral attitudes.

high places Senior ranks (of Government, organisation, etc.)

high-sounding Pompous; magnificent.

• *He's talking a lot of high-sounding nonsense.*

high spot Outstanding attraction.

• *The high spot of the evening was the firework display.*

highly strung Tense. Unusually sensitive.

high time Fully time; applied to an event already due, if not overdue.

• *Look at the clock; it's high time you went to bed.*

highway
Queen's highway All public roads and thoroughfares along which the public has a right to travel (but, legally, only to travel, not to linger upon, or to obstruct).

hill
old as the hills Very old.
over the hill Past one's best.

hinge
hinge upon Depend on.
- *The whole play hinges upon the success of his performance.*

hint
broad hint A stressed, an obvious hint.
drop or throw out a hint Hint in a casual manner.
- *I still haven't received the boss's reply; will you drop a hint to her secretary?*
take a or the hint Understand what is being suggested indirectly.

hit
hit back Retaliate.
hit below the belt 1. [LIT] Commit foul in boxing.
    2. [MET] Behave unfairly.
hit it off Agree.
hit or (and) miss Indiscriminate.
hit the (right) nail on the head Guess or judge correctly.
hit upon Discover (usually unexpectedly).

hither
hither and thither Here and there; in this direction and in that direction. [Old f.]

hive
hive off Take away (responsibility, work, etc.) and give to another.

hoary
hoary age Age when one's hair has turned white, or hoary; very old.
- *He died at the hoary age of ninety.*
(Note—Hoary is often used to mean 'very old' in connection with other matters, e.g. *a hoary joke*.)

139

hobby
See under **horse**.

Hobson
Hobson's choice See under **choice**.

hocus-pocus The words traditionally uttered by a conjuror as he performs a trick; hence, gibberish, a swindle.

hog
go the whole hog Go to the fullest possible extent. Complete a matter.

- *If we're going to the cinema, why not go the whole hog and have a meal out as well.*

hoist
hoist with one's own petard Beaten with one's own weapons; caught in one's own trap.

hold
hold (something) against Blame for.

hold cheap Regard as having little value.

hold dear Cherish.

hold down Hold (job).

hold it against (one) Blame (one).

hold the fort [LIT] Defend a fortress. [MET] Remain on duty, in charge, at work, in supervision, etc.

hold forth Discourse; orate.

hold good Remain unaffected and unaltered.

- *My promise to visit you next summer holds good.*

hold off Delay.

hold or *stand one's ground* Not yield.

- *Despite the Opposition's abuse, the Minister stood his ground.*

hold (oneself) in Restrain (oneself).

hold one's horses Restrain oneself.

hold on 1. [LIT] Continue one's grasp.
  2. [MET] Wait.

hold one's own Maintain successfully one's opinion, argument, or position.

hold out 1. As *hold on* (1).
  2. Extend, offer.

hold over 1. Keep back; reserve.
  2. Use some knowledge as a threat.

hold to Adhere to.

hold together Remain undivided; not separated.

hold up 1. Delay.
    2. Support.
    3. Exhibit.
hold water See under **water**.
hold with Concur; agree with.
    ● *I don't hold with allowing children too much freedom.*
no holds barred Without restraint.
there's no holding one One is difficult to restrain.

hole
be in a hole Be in an awkward situation.
hole-and-corner Furtive; secret.
make a hole in Use a sizeable part of.
pick holes in Find fault with.

hollow
hollow laugh Mirthless laugh.
hollow promises False promises.

holy
holier-than-thou Sanctimonious.

homage
pay or give homage to Show respect and reverence.

home
at-home An evening party, usually informal.
bring a thing home to a person Compel him to realise it.
    ● *Perhaps the accident will bring home to him his stupidity in driving so fast.*
broken home Family with divorced or separated parents.
come home to roost Recoil disadvantageously against originator.
home and dry Finally successful.
home from home Place which is not one's home but where one feels at home.
home truth Plain fact, however unpalatable.
make oneself at home Behave informally, as though the house was one's own.
    ● *Do sit down and make yourself at home.*

honest
earn (turn) an honest penny Earn money honestly.
honest broker Impartial mediator.

honour

a debt of honour a debt which cannot be legally enforced—e.g. a gambling debt, or one which is purely moral.

do the honours Act as host or hostess.

honour among thieves Mutual help or trust even among people normally considered incapable of either. Similar to *dog doesn't eat dog*.

honours are even Neither side has won or lost.

in honour of To celebrate.

(in) honour bound Compelled by one's sense of duty or correctness.

a point of honour Conduct arising from one's own particular sense of self-respect.

hook

by hook or by crook By any method, right or wrong; without scruples.

hook, line and sinker Completely and utterly.
- *I put the plan a different way, and they fell for it (swallowed it) hook, line and sinker.*

off the hook Out of a difficulty.
- *It's his own fault for getting himself into this situation, but we'll have to think of a way to get him off the hook.*

hoop

go or *be put through the hoop(s)* Suffer an ordeal.

hope

hope against hope Continue to hope despite unfavourable conditions.

raise one's hopes Give one reason to expect.

horizon

on the horizon [MET] Likely to occur in the remote future.

horn

draw in one's horns Withdraw, alter or abandon (plans, etc.).

hornet's nest

stir up or *put one's hand in a hornet's nest* Create trouble by interfering unwisely.

horse

a dark horse A person whose qualities and possibilities are unknown.

change horses in midstream Change plans, allegiance, etc. at an awkward moment.

eat like a horse Have a good appetite.

flog a dead horse Make useless effort.

hobby-horse 1. Favourite notion or private idea which one is constantly referring to.
- *The foreman's been riding his hobby-horse about efficiency again.*
2. Abbreviation *hobby.* Spare-time occupation. Pastime.

horse sense Common sense.

look a gift horse in the mouth Examine too critically anything which is a present.

on one's high horse Assuming a haughty or superior attitude. Stand-offish. Also *trying to ride the high horse.*

put the cart before the horse Do things in the wrong order.

(straight) from the horse's mouth (Of information received) direct, not through an intermediary.

take a horse to the water Only go so far.

wild horses wouldn't (make one) Nothing would.
- *Wild horses wouldn't make me go swimming in the sea today.*

hot

hot air Excited, boastful, meaningless talk.

hot and bothered Flustered.

hot favourite Very popular. Strongly recommended.

hot line Rapid means of communication.

hot seat Difficult position or post.

hot under the collar Angry.

hot water See under **water.**

hour

improve the shining hour Take advantage of an opportunity.

keep regular hours Always go to bed and get up at the same times, usually early ones.

the small hours The early hours of the morning, i.e. between 1 and 4 a.m.

the witching hour Midnight. [Old f.]

till all hours Until very late.

house

bring down the house Give a tremendously popular performance, not necessarily in a theatre, of any type.

house-warming A dinner-party, etc., given to celebrate the settling down in a new house, a return after a long absence, or any similar occasion.

keep open house Welcome visitors, without invitation, at any time. Be generous and frequent with hospitality.

like a house on fire Vigorously. Extremely well. Successfully.

on the house Free.

put one's house in order Organise one's affairs in an orderly way.

safe as houses Very safe.

how

how about I suggest.

how comes it?; how is it? How or why does it happen?

- *How comes it that you are always late on Monday?*

how do you do? The usual formal greeting.

how is ——? Abbrev. for How (= in what state) is the health of ——?

hue

hue and cry Noise of pursuit. Outcry (against).

- *Some MPs are raising a great hue and cry about the amount of money being spent on defence.*

huff

in a huff Showing anger or sulkiness.

hum

hum and haw Hesitate; procrastinate.

hunt

hunt down Find after careful search.

hunt up Search for.

- *You'll have to hunt up the word in the dictionary.*

hurl

hurl defiance Openly and loudly defy. Frequently used facetiously.

hurly-burly

Tumult; the noise and struggle of crowds.

hurry

hurry on with; hurry up Hasten.

- *Hurry up, or we shall miss the train.*

in a hurry Hastening. Not reluctantly.

- *We can't go to that restaurant again in a hurry.*

husband
husband one's resources To 'husband' is to take care of, to use economically. 'Resources' are all the means one has.

hush
hush-hush Secret.
hush up Suppress mention of.

I

ice

break the ice Overcome reserve.

cut no ice Fail to impress.

on ice In reserve. Waiting for later attention.

be or skate on thin ice Take risks.

tip of the iceberg Small part of much bigger and hidden problem.

idea

what's the big idea? What folly have you in mind?

ilk

that ilk The same name. The same nature.

ill

ill-assorted Incompatible; badly matched.

ill-at-ease Uncomfortable; in a state of embarrassment.

ill-gotten gains Money, reward (etc.) gained improperly.

it's an ill wind that blows nobody good It is a specially disastrous matter if nobody whatsoever derives any benefit from it.

speak ill of Disparage.

image

the image; the very image; the spit and image; the spitting image Exactly alike.

- *The baby is the image of his father.*

imagination

flight or stretch of imagination Imaginative effort.

impression

be under the impression Have the notion or (vague) belief.

- *I was under the impression that today was Friday.*

give or *create a false impression* Mislead by a statement or action.

- *The story she has told gives a totally false impression of what really happened.*

make a good impression Behave in a manner which will create admiration and respect.

- *He made a very good impression when he applied for the job.*

in

be in on Know.

in at Present at.

in for (it) Likely to experience (trouble).

in with On intimate or friendly terms with.

ins and outs Details.

not much in it Little difference (between various arguments, competitors etc.).

inch

every inch Completely; entirely.

- *John looks every inch a golfer.*

inch by inch By small degrees.

within an inch Close to.

incline

be inclined to Have a tendency to; be in favour of.

- *I am inclined to forgive him because of his youth.*

incumbent

incumbent upon one An essential duty for one.

inference

draw an inference Assume; infer.

- *From his manner, we drew the inference that he was satisfied with the results of his visit.*

influence

under the influence In full, 'under the influence of intoxicating liquor'.

iniquity

sink of iniquity Any place with a bad reputation. (Frequently used facetiously).

initiative
on one's own initiative Without prompting.
take the initiative Be the first (to do something).

in-laws
The relations of one's husband or wife—*mother-in-law, sister-in-law,* etc.

innings
have a good innings Spend a long time. (E.g. said of someone who has lived to old age.)

ins-and-outs
the ins-and-outs All the details.

instance
for instance As an example; to explain or elaborate one's meaning. Similar to *for example.*
in the first instance To begin with.

insult
add insult to injury Be offensive twice over.

intent
to all intents and purposes Apparently. As far as one can see.

interim
in the interim Between now and some specified event.
 • *We leave next week; in the interim we shall be visiting friends.*

interval
at intervals At irregular periods of time.
 • *The discussion continued; at intervals the speakers stopped for refreshment.*

iota
one iota The smallest possible quantity.
(*Note*—This idiom is always used in the negative.)

iron
iron out Remove difficulties from.
irons in the fire Matters of interest or importance which may prove profitable.

issue
confuse the issue Confuse the final analysis or result; bring forward irrelevant arguments.
force an issue Compel a decision to be reached.

join issue (with someone) (on something) Proceed to argue.
make an issue of Argue about.
take issue Disagree.

it
this is it What has been expected has arrived.

ivory
ivory tower State of detachment from ordinary life.

J

jack
every man jack Every single man.

hit the jackpot Enjoy great success (esp. financial).

jack of all trades (and master of none) One capable of undertaking a variety of jobs (but who is expert at none of them).

before you can say Jack Robinson Extremely quickly.

  - *He knocked, and before you could say Jack Robinson the door opened.*

jaundice
view with a jaundiced eye; take a jaundiced view of Regard with jealousy, envy, suspicion or distrust.

jib
the cut of one's jib One's personal appearance and manner.

job
a good job Fortunate.

  - *It's a good job it's not raining.*

give up as a bad job Stop doing (something) because of lack of success.

have a job to Have difficulty in.

Job's comforter One who comes nominally to console and comfort a person, but who actually adds to his distress by being pessimistic and reproachful.

just the job Exactly what is required.

make a good job of Succeed at.

make the best of a bad job Do one's best in unfortunate circumstances.

try the patience of Job Be vexatious.

jog

jog along To 'jog' is to proceed at a slow, regular pace. Used almost always metaphorically to indicate quiet, routine and unexciting progress.

jog-trot Progress as above.

jog a person's memory Remind, in order to prevent something being forgotten.

joke

crack a joke Make a joke; tell a humorous story.

it's no joke It is a serious matter.

joking apart Seriously.

practical joke Trick played on a person to gain a laugh at his expense.

Jones

keep up with the Joneses Try to reach same standards (especially of material comfort) as everyone else, or one's neighbours.

jot

jot or tittle Jot is a corruption of 'iota' (see **iota**); 'tittle' also means something tiny. (The expression is always used negatively.)

jot down Note briefly and quickly.

judgement

Against one's better judgement Contrary to what one really feels to be best.

sit in judgement on Judge.

juggle with

Rearrange. Misrepresent.

juice

stew in one's own juice Endure the consequences of one's own actions.

jump

jump at Take a quick advantage of; seize an opportunity.
- *The house is a bargain, and you should jump at the offer.*

jump down one's throat Speak with unexpected violence to one.
- *I only asked him if I could use his telephone, and he jumped down my throat.*

jump in Get in (car).

jump the gun Start before the proper time.

jump the queue Take place in queue ahead of others already there.

jump to it! Hurry!

the high jump Serious trouble.

- *When David comes back home, he's for the high jump.*

jungle

law of the jungle Lawlessness. State of vicious competition.

just

just in case As a precaution.

just so 1. Very orderly.

- *Everything in his kitchen is just so.*

2. (Exclamation of agreement). Precisely.

justice

do justice to Treat justly or fairly; appreciate fully (used frequently in reference to food).

do oneself justice Show one's abilities to their good advantage.

- *Did you do yourself justice in the driving-test?*

poetic justice Justice that is specially pleasing.

rough justice Justice that is not impeccable.

K

keel
on an even keel Calm.

keen
keen as mustard (on) Very enthusiastic (about).

keep
keep abreast of Keep level with.
- *We do our best to keep abreast of modern improvements.*
Similar to *keep pace with.*
keep aloof Remain distant from, physically or in manner.
keep at Persist or continue with.
- *You'll never learn to paint unless you keep at it.*
keep back Conceal. Slow down the progress of.
keep company Associate with.
keep cool Remain calm.
keep dark Conceal; refrain from mentioning.
keep one's counsel Remain silent and reticent.
keep one's distance (Originally) Maintain one's correct and formal attitude. (Now more frequently) Remain away from.
- *The dog's rather wild, so I should keep your distance.*
keep one's end up Not slacken. Acquit oneself well.
keep an eye on Watch; act as temporary guardian to.
- *I would be glad if you'd keep an eye on the children while we're away.*
keep at arm's length Avoid familiarity with.
keep going Continue (at one's work or routine, etc.).
- *He looks ill; I don't know how long he'll be able to keep going.*
keep guard Watch; act as sentinel.

keep one's hand in Continue to practise, in order to retain one's skill.

keep one's head Not allow oneself to become flustered.

keep house Act as the manager of a household.

- *When his wife died his sister went to keep house for him.*

keep in touch (with) Remain in contact or in communication (with).

keep in with Remain on good terms with, usually with some definite motive.

keep it up Continue in the same manner.

keep off Avoid.

keep on Persist in; repeat one's present actions.

keep one's word Do as one promises.

keep (oneself) to oneself Remain aloof and uncommunicative.

keep order Control.

keep out Refuse admittance to.

keep out of the way Absent or efface oneself.

keep pace with [LIT] and [MET]. Move at the same speed as.

- *My horse couldn't keep pace with the rest of the field.*
- *I can't keep pace with all the changes in tax law.*

keep the ball rolling Maintain impetus.

keep the peace Maintain peace.

keep secret Similar to *keep it dark*.

keep to Adhere to.

keep something to oneself Fail to disclose or share something.

keep a stiff upper lip Not allow one's lip to tremble with emotion; be firm and brave.

keep a straight face Refrain from laughing.

keep up Continue.

- *He wrote frequently at first, but I hadn't enough time to keep up the correspondence.*

keep up with Similar to *keep pace with* [LIT] and [MET].

- *I can't keep up with you—you walk too fast.*
- *It is difficult to keep up with all these new inventions.*

keep watch Act as look-out.

in keeping with (negative form = out of keeping with) Appropriate to; suitable to.

key

low key Subdued.

kick
kick over the traces Be insubordinate. Act independently.
kick up a fuss Cause a violent disturbance; quarrel.

kill
dressed or got up to kill Dressed in a manner designed to attract
 maximum attention.
kill oneself Exert oneself unduly.
kill the fatted calf Entertain lavishly.
kill with kindness Harm with too much kindness.

kin
next of kin Nearest relations.

kind
in kind In the same way.
nothing of the kind Nothing like that.
two of a kind Two similar people or things.

kindly
take kindly to Be well disposed towards.

kiss
kiss goodbye to Regard as lost.
kiss of death Something sure to cause failure, destruction, etc.

kitchen
everything but the kitchen sink Everything that can be
 imagined.

kite
fly a kite Act so as to test people's opinion, reaction etc.

kith
kith and kin Acquaintances and blood relations. (Used loosely
 to refer to members of same race.)

knee
bring person to his knees Cause him to submit.

knife
get one's knife into Behave vindictively to.

knight
knight errant Chivalrous man who, without expecting reward,
 helps and protects a weak or helpless person.

knit

knit one's brows Frown; regard in a puzzled way. ('Knit' here means to draw towards one another.)

knock

knock about 1. Wander, gaining experience in the process.
- *I've knocked about the world for forty years.*

2. Injure physically. Treat roughly.
- *I got knocked about a bit playing football yesterday.*

3. *knock-about* (Adjective) Noisy, boisterous, rowdy.

knock back Drink (esp. quickly or to excess).

knock down Strike a person so violently that he falls.

knock-down prices The cheapest possible. The best available (as in an auction. See *knock down to*).

knock down to Sell to a person who has made a final bid at an auction sale.

knock for six Overwhelm.

knock into a cocked hat Defeat easily. Be very much superior to.

knock into shape Put into good order.

knock off 1. Cease work for the day.

2. Steal.

knock on the head Destroy.
- *We'll soon knock his scheme on the head.*

knock out (Verb) Render incapable of further fighting.

knock over 1. [LIT] Overturn; upset.

2. [MET] Completely overwhelm.

knock the bottom out of Destroy.

knock together Create hastily.

knock up Rouse from sleep by knocking at the door.

take a knock 1. Receive a slight injury.

2. Suffer (slightly).

knot

Tie (up) in knots Baffle. Confuse.

know

I don't know him from Adam Exaggeration for 'I don't know him'.

in the know Having (private, secret, etc.) information.

know the ropes See under **ropes**.

not want to know Be uninterested or unconcerned.

knuckle

knuckle down Work hard. Begin to work.

- *If I can get a chance to knuckle down to it, I'll soon finish painting the bathroom.*

knuckle under Surrender.

rap on the knuckle See under **rap.**

L

labour

labour of love Work performed from affection or regard, and without expectation of payment.

labour a point Over-stress a point in one's argument.

labour under an affliction Suffer from some handicap or inconvenience, usually permanent.

labour under a delusion or illusion Be influenced by some false idea.

lady

Lady Bountiful A generous and kindly woman; now often applied derogatorily to a person who is too prominent in works of charity.

ladies' man One who makes special efforts to charm or please women.

laid

laid up 1. In bed through illness or accident.
2. Nautical. In harbour for repairs, etc.

lamb

like a lamb Without resistance.

might as well be hanged for a sheep as (for) a lamb As one is taking risks (in trouble, doing wrong, etc.) one might just as well be bold.

lame

lame duck Person or business unable to function effectively.

land

land on one's feet Enjoy fortunate success.

land up Find oneself in certain place.

land with Give something unwanted or unpleasant.

see how the land lies Discover the state of affairs; make discreet enquiries.

the land of the living Among living people.

the lie of the land How matters are.

landslide

(*political*) A sudden complete change of political popularity and, as a result, political power in an election. (Hence *landslide victory.*)

language

speak the same language Have similar outlook.

lap

lap of luxury Extreme richness.

- *This flat is hardly the lap of luxury, but it suits us.*

large

at large 1. Free after escaping.

2. In general.

lark

rise with the lark Get up early.

last

at last Eventually; after a long time has passed.

at long last As above, but more emphatic.

at one's last gasp In an utterly exhausted, or almost dying, condition.

last but not least Last to be mentioned, but not last in importance.

last out Survive, be available or serviceable, for as long as is necessary.

last person Very unlikely.

- *He is the last person you would expect to take risks.*

on one's last legs Almost, though not quite, exhausted. (The idiom is also applied to any affair, etc., which is on the verge of failing.)

stick to one's last Confine oneself to what one does well. Not meddle in another's business.

the last straw See under **straw**.

the last word 1. The final contribution to an argument.

- *He's a difficult man to negotiate with – always insists on having the last word.*
2. [MET] The culminating achievement, that which nothing can better. (Usually exaggeration).
- *This is the last word in electric cookers.*

late
sooner or later Eventually.

laugh
laugh away or off Dismiss (or conceal) something by laughing.
laugh in person's face Show open contempt for person.
laugh on the other side of one's face Be the reverse of amused; be depressed or unhappy.
laugh out of court Fail to be taken seriously.
laugh up one's sleeve Be amused secretly; hide one's laughter in contempt.
laughing-stock Object of ridicule.
no laughing matter A serious matter.

launch
launch out Depart from one's normal habits or occupation.

laurels
(win) laurels (Acquire) honour.
look to one's laurels Beware of losing one's place.
rest on one's laurels Cease to strive further.

law
arm of the law Criminal law, personified by the police.
the eyes or eye of the law A legal stand-point.
- *In the eyes of the law, you are now an adult.*
have the law on Prosecute in a court of law.
law-abiding Observing the law.
a law unto oneself One who follows his own inclinations, regardless of custom.
lay down the law Speak very firmly; use one's authority; insist on proper observance.
- *The doctor laid down the law, and told me to eat less.*
take the law into one's own hands Ignore the legal method of obtaining justice, and act entirely as one considers suitable and just.

lay
lay about one Strike out violently in every direction.

lay or *put aside; lay by* 1. Abandon, usually for a short time.
2. Put away for future use.

lay bare Reveal.

lay a bet Place a bet or wager.

lay at one's door or *to one's charge* Place the blame or responsibility on one.

- *The death of the patient was laid at the hospital's door.*

lay off Cease to employ (person).

lay one's hands on Find. Obtain possession of.

- *I can't lay my hands on my umbrella.*

lay hold of Grasp.

lay in or *up* Store for future use.

- *We must lay in some candles in case there's an electricity strike.*

lay into Attack.

lay on thick Exaggerate greatly (usually blame, or praise).

lay oneself open (to) Expose oneself (to); lead to an unfavourable assumption.

- *If this party goes on much longer, we'll lay ourselves wide open to complaints from the people next door.*

lay out 1. Spend.
2. Present to view.
3. Knock unconscious.

lay stress (weight, emphasis) on Emphasise.

- *The Chancellor laid stress on the need for economy.*

lay waste Ravage.

lead

give a lead 1. Provide an example by doing something first.
2. Provide a clue.

lead a dance Cause considerable trouble and activity.

- *The chicken led us a dance before we caught it.*

lead astray Mislead. Encourage to do wrong.

lead by the nose Control a person as completely as if he were a horse being led by a rope.

lead off Act as the leader in beginning any function (dancing, singing, etc.); start.

lead on Encourage to go further than was intended.

- *He's normally good, but sometimes others lead him on.*

lead one a dog's life Make one's life miserable.

lead the way Similar to *lead off*, but also frequently used in the literal sense of going first to point the way.

lead up to Progress gradually towards.

leading light Prominent person.

take the lead or *leading part* Act the most important part. Show initiative.

- *Someone will have to take the lead in forming a committee.*

leaf

take a leaf out of a person's book Copy; take as an example.

- *I wish you'd take a leaf out of Peter's book, and get up early.*

turn over a new leaf Alter; change; make a fresh and better beginning.

- *She has promised to turn over a new leaf, and be more punctual.*

league

not in the same league as Nowhere near as good as.

lean

lean over backwards Use all one's best endeavours.

leap

by leaps and bounds With extreme rapidity.

- *Their prosperity is increasing by leaps and bounds.*

a leap in the dark An action the result of which is uncertain or unknown.

learn

learn by heart Memorise.

lease

a new lease of life Fresh reserves of energy.

leash

straining at the leash Keen to start.

least

at least As the minimum.

- *If we can't afford a new car, at least we can get the old one repaired.*

in the least In the smallest degree.

least said, soonest mended The less one says, the better.

to say the least of it To minimise; express as mildly as possible.

- *His bluntness was, to say the least of it, unlikely to make him popular.*

leave

beg leave Ask permission. [Old f. Formal.]

leave alone Do not interfere (with).

leave behind 1. Forget.

- *John has left his spectacles behind.*
2. Deliberately discard.
- *I've left my umbrella behind; it isn't going to rain.*

leave in or *out in the cold* Ignore; to take no notice of, or interest in.

leave in the lurch Abandon in circumstances of danger and difficulty.

leave it at that Take no further action. Make no further comment.

leave much to be desired Be far from satisfactory.

leave off 1. Cease to wear a garment.

2. Cease; stop what one is doing.

leave out Omit.

leave over Defer.

- *I can't do it now; I'll leave it over till tomorrow.*

leave a person to it Leave a person alone to continue in his own way.

- *If you think you can finish it on your own, I'll leave you to it.*

leave at the post See under **post.**

leave one cold Fail to excite, interest, etc.

- *That sort of book just leaves me cold.*

leave to oneself Leave in solitude, without interference.

- *If you leave him to himself, he'll be quite happy.*

leave standing Make more rapid progress than.

leave well alone Emphatic form of *leave alone.*

leave word Leave a message, verbal or written.

take French leave Abandon one's work or post without obtaining the necessary permission from one's superior.

take leave Venture.

take leave of one's senses Go mad.

take one's leave (of) Depart; say farewell (to).

without so much as a by your leave Without even asking permission.

leeway

make up leeway Compensate for time which has been lost.

left

have two left feet Be clumsy.

left-handed compliment One which is the reverse of complimentary.

left, right and centre In or from all directions.

leg

give a leg-up [LIT] Help a person to mount horse, etc. [MET]
Help generally.

not a leg to stand on Having nothing effective in support of an
argument.

on one's last legs Close to exhaustion or to the limits of use-
fulness.

pull one's leg Deceive jocularly. Trick. Befool.

    • *He takes everything so seriously: I can't resist pulling his leg.*

stretch one's legs Take a walk for exercise.

lend

lend a hand Help.

lend itself to Be suitable for.

length

at great length For a long time.

    • *She spoke at great length about nothing at all.*

at length After considerable time; eventually.

go to any lengths Ignore every impediment that may get in one's
way.

leopard

leopard cannot change its spots Person's nature cannot be
altered.

less

in less than no time Very quickly.

lesson

teach one a lesson Do something which will act as a reprimand
to one and show up one's fault.

let

let alone 1. Refrain from interfering with.

    2. In addition to being (or having).

let be Same as *let alone* (1).

let the cat out of the bag Reveal a secret (usually accidentally).
Create trouble (usually by tactlessness).

let down Betray; fail to support when support was needed.

    • *My brother promised to give me a lift, but he let me down.*

let fall (applied to speech) Remark casually.

let fly 1. [LIT] Propel swiftly.

    2. [MET] Abandon control.

    • *He lost his temper, and let fly.*

let go Release one's hold.
- *He let go of the rope, and crashed to the ground.*

let someone in 1. Admit.
- *John knocked, and I let him in.*

2. Involve a person without his or her knowledge or consent; make responsible for.
- *His tactlessness lets me in for a lot of embarrassment.*

let loose Release.

let off 1. Allow to go free and unpunished.
- *The prisoner was let off with some good advice.*

2. Explode.
- *We let off fireworks on November 5th.*

let on Reveal. Pretend.

let oneself go Give way to one's impulses, enthusiasms, etc.

let out 1. Release; set free.
- *I'll open the cage and let out the bird.*

2. Disclose; reveal.
- *I'll tell you a secret, but you mustn't let it out.*

let pass Ignore.
- *What the newspaper said isn't at all accurate, but let that pass.*

let someone have it Speak bluntly or angrily to someone. Strike person.

let sleeping dogs lie Avoid anything (usually people) which might stir up trouble.

let slip Inadvertently release (e.g. a remark). Miss (an opportunity).

let well alone Refrain from interfering, because it may do more harm than good.

letter

to the letter Exactly; precisely.
- *His report was correct to the letter.*

the letter of the law Exactly in accordance with the rules and regulations of the law.

level

do one's level best Do one's utmost; use all one's efforts.
- *I'll do my level best to be at the concert.*

keep a level head Remain calm and sensible. Keep control of oneself.
- *In these exciting times, it isn't always easy to keep a level head.*

level-headed Sensible.

level-pegging At the same level; in the same state.

on the level Truth(fully), honest(ly).

liberal

liberal education One planned on broad principles.

liberty

at liberty Free; unrestrained. Permitted or invited to do something.

- *You are at liberty to wander anywhere in the park.*

take the liberty Act as though one possessed a right which in fact one does not; presume.

- *I have taken the liberty of switching off your car-lights.*

take liberties Go beyond the normal limits of convention or good manners. Be unduly familiar (with).

lick

lick into shape Make efficient or presentable. Mould.

lick one's boots Be sycophantic to one.

lick one's wounds Consider consequences of one's defeat.

lid

take or blow the lid off Expose.

lie

give the lie to Completely deny; disprove.

has made one's bed and must lie on it Must endure the consequences of one's action.

lie at one's door Become one's responsibility.

lie in one's teeth Tell serious lies.

lie low Remain unobtrusive.

lie up Lie in bed as the result of an illness or accident.

white lie A harmless lie told only with the object of helping or comforting someone.

lieu

in lieu of Instead of; in place of.

life

as large as life [LIT] In person. [MET] Prominent. Unmistakable. (This idiom is used in a general rather than an exact and literal sense, as emphasis.)

breath of life Absolutely essential.

come to life Become alive; give an indication of being alive.

- *I seldom come to life before mid-morning.*

for the life of me. For dear life. [LIT] 'Even if what I am saying meant the loss of my life.' Used merely for emphasis.

- *For the life of me I can't understand what you're worrying about.*

have the time of one's life Enjoy oneself thoroughly.

large as life In person.

life and soul of the party A vivacious person.

matter of life and death Desperately serious matter; of crucial significance.

new lease of life Fresh possibilities of continued existence.

- *Since he got back from holiday he's taken on a new lease of life.*

not on your life! Certainly not!

prime of life The most fully developed period of life (usually supposed to be about forty).

take one's life in one's hands Take bold risk.

to the life Exactly; with complete realism.

true to life Accurate.

lift

lift a finger Make a slight effort. (Usually used in negative.)

- *He never lifted a finger to help me.*

lift one's hand against Strike.

light

bring to light Reveal.

come to light Be revealed, exposed.

in a good light Favourably.

in the light of In view of. With the help given by.

light-fingered Thievish.

light upon Discover by chance.

make light of Treat as of little consequence.

shed or throw (a flood of) light on 1. [LIT] Light brilliantly.
2. [MET] Make clear and plain. Help to explain.

see the light Come round to one's point of view.

see the light of day Come into being.

strike a light Ignite a match.

the lighter side The more enjoyable or amusing aspect.

like

like; the like a similar object; anything strongly resembling another of the same class.

- *Apples, pears, and the like.*

like father, like son The son is like (or as bad as) his father.

like-minded Similar in their attitudes, views, etc.

nothing like 1. Emphatic form of 'unlike'.

- *The picture is nothing like him.*

2. Not nearly.
- *There were nothing like as many people as we expected.*

likelihood
in all likelihood Very probably.

likely
a likely story Something unlikely to be true.
not likely! Certainly not!

lily
gild or *paint the lily* Improve what is already satisfactory.

limit
within limits To some extent.

line
all along the line In every way.
along or *on the lines of* Similar to.
bring into line Cause to agree.
come into line Agree. Co-operate.
end of the line Point beyond which it is useless to go.
hard line Uncompromising attitude.
in line for Likely to receive.
in line with In accordance with.
in the line of duty As part of one's duty.
in one's line Within one's knowledge, experience or interests.
step out of line Fail to conform.
toe the line Conform.

linen
wash one's dirty linen in public Reveal discreditable matters
about oneself.

lion
the lion's share The greatest or most valuable portion.

lip
lick one's lips Express pleasure in anticipation of something.
pay lip-service (to) Pretend to agree (with).
smack one's lips Show eager anticipation.
stiff upper lip Fortitude.

little
little by little, inch by inch, etc. A small amount of distance,
repeated until a large total is reached.
- *Little by little the truth is being made public.*

live

live down By good conduct, etc., enable people to forget some past failure.

- *If I fail, I shall never live it down.*

live and learn Way of greeting some new fact or piece of knowledge, etc.

live and let live Be sympathetic to the failings of others.

live up to Prove oneself worthy of.

live wire Lively and energetic person.

within living memory Within the memory of people still alive.

lo!

lo and behold! an exclamatory introduction expressing surprise.

- *And lo and behold, he changed his mind.*

load

loaded question Question with dangerous implications.

take a load off one's mind Relieve one of anxiety.

lock

lock, stock and barrel Entirely; wholly.

under lock and key Secure.

log

sleep like a log Sleep very soundly.

loin

gird up one's loins Prepare.

loggerheads

at loggerheads Disagreeing; quarrelling.

long

in the long run At the end; after a number of other things have happened.

- *In the long run, honesty is always the best policy.*

long arm of coincidence Applied to coincidences in general, the 'long arm' referring to the surprising and abnormal way in which they occur.

- *I hadn't seen him for years, but by the long arm of coincidence we met on a train journey.*

long-drawn (out) Long continued or sustained.

- *a long-drawn cry sounded across the sea.*

long odds Unfavourable chances; an improbable event.

the long and the short of it The whole position or situation briefly stated.

long shot See under **shot.**

long-standing Existing for a long time.

long-suffering Patient and enduring.

long-term plans Plans which extend a long way into the future.

long in the tooth Old.

long-winded Verbose; wearingly talkative.

look

look about or *around one* Study one's surroundings and prospects.

- *I want to look around for a month or two before I start at university.*

look after Take care or charge of.

- *We promised to look after the cats while the family was abroad.*

look back Contemplate the past.

- *If we look back, we realise the changes war has made.*

look bad Appear discreditable.

look before you leap Take care before committing yourself to action.

look daggers Regard fiercely and bitterly; look at with fury and hatred.

look down upon or *down one's nose at* Scorn; regard with contempt.

look for 1. Search for.

- *She looked for the missing money.*

2. Expect.

- *I look for a number of improvements when the Government changes.*

look for a needle in a haystack Look for a small object in a large place, or for one person among many, etc.

look forward to Regard some future event with pleasure.

- *I look forward to your visit next week.*

look a gift horse in the mouth See under **horse.**

look good Appear creditable.

look into Examine; scrutinise.

- *He promised to look into my complaint.*

look on the bright side Regard cheerfully; see the best in any situation.

look one in the eye or *face* Not be ashamed.

look one's age In appearance to give impression of being as old as one actually is.

look the other way [LIT] Turn one's head. [MET] Refrain from noticing.

look out! *(exclamation)* Beware, be careful!
- *Look out, or you'll be run over!*

look out; keep a sharp lookout for Watch for.

look-out (Noun) Affair; concern; business.
- *Joan has decided to go to South America. What happens there is her own look-out.*

look over 1. [LIT]
- *He looked over the wall.*

2. [MET] Scan; examine.
- *I'll be glad if you'll look over these letters.*

look sharp Hurry up.

look small Appear insignificant.

look to it Note; take careful action.

look up 1. Refer to books, etc., to ascertain some fact.
- *I'll look it up in the encyclopaedia.*

2. Visit an acquaintance whom one hasn't seen for some time.

3. Improve; appear more cheerful.
- *The business is beginning to look up.*

look up to Regard with awe or respect.

not much to look at Unattractive.

not to get a look-in Be excluded.

not to like the look of something Find something alarming.

loose

(play) fast and loose Act irresponsibly.

at a loose end Idle; having no definite object.

loosen person's tongue Make person talk freely.

lord

drunk as a lord Very drunk.

lord it over Behave arrogantly, as a person of importance.

lose

lose face Be humiliated. Lose reputation or credibility. Hence *loss of face.*

lose ground Suffer, by degrees, loss of reputation, health or position.

lose heart Become discouraged.

lose one's head Suffer panic or loss of control.

lose one's nerve Become frightened.

lose oneself in Be preoccupied by.

losing battle A hopeless cause.

loss; lost

at a loss 1. For less than the cost price.
- *I sold the goods at a loss.*

2. Temporarily unable to act or reply; undecided.
- *I was at a loss to answer him.*

a lost cause a movement, project or agitation, etc., which has no longer any chance of becoming effective.

lost for words Too surprised (etc.) to speak.

lost in admiration So overcome with admiration that one cannot express one's emotions.

lot

throw or cast in one's lot with Decide to join, or to share the fortunes of.

draw lots or cast lots Decide by throwing dice or by some similar method of chance.

the whole lot The whole number.

love

calf-love Adolescent love; a young man's first love affair; usually not very serious.

labour of love Work done out of love for someone or something, rather than for money.

for love or money By any means.
- *I've tried all the shops, but I can't get any cream for love or money.*

no love lost Dislike, unfriendliness.

lovely

lovely and Very.
- *The sun's lovely and warm.*

low

at a low ebb [LIT] A condition existing when an ebbing tide has left the water in a river at its lowest point. [MET] Feeble, almost exhausted.

in low spirits Depressed.

luck

as luck would have it Unfortunately.

down on one's luck In an unfortunate state.

hard luck Unfortunate.

push one's luck Take more risks than necessary.

run of luck A series of lucky events. Used also in the opposite sense—*a run of bad luck.*

take pot luck Accept impromptu hospitality without a definite invitation. Dine on whatever happens to be cooking in the pot. Take any sort of risk.

tough luck Bad luck.

try one's luck Attempt success.

with luck If all goes well.

worse luck! Unfortunately!

lumber

get lumbered with Be given, against one's will.

lump

a lump in one's throat A sense of pity, producing a desire to weep.

if you don't like it, you can lump it You must tolerate it whether you like it or not.

lump sum The whole amount at once.

● *They paid him in a lump sum all that was owing.*

lump together Merge.

● *If we lump all our money together, we shall have over £50.*

lying

refuse to take something lying down Object strenuously to something. Resist something strongly.

M

mad

drive or send mad Cause to become mad.

- *The noise of that radio is driving me mad.*

hopping mad Very angry.

like mad With tremendous energy.

- *He ran like mad.*

mad as a march hare Utterly and completely mad.

mad about Infatuated with.

mad on Extremely or wildly interested in.

- *My daughter's mad on dancing.*

made

made for Ideally suited to.

maiden

maiden name The surname of a woman before she was married.

maiden speech The first speech made in Parliament by a member.

maiden voyage The first voyage made by a vessel in the sea or air.

main

in the main Chiefly.

main chance; have an eye to the main chance Be alert to one's own interests.

majority

attain one's majority Reach the age at which one is legally regarded as an adult.

made

made for Ideally suited to.

self-made man or woman One who has made own success (in life, business).

make

be the making of Ensure success of.

have the makings of Have the ability for becoming.

in the making Being formed.

make after Follow quickly.

make as if Pretend.

make-believe Pretence.

make do Use as the best substitute available.

• *We hadn't time for lunch, but we made do with sandwiches.*

make fast Secure; fasten firmly.

• *They made fast the boat to the pier.*

make for 1. Set out, usually quickly, in a particular direction.

• *The ships made for the harbour because of the storm.*

2. Help to make or maintain.

• *The minister's speech does not make for peace.*

make good 1. Repair; put back something that has been destroyed; restore.

2. Recover a lost reputation.

make a habit of doing Become accustomed to do.

make it Succeed.

make it up Become friendly again after a quarrel, or agree after a dispute.

make money Earn money. Show a profit.

make the most of Put to the best use possible.

make much of Make special efforts to please; treat with conspicuous kindness and respect. Very similar to *make a fuss of.*

make nothing of 1. Treat as trivial or of no importance. Similar to *make little of.*

2. Completely fail to understand.

what do you make of it? What do you deduce from it? Do you understand it?

make off Run away (usually as the result of some guilty act).

make oneself scarce Disappear quickly; efface oneself.

• *We decided that it would be tactful to make ourselves scarce.*

make or break Succeed or fail. Also *make or mar.*

make out 1. Comprehend; decipher.

2. Inscribe, write.

3. Imply; indicate.

make over Make a formal gift of property.

make so bold as to Take the liberty of. [Rather formal and old f.]

- *May I make so bold as to suggest a compromise?*

make time for Act to provide an opportunity for discussion of, attention to, etc.

make up 1. Invent; originate.

2. Complete.

3. Compensate for.

See **make it up.**

make-up Cosmetics.

make up for Compensate for.

make up to Flatter, attempt to please, in order to obtain favours.

on the make Trying to make money.

makeshift

makeshift Inferior or temporary; substitute.

- *We will put up a makeshift roof till the other is mended.*

man

as one man Unanimously.

be one's own man Be independent.

every man-jack Everyone.

hit a man when he is down Punish person who is already at a disadvantage.

man-about-town Man with active social life.

man and boy Since childhood.

man in the street Ordinary man.

a man of letters An author; one whose profession is that of a writer.

a man of straw A worthless person.

a man of his word One who is truthful and trustworthy, who does not break promises.

man of few words Reticent man.

man of the moment Person currently prominent or successful.

a man of the world One with worldly knowledge and experience.

man to man Without prevarication.

sort out the men from the boys Determine who is mature, brave, competent etc. and who is not.

to a man Everyone, without exception.

manner

all manner of All kinds of.

by no manner of means See under **means**.

in a manner of speaking So to say. As it were.

to the manner born As if naturally or instinctively fitted for a position, etc.

many

a good or great many Very many.

many a long day A long time.

many's the time or many a time Frequently.

map

put on the map Make well known.

march

marching orders, get one's Be dismissed.

mare

mare's nest Something which does not exist; a mere effort of the imagination.

mark

beside the mark Unconnected with the subject being discussed.

make one's mark Establish a reputation.

mark down Reduce price.

a marked man One who has become notorious through his connection with some particular incident.

mark my words Take particular note of what I am saying.

mark time Deliberately wait, without progressing.

mark-up Sum added to ensure profit.

overstep the mark Go beyond what is proper. Also *overshoot the mark.*

quick off the mark Quick to take action.

up to the mark In a normal state of health; well. (This idiom is generally used in the negative.)

wide of the mark Very inaccurate.

  • *His guesses were all wide of the mark.*

market

be in the market for Be interested in buying.

be on the market Be available for sale.

put on the market Offer for sale.

marrow

to the marrow All the way through.

martyr

be a martyr to Suffer severely from.

mass

masses of A large number of.

master

mastermind (Noun) Chief planner, thinker or originator. (Verb) To be in control as mastermind.

master of oneself Capable of self-control; able to think and act coolly and logically.

master-stroke An exceptionally shrewd or clever action.

match

be a match for Be as good as.

meet one's match Meet one's equal.

matter

for that matter As far as that is concerned.

matter of course An affair of normal routine; regularly.

matter of fact Something which is established as truth (as opposed to opinion). Hence *as a matter of fact*: emphatic phrase stressing truth of an expression.

matter-of-fact (Adjective) Commonplace; ordinary.

a matter of life and death Of vital and extreme importance.

the matter in question The affair being discussed or referred to.

no matter 1. In spite of.

- *I shall go, no matter what the weather may be.*

2. Immaterial; having no importance.

- *I had something to say, but it's no matter (it doesn't matter).*

what's the matter What is concerning or occupying you?

what's the matter with it? What is wrong with it?

may

be that as it may Even so.

that is as may be That may be so.

meal

make a meal of Find or create undue difficulties in; take a long time doing.

mealy-mouthed Applied to one who is a hypocrite or coward, and is afraid to speak honestly.

square meal A full, complete meal.

mean

mean well Possess good intentions.

means

by all means 1. Indication of cordial assent.

- *Shall I ask him to come in? By all means.*

2. By exerting every effort.

- *Try by all (or every) means to persuade him to come.*

by all or *no manner of means* Indicating emphatic assent (or dissent).

by fair means or foul In any way possible.

by no means; not by any means Elaborated forms of 'not'.

by what means? By what method? How?

means to an end An action merely leading to one's real object.

meantime; meanwhile

in the meantime; meanwhile The period during which an event has occurred; while this was happening; during the intervening time.

Similar to *for the time being* (under **time**).

measure

for good measure To add something more than necessary.

get the measure of Estimate the quality of.

in some measure To some extent.

measure one's length Fall flat.

- *He staggered, and measured his length on the pavement.*

take measures to Take suitable action to.

take person's measure Estimate the sort of person someone is.

measure up to Reach the level or standard of.

- *Does the scenery measure up to your expectations?*

meat

meat and drink Very easy. Very enjoyable.

one man's meat is another man's poison What one person enjoys may be disliked by another.

medicine

a dose of one's own medicine Treatment that one is accustomed to give (rather than receive).

take one's medicine 1. [LIT]

2. [MET] Suffer one's just deserts.

meet

meet half-way Compromise.

meet the case Suffice.

meet one's Waterloo Meet defeat after period of success.

meet with 1. Receive.

2. Be received with.

more than meets the eye Something suppressed or hidden.

melt

in the melting-pot Under reconsideration, and likely to be completely changed.

melt away 1. [LIT] Disappear or change form by melting.

2. [MET] (Of person) Depart unobtrusively.

melt down Reduce to a single mass by heating until it becomes fluid, and then allow to harden.

memory

burden one's memory Cause to become a weight or burden on one's memory.

commit to memory Similar to *learn by heart* (under **heart**).

within living memory During the lifetime of people now alive.

mend

mend one's ways Improve one's behaviour.

on the mend Recovering from illness, injury or a period of weakness.

mention

not to mention In addition to; distinct from.

don't mention it A polite dismissal of apology or thanks.

- *'I am sorry to have troubled you.' 'Don't mention it.'*

mercy

at the mercy of Dependent upon; controlled by; in the power of.

- *The ship was at the mercy of the waves.*

left to the (tender) mercies or mercy of Abandoned to the (unpleasant) effect of.

thankful for small mercies Grateful for small matters.

merry

make merry Rejoice.

make merry at Make fun of. Laugh at.

merry-making Rejoicing and festivities upon some special occasion.

play merry hell with Cause considerable upset to.

mess

make a mess of Bungle.

mess up Bring muddle to.

message
get the message Understand.

mete
mete out Distribute; give out. (Frequently applied to justice, punishment, etc.)

method
there's method in his madness What he says, plans, does (etc.) is not as mad as it appears.

mettle
on one's mettle Roused to the use of one's best efforts; prepared to do one's utmost.

middle
middle-of-the-road Avoiding extremes.

midsummer
midsummer madness [LIT] Temporary madness, brought on by the conjunction of the full moon at midsummer and the heat of the season. [MET] Applied to any sort of crazy idea or plan.

might
might and main All one's powers or strength.

mildly
put something mildly Make a deliberate or ironic under-statement.
- *When the telephone rang in the middle of the night, I was rather irritated, to put it mildly.*

mile
a mile away or off Easily.
- *You could see a mile off that the accident would happen.*
stick out a mile Be very obvious.

milk
milk-and-water Feeble; weak.
milk of human kindness Genuine and natural kindness towards one's fellow-creatures.
no use crying over spilt milk Useless to bewail mistake that cannot be put right.

mill
go or be put through the mill Undergo any rigorous experience, usually at someone's hands.

mill-stone round one's neck Liability.

million
one in a million Very special.

mince
not to mince matters or words Not to speak tactfully or politely; to be plain and direct.

• *I told him, without mincing matters, that I wasn't satisfied.*

make mincemeat of 'Mincemeat' consists [LIT] of ingredients chopped (or minced) into very small pieces for cooking. The phrase is used [MET] to indicate the destruction of arguments, plans, etc.

mind
apply or give one's mind to Consider carefully; concentrate one's attention upon.

bear or keep in mind Retain in one's memory; remember.

be in two minds Be undecided.

be of the same mind Agree.

call to mind Recollect. Remember.

cast one's mind back Recall the past.

change one's mind Adopt new opinion.

come into one's mind Be remembered.

do you mind? Don't do or say that.

go out of one's mind 1. Forget.
 2. [LIT] Go insane. [MET] Become intensely irritated, confused, etc.

give one's mind to See *apply one's mind.*

give a piece of one's mind Blame; express one's opinion candidly (and, usually, critically or adversely).

have a good mind to Be much inclined to.

have a mind of one's own Be able to form one's own opinions.

have half a mind to Be strongly disposed to do something, but unlikely to do it.

have it in mind to Intend to.

have on one's mind Be preoccupied by.

in one's right mind Sane. Generally used negatively, an alternative being *out of one's mind*

in two minds Undecided.

keep one's mind on Think constantly about.

know one's own mind Have clear and fixed opinions.

make up one's mind Come to a decision.

mind 1. Take into one's care or charge.
- *The mother asked the girl to mind the baby for an hour.*
2. Show care about; be careful of.
- *Mind the wet paint.*
3. Regret; object to.
- *I hope you won't mind my going out.*

mind's eye Imagination.

mind one's own business Do not concern oneself in other people's affairs.

mind (out for) Be on one's guard against.

a mind to A liking or desire to.

of one or the same mind Having the same opinions.

one-track mind A mind, or personality, exclusively committed to one preoccupation (e.g. money, work, sex, etc.).

out of one's mind See **in one's right mind.**

out of sight, out of mind That which cannot be seen may be forgotten.

presence of mind Mental alertness and an immediate response to an emergency.

prey on one's mind Cause deep and prolonged mental distress.

put one's mind at rest Free one from worry.

put one's mind to Concentrate on.

put out of one's mind Take no account of.

put person in mind of Make person remember.

read one's mind Know what one is thinking.

set one's mind on Wish to attain.

speak one's mind Give one's frank opinion.

take one's mind off Divert one's attention from.

to my mind In my opinion. According to my judgement.

mine

mine of information Source of much information.

mint

in mint condition As new.

mint of money A very large sum of money.

mischief

do (person) a mischief Hurt (person).

make mischief Intentionally cause discord and unhappiness.

miss

give a miss Avoid.

miss is as good as a mile If one fails, the degree of failure is immaterial.

not miss much 1. Be absent from something uninteresting.
2. Be alert.
Also *never miss a trick*

mistake
and or make no mistake! An idiom used entirely for emphasis.
there's no mistaking It is impossible to mistake.

mix
mixed bag Varied collection.
mixed blessing Having advantages and disadvantages.

moment
at the moment At present.
half a moment A very short time.
have one's moments Be good at times.
in a moment In a short while.
moment of truth Critical or decisive moment.
unguarded moment A moment in which one has forgotten to be careful in speech or action.

money
hush-money Money paid to prevent a secret being revealed.
money for jam or old rope Money easily obtained.
money is no object The shortage of money is no hindrance.
money to burn Large amounts of money.
pin-money Money supplied for minor pleasures and amusements.
pocket-money Small sums for personal expenditure.
spend money like water Spend extravagantly.

month
month of Sundays A long and indefinite period.

moon
moonshine Unreal, fantastic and untrue statement, ideas, plans, etc.
moon-struck Dazed, incapable of thought.
once in a blue moon Very infrequently.

morning
morning coffee Coffee drunk halfway through the morning, i.e. about eleven o'clock.
morning dress Official and formal clothing worn by men during

the day (as opposed to evening dress), i.e. black coat with short 'tails', black waistcoat and dark grey trousers.

most

at the most; at most At the highest; as the limit.
for the most part In most circumstances; usually,
  ● *For the most part, we go away at weekends.*
make the most of Take full advantage of.

mother

mother earth The ground.
mother-tongue The language spoken in one's native land.

motion

go through the motions Do something without serious purpose.
set (the wheels) in motion Begin.

mount

mount up Increase; accumulate.
  ● *I'm afraid our expenses are mounting up rather fast.*

mountain

make a mountain out of a molehill Make much out of very little; greatly exaggerate.
move mountains Make every effort.

mouth

by word of mouth By speech; orally.
down in the mouth Depressed; despondent.
have a big mouth Be indiscreet or boastful.
make one's mouth water Create pleasurable sense of anticipation.
shoot one's mouth off Boast. Blab.
take the words out of someone's mouth Say what someone was about to say.

move

get a move on Hurry.
make a move Go.
move heaven and earth Make every possible effort; use every available means.
move off Depart.
move on Change one's position.

mow

mow down Cut, with wide sweeping strokes, as wheat, etc., is cut with a scythe.

much

be too much for Overwhelm.

not come to much Have little success.

not much to look at Insignificant. Not striking or attractive.

mud

mudslinging Throwing insults.

one's name is mud One is in disgrace.

muddle

muddle through Achieve one's objectives without showing very much skill in doing so.

music

face the music Be prepared to accept criticism, usually as consequence of one's own actions.

music to one's ears A pleasure to hear.

must

it must needs be It will inevitably be. [Old f.]

- *It must needs be some weeks before we receive a reply from Australia.*

needs must when the devil drives If this is inevitable, I must accept it as such.

mustard

keen as mustard (on) Very eager (about).

muster

pass muster Be accepted as adequate.

N

nail

hard as nails Very tough. (Applied to people.)

hit the nail on the head See under **hit**.

nail-biting Such as to cause nervous anxiety.

nail in one's coffin Something that will shorten life—drink, anxiety, etc.—or destroy one's reputation.

nail one's colours to the mast Publicly demonstrate one's allegiance. Refuse to surrender or modify one's opinions or principles.

on the nail Promptly; immediately.

- *He pays his debts on the nail.*

namby-pamby

feeble; effeminate. Insipid.

name

clear one's name Prove one's innocence.

give a bad name to Damage the reputation of.

have to one's name Own.

make a name for oneself Gain a reputation.

name-dropping Mentioning the names of important people to impress others.

no names, no pack drill If no names are mentioned, there can be no question of offence or punishment.

take one's name in vain Refer to one lightly.

you name it No matter what.

nap

catch napping See under **catch**.

narrow

a narrow escape, majority, etc. One which nearly did not occur.

- *I had a narrow escape from being run over by a bus this morning.*

a narrow margin Very little (space, etc.).

- *John passed the examination by a narrow margin.*

a narrow squeak A success or escape only just attained.

- *We won the game, but it was a narrow squeak.*

narrow-minded Having an illiberal mind and attitude.

nature

in the nature of things Part of normal circumstances, routine, instinct, etc.

- *It's in the nature of things for children to behave in that way.*

near

near by or near at hand Close; a short distance away.

near the mark Nearly or approximately correct.

near miss Narrow failure to strike, hit, collide etc.

a near or close thing A success which was very nearly a failure.

- *I ran all the way and caught the train, but it was a near thing.*

nearest and dearest Closest relatives.

necessity

make a virtue of necessity See under **virtue.**

necessity is the mother of invention New ways of doing things are usually contrived because of a pressing need.

of necessity Unavoidably.

neck

get it in the neck Get into trouble.

neck and crop Entirely.

neck and neck Side by side; level.

- *It was a neck and neck race.*

neck or nothing Desperate; risking everything.

up to one's neck Very involved.

needle

needle in a haystack Thing impossible to find because of its concealment among many other things.

sharp as a needle 1. [LIT] Very sharp.

2. [MET] Acute.

needless

needless to say It is unnecessary to say.

negative
in the negative No.

neither
neither here nor there See under **here.**

nerve
bundle of nerves Very nervous person.
get on one's nerves Irritate (usually by the repetition of some annoying action, usually slight).
have the nerve to Have the courage, or impertinence, to.

nest
feather one's nest See under **feather.**
nest egg [LIT] An artificial egg left in the nest to encourage the hen to further laying. [MET] Money saved for one's old age or for some specific purpose in the future.

nettle
grasp the nettle Tackle a disagreeable problem.

never
never mind Do not trouble or concern yourself.
never say die! Never give up hope of success.
well I never! Expression of surprise.

new
be a new one on Be unfamiliar to.
new broom A newcomer who intends to demonstrate his efficiency, ideas, etc.
new-fangled A slightly contemptuous term applied to any new invention or method, usually of a minor type.

next
next door to [LIT] In the adjoining house. [MET] Any form of nearness.
  ● *Her statements are next door to lying.*
next to nothing Practically nothing.
what(ever) next? Expression of surprise, literally suggesting 'What can occur subsequently which can possibly be more absurd, surprising, shocking, etc.?'

nick
in the nick of time Just in time, at the right and vital moment.

night

have a good or *bad night* Sleep well (or badly).

night out Evening (not night) away from home, for enjoyment.

overnight [LIT] The period between one day and the next. [MET] In a very brief time.

- *He became famous overnight.*

stay the night Remain until following day.

nine

dressed up to the nines Elaborately dressed.

nine day's wonder See under **wonder**.

nine times out of ten Nearly always.

nine to five Normal hours of work.

nineteen to the dozen Very vigorously.

nip

nip and tuck Same as *neck and neck.*

nip in the bud End any project before it has a chance of maturing.

nit

nit-picking Trivial and irritating fault-finding.

nitty-gritty Basic practical details.

no

no one else No other person.

no such thing An emphatic negative.

- *He said I had promised to go, but I told him I had done no such thing.*

no way (Under) no circumstances.

there's no accounting for taste Some people have very unexpected or odd likes and dislikes.

will not take no for an answer Persist, despite refusals.

nod

nodding acquaintance Slight acquaintance with person, or slight knowledge of thing.

on the nod Without objection.

- *The committee approved the whole plan on the nod.*

noise

big noise Important person.

noise abroad Cause to be widely known.

nose

cut off one's nose to spite one's face Commit, through revenge or spite, some foolish action which injures oneself.

follow one's nose Go straight forward.

keep one's nose clean Avoid trouble or risk.

keep one's nose to the grindstone Make one work incessantly.

lead by the nose See under **lead.**

look down one's nose at Scorn.

nosey-parker Inquisitive person.

pay through the nose Pay far too much; pay extortionately.

- *You'll have to pay through the nose if you stay at that hotel.*

plain as the nose on one's face Very obvious.

put one's nose out of joint Offend one.

rub person's nose in it Punish person (excessively). Humiliate person by reminding him of mistake.

thumb one's nose at Express or show scorn for.

under one's (very) nose In a near and obvious place.

not

not in the least; not a bit Not to any degree whatever.

- *I was not in the least afraid.*

not so No; a general negative.

note

strike a wrong note Be inappropriate.

strike the right note Act suitably.

take note (of) Pay attention (to).

nothing

can make nothing of Cannot understand.

count for nothing Not be appreciated. Carry no influence.

for nothing 1. Without payment.

　2. Without result.

have nothing to do with Not be concerned with.

make nothing of Not understand.

nothing to choose between them; nothing in it Practically equal.

- *Both brothers are clever; there is nothing to choose between them.*

nothing for it No option; no other choice.

- *If I fail to get this job, there'll be nothing for it but to emigrate.*

nothing like as or so good as In no way as good as.

nothing more nor less; nothing short of Completely; absolutely.

- *The film was nothing more nor less than a disaster.*

nothing to write home about Nothing very special.

there's nothing to it It is easy.
to say nothing of Not to mention.

notice

at short notice At the end of an unexpectedly short period.
- *We have to leave for America at short notice.*

till further notice Until a future time to be decided.

now

as of now From this time on.
(every) now and again or and then From time to time.
for now Until later.
just now Almost, but not quite at the present time.
now or never the unique opportunity.

null

null and void Non-existent and consequently non-effective.

number

number one Oneself.
one's number is up One is about to be defeated.
opposite number Person doing similar job in another firm.

nut

a hard nut to crack A difficult problem or person to deal with, or matter to decide.

nutshell

in a nutshell Stated very briefly.
- *This book will explain the whole problem in a nutshell.*

O

oar
put in one's oar Intervene; interfere.
rest on one's oars Cease work for a time.

oats
sow one's wild oats Commit the usual follies of youth.

obligations
discharge one's obligations Repay what is due.
under an obligation Compelled, either by law or by one's sense
of duty.
  • *Please don't feel under any obligation to come.*

oblivion
fall or sink into oblivion Become completely forgotten.

occasion
have occasion Have need, reason, justification.
if the occasion arises If there is reason, opportunity.
on occasion Sometimes; when necessary.
rise to the occasion Show the required qualities.
take the occasion to Seize the opportunity to.

occupy
occupy one's time, energies, talents, etc. 'Occupy' here used in
the sense of 'employ', 'use'.

occur
it occurs to me; it has just occurred to me The idea has come to
me; I have just realised.

- *It occurs to me that if we go to the concert tonight we won't get back in time.*

odd

be at odds Be in disagreement.

make no odds Be unimportant.

odd is added to numbers to indicate additional unspecified amounts of lower denomination. Thus *Forty-odd chairs* means any number between forty and fifty; *five pounds odd* means five pounds and some pence.

odd man out Person unlike others in a group.

odds the terms upon which one may bet. *'Long odds'* means that the chances of winning are considered very slight, and the phrase is used to indicate improbability.

- *It's long odds against Arthur coming home from Australia this year.*

'the odds', on the other hand, may imply the reverse, a probable event.

- *The odds are that Jim will be able to come.*

what's the odds! What does it matter!

odds and ends Small, unclassified objects; what remains when more important things have been dealt with.

odds-on Likely to succeed.

over the odds More than the normal price.

odour

in bad odour Unpopular; regarded unfavourably.

odour of sanctity (Disagreeable) sense of one's holiness.

off

badly off Poor.

be off 1. An imperative order to depart.

2. Depart.

- *I must be off to catch my train.*

3. Be unfit to eat or drink; stale. (Also *go off*.)

- *Don't eat that meat—it was bought last week, and must be (have gone) off by now.*

in the offing About to happen.

off and on From time to time.

off one's food Disinclined to eat; without an appetite.

off one's guard In a state of relaxation and unawareness.

off-hand 1. Without preparation; impromptu.

- *I can't give you figures off-hand; I shall have to look them up.*

2. Casual and irresponsible.

offshoot A branching-off; a lesser concern or business which has developed from the original one.

well off 1. Rich.

2. In comfortable and satisfactory circumstances.

- *You shouldn't grumble about the house; you don't realise when you're well off.*

on the off chance In the hope (usually faint).

office
through the good (kind) offices of With the help of.

often
as often as not Occurring on about half of the possible occasions.

every so often Occasionally.

more often than not Usually.

once too often In a way bringing failure.

oil
burn the midnight oil Stay up late to work or study.

oil and water Applied to two dissimilar or irreconcilable things, people, points of view, etc.

oil the wheels Make things work well.

ointment
fly in the ointment See under **fly**.

old
any old how Carelessly.

of old Belonging to the distant past.

old boy network Means of help through contacts with influential friends or acquaintances.

an old hand or stager Person very skilled or experienced at something.

old head See under **head**.

old maid An elderly spinster, or one with fixed habits.

old timer Person who has been doing something for a long time.

olive
olive-branch A gesture of peace.

on
on and off Intermittently; occasionally.

once
all at once 1. Suddenly.

2. All together.

just this once On this occasion (and no other).

once and for all Finally.

once in a blue moon Very rarely.

once in a way or *while* Occasionally, but not often.

once-over Brief examination.

once upon a time At some period in the past.

one

one and all Everyone.

one by one Singly.

one of those things Something that cannot be avoided.

one-off Occurring only once. Intended to happen only once.

one-sided Made from one point of view and for the advantage of one party only.

one up on Better than.

open

open and above-board Entirely frank and candid.

- *He was entirely open and above-board in his statements.*

open (a discussion, proceedings) Begin.

open one's eyes to Make one aware.

open the door to Lead to; encourage; result in.

open mind Willingness to listen or be persuaded.

open-mouthed Showing surprise.

open secret A fact supposed to be secret, but known to everybody; no secret at all.

open sesame Any simple and miraculous method of solving a problem.

- *The Chancellor thinks that taxing the rich is the open sesame to universal prosperity.*

open and shut Easily decided.

open to Ready to receive.

open with Frank and honest in dealings with.

with open arms Enthusiastically. Heartily.

- *The hotel welcomed us with open arms.*

with (one's) eyes open Aware of the consequences, implications, etc.

opinion

be of the opinion Believe; consider.

golden opinions Very great admiration; general praise.

- *The new President has already won golden opinions, even from his political opponents.*

matter of opinion Subject for dispute. Opposite of *matter of fact.*

pass an opinion Express an opinion or view.

- *I don't know enough about paintings to pass an opinion.*

opportunity
take or seize the opportunity Make use of a particular moment.

- *May I take this opportunity of expressing our gratitude for your kindness.*

opposition
meet with opposition Be opposed.

option
have no option but to Must.
keep or leave one's options open Refrain from committing oneself.

order
order about Domineer by giving orders.
order of the day The current fashion.
in good order Fit for use.
in order 1. In succession; as pre-arranged plan.

- *The candidates will be interviewed in alphabetical order.*

2. Tidy, neat.

- *Please see that this room is in order when the visitors arrive.*

3. Officially correct.

- *You will be in order if you speak after the chairman.*

in working order Ready for use.
on order Requested from the manufacturer but not yet supplied.

- *Our new cooker has now been on order for five weeks.*

out of order 1. The reverse of *in order* (2).

- *All these papers are out of order.*

2. The reverse of *in order* (3).

- *You will be out of order if you interrupt the Chairman.*

take orders from Obey orders given by.
take (holy) orders Become a clergyman.

ordinary
in the ordinary way Normally.
ordinary run of things (or *course of events*) Events which may be expected to happen normally.

- *In the ordinary run of things I play tennis nearly every weekend.*

out of the ordinary Unusual; exceptional.

- *It is quite out of the ordinary for snow to fall during the summer in Britain.*

other
on the other hand On the contrary.

the other day Recently; not long ago.

out
all out Using all one's speed or effort.
be out 1. Be mistaken in one's judgement.
    2. Not at home.
- *I am sorry we were out when you called.*

flat out At full speed. Using all one's energies.
have it out See under **have.**
out and about Outside, in motion.
out-and-out Thoroughly, completely.
out for Engaged in seeking.
- *He's out for all the credit he can get.*

out of 1. From.
- *He did it out of kindness.*
2. Without any (applied to something normally available).
- *The grocer was out of coffee.*

See *out of stock.*
3. Having no share or part in.
out of character Not typical.
- *His behaviour yesterday was very out of character.*

out of doors In the open air; exposed to the weather.
out of it Not part of (activity, group, etc.).
out of joint Restless, uncomfortable, and generally unsatisfactory.
out of one's mind [LIT] Insane. [MET] Extremely foolish or rash.
out of place See under **place.**
out of pocket See under **pocket.**
out of print Term applied to a book when all copies are sold and no more will be printed.
out of sorts See under **sort.**
out of the question See under **question.**
out of stock Not available, owing to supplies being exhausted.
- *I am sorry, but that brand of cigarette is out of stock.*

Similar to *out of* (2).
out of one's way 1. On a detour.
- *It's a little out of my way, but I'll drive you there.*
2. To some trouble, inconvenience.
- *The neighbours went out of their way to be helpful when we first came to live here.*

out of the way 1. Unusual.
- *It was an out-of-the-way request.*
2. Remote.

- *The house was in an out-of-the-way village.*
3. In a position which causes no obstruction.
- *Please put the cushion out of your way.*

out of work Without employment.
out to Striving to.
out with it! Say what you want to say or ought to say.
will out Will be discovered.

over
all over See under **all.**
go overboard Be very or too enthusiastic.
over and above In addition to; extra to.
- *I've been given a week's holiday over and above my normal entitlement.*

over and done with Finished.
over and over (again) Repeatedly; many times.
over one's head Beyond one's comprehension.
overshoot; overshoot the mark Go too far; exceed; exaggerate

owe
owe it to oneself Consider it necessary to one's self-respect or happiness.
- *I owe it to myself to explain how it all happened.*

own
come into one's own Reach position where one is properly appreciated.
do one's own thing Do what one likes or is good at.
get one's own back on Revenge oneself on.
hold one's own Maintain one's position.
- *He can hold his own in most sorts of argument.*

on one's own By oneself; without companionship or assistance.
off one's own bat On one's own initiative or responsibility.
own up Make a confession.

P

pace
keep pace Keep level; [LIT] Go at the same speed. [MET] Maintain knowledge or understanding.
put through one's paces Test a person in order to discover his knowledge or ability.
set the pace Establish speed of progress.
show one's paces Demonstrate one's ability.
stand the pace Maintain equality with others.

pack
packed like sardines Crowded as closely together as sardines are in the tins in which they are sold.
packed out Very crowded.
pack it in Stop whatever one is doing.
pack of lies Many lies.
pack one's bags Get ready to depart.
pack up Finish. Go out of action.

paddle
paddle one's own canoe Manage one's own affairs without help or interference.

pain
be at or take pains to Take trouble to.
  • *I was at great pains to make the occasion a success.*
get for one's pains Receive for one's exertions or trouble.
  • *All he got for his pains was ingratitude.*
pain in the neck Annoying person or thing.
on pain of Incurring punishment by.

paint
not so black as is painted Not as bad as represented.
paint the town red Go out and have a good time.

pale
beyond the pale Outside the normal limits of acceptable behaviour.

palm
grease one's palm Bribe one.
in the palm of one's hand Under one's control.
palm off on Substitute something of inferior value.
  • *I asked for butter, but they palmed off margarine on me.*
palmy days Times of great prosperity.

paper
commit to paper Write, with the special object of keeping a record.
on paper By report. Hypothetically. To judge from what is written down, as distinct from what is known in practice.
  • *On paper, these policies seem very sound.*
paper over the cracks Thinly conceal deficiencies.
put pen to paper Begin to write.

par
below par Below the expected standard.
on a par with On the same terms as.
  • *That remark is on a par with his normal behaviour.*
par for the course What is to be expected.
up to par At the expected level.

parallel
draw a parallel Compare to indicate similarity.

parcel
parcel out Divide and distribute in portions.

pare
pare down Reduce by degrees.
  • *We have pared down expenses to the limit.*

parlour
parlour tricks Minor social accomplishments—amateur singing, playing, etc. Now used ironically to mean minor roguery or incompetence.

parrot-fashion
As a parrot talks; from memory, with little or no regard to the real meaning.

part
for my part As far as I am concerned.
for the most part In most cases.
many parts Many abilities.
on the part of Coming from.
part and parcel An essential and necessary part.
part with Surrender.
take (someone's) part Support. Back up.
take part in Participate in.

Parthian
a Parthian shot A parting retort.

partial
be partial to Like; enjoy.
  • *I am rather partial to duck and green peas.*

particular
in particular Especially.

parting
parting shot Remark made when one is leaving (usually sign of defiance, or so that no response is possible).
parting of the ways Point at which people disagree.

partner
partner in crime 1. [LIT] Person with whom one commits crime. 2. [MET] (Usually jocular) Companion. Friend.
Sleeping partner Fellow-owner (of firm) who does no work (i.e. is merely investor).

party
party line Official policy.

pass
in passing Incidentally.
let pass Ignore.
make a pass Make a threatening movement or gesture towards.
make a pass at Make amorous approach to.
pass (at cards) Refrain from playing at that particular moment of the game.
pass away, over Formal and rather old-f. phrase for 'die'.

pass by Go past.

pass by on the other side Ignore a problem.

pass for Be accepted as.

pass one's comprehension Be more than one can understand.

pass judgement Express a final and definite opinion.

pass muster Be regarded as up to the necessary standards; just good enough.

pass off 1. Ignore; treat as if it were unimportant.
  - *He hated his familiarity, but passed it off as a joke*
  2. Intentionally convey a false impression concerning some person or object.
  - *The boy was only twelve, but liked to pass himself off as much older.*
  3. Disappear by degrees or stages.
  - *There was a thick mist at first, but it soon began to pass off.*

pass on 1. Go on.
  2. Die.
  3. Hand on.

pass one's eye over Read quickly.

pass out 1. Finish military training successfully.
  2. Faint.

pass over 1. Ignore.
  2. Forgive; excuse.
  3. Die.

a pretty pass or mess! A fine state of affairs! (Always used ironically.)
  - *Things have come to a pretty pass!*

pass the time Spend or use up time.

pass the time of day Spend a few moments in conversation.

pass a remark Utter; make a remark.

pass up 1. Hand over.
  2. Ignore. Refuse.

past

not put it past (a person) to do Not be surprised if (a person) did. Regard (a person) to be (normally) capable of doing.

past-master An expert; a highly experienced person.

pat

pat on the back Expression of congratulation.

patch

a good or bad patch A period of good (or poor) luck, success, etc.

- *The school's football is going through a bad patch this season.*

hit or *strike a bad patch* Experience period of difficulty.

in patches In places or at certain times.

not be a patch on Not be as good as.

patch up (a quarrel, etc.) Repair. Set to rights (usually hastily or temporarily).

patience

out of patience; having lost patience With no patience left; exasperated.

try the patience of a saint Cause extreme annoyance.

pause

give (one) pause Make (one) hesitate.

pave

pave the way to (for) Lead to; result in.

- *This treaty will pave the way to peace.*

paved with good intentions Well-meaning.

pay

the devil to pay Tremendous trouble; a general upheaval; serious consequences.

- *If you don't post that letter tonight, there'll be the devil to pay.*

pay attention Listen and observe intently and carefully.

- *Pay attention to your teachers, and don't waste your time.*

pay back 1. Return what has been lent or given.

2. Punish, in return for some injury.

pay for 1. Hand over money in payment for.

2. Be punished for.

pay off 1. Pay the whole of what is due.

2. Naval. A ship is said to be 'paid off' when she returns to port and discharges her crew.

3. Succeed.

pay out 1. [Nautical.] Slacken or loosen a rope.

2. Pay; disburse money.

pay the earth Pay a large sum of money.

pay the piper Pay whatever the cost, financial or otherwise, may be. Be in a position of power because one has the authority (especially financial) to demand obedience.

pay one's way Pay expenses out of one's income.

- *I doubt if that shop will ever pay its way.*

pay up Pay what one owes.

put paid to Finished. Settled.

- *A broken leg put paid to his walking holiday.*

peace
hold one's peace Remain silent.
keep the peace Refrain from quarrelling, or causing any other disturbance.
make one's peace with Re-establish friendly relations with.
peace of mind Freedom from worry.

pearl
cast pearls before swine Present or introduce something of value or beauty to those who are entirely unable to appreciate it.
pearls of wisdom Wise sayings, advice, etc.

peck
keep one's pecker up Remain cheerful.
pecking order Hierarchy.

pedal
soft-pedal Refrain from stressing.

pedestal
put on a pedestal Admire. Respect.

peg
off the peg Ready-made.
peg away Continue steadily; persevere.
 - *If you peg away long enough, you'll be able to learn any language.*
peg down Confine to a certain level.
take one down a peg or two Humble someone.

penalty
pay the penalty Suffer what is due and inevitable as the result of an action.

penny
in for a penny, in for a pound (Frequently abbrev. to 'In for a penny'.) Being slightly involved, one may as well be involved still further.
in penny numbers In small quantities.
like a bad penny Occurring or reappearing frequently when not wanted.
penny-dreadful An old-f. term for cheap and sensational magazines.

a penny for your thoughts A facetious offer, made to arouse someone who has been silent and withdrawn.

not cost a penny Cost nothing.

not have a penny to one's name Have no money.

penny-pinching Mean(ness).

penny wise Careful in saving small sums, but wasteful in large matters.

a pretty penny A large sum of money.

take care of the pennies (and the pounds will take care of themselves) Care of small matters will reduce problems with large ones.

the penny dropped He (etc.) suddenly understood.

turn or earn an honest penny Earn money (usually by extra work, or unusual methods).

two (ten) a penny Common.

pep

pep-talk A talk intended to improve a person's performance, spirits, enthusiasm, etc.

period

at no period At no time; never in the past.

perish

perish the thought I do hope that that will not happen.

person

in person Personally.

perspective

put something in perspective Place it in its context; view in relation to other factors.

pet

pet aversion Person or thing disliked above all else.

pick

pick and choose Select carefully.

pick holes in Criticise. Show the faults in.

pick-me-up A quick restorative, after weakness or fatigue.

pick of the bunch Best of those available.

pick on Select from others, for special treatment.

pick up Acquire by chance; obtain casually.

pick one's way or one's steps Walk deliberately and carefully among difficulties and obstructions.

pick one's words Select carefully what one says.

piece

all of a piece All part of, or connected with.

a piece of one's mind One's candid opinion. A rebuke.

go to pieces Deteriorate completely. Opposite, *pick up the pieces*: correct a damaged situation.

in one piece 1. [LIT] Unbroken.
   2. [MET] Unharmed.

pull to pieces Analyse; examine closely with the object of finding fault. Similar to *pick holes in.*

say one's piece Say what one must say.

pig

make a pig of oneself Eat too much.

make a pig's ear Make a mess.

pig in a poke Something acquired without knowing its value, and without previous examination or knowledge. Usually used with the verb 'buy'.

pig(gy) in the middle Person between two conflicting sides.

pigs might fly Wonders might occur. (Used ironically.)

pile

pile it on Exaggerate.

pile on the agony Increase or intensify distress or discomfort.

pill

a bitter pill An unpleasant, humiliating or intensely disappointing fact.

sugar or *sweeten the pill* Do something to make an unpleasant task, statement, piece of news, etc., less so.

pillar

from pillar to post From one predicament or resource to another.

pin

pin back one's ears Listen.

pin down 1. [LIT] Fix; fasten firmly.
   2. [MET] Compel to deal with some particular fact or substantiate a statement.
   • *The plumber promised to come, but it was difficult to pin him down to an exact time.*

pin one's faith on Believe in completely; trust absolutely.

pin one's hopes on Attach one's hopes to; concentrate one's hopes on.

- *We are pinning our hopes on having a longer holiday next year.*

pin something on someone Prove someone guilty of something.

pin-money See under **money**.

pins and needles The tingling sensation felt in a limb which has become stiff and numb.

pin-prick Small irritation.

you could hear a pin drop It was very quiet.

pinch

at a pinch In an emergency; if absolutely necessary.

feel the pinch Be short of money.

where the shoe pinches Where the difficulty lies.

pink

pink of perfection Absolutely and completely perfect.

tickled pink Very pleased.

pipe

pipe up Speak. Interrupt.

in the pipeline In preparation. About to arrive.

piping

piping hot [LIT] Very hot.

pistol

hold pistol to one's head Threaten one.

pit

pit against Place in competition against; compel to fight.

pit one's wits against Set about planning to defeat one by exercise of wits.

pitch

pitch black Very black.

pitch darkness Extreme darkness.

pitch one's tent [LIT] To 'pitch' a tent is to erect it, usually for a limited period. [MET] To settle anywhere.

pity

what a pity or shame! A general expression of regret.

- *What a pity that you won't be able to come to the party.*

more's the pity That makes matters worse.

take pity on Feel sympathy for.

place

go places Be likely to succeed.

in the first place Firstly, at the beginning.

- *In the first place, I must explain that I can't speak English very well.*

(Similarly second, third, etc., place.)

in place In the correct position.

in place of Instead of.

in places At some points (but not at others).

know one's place Know how to behave.

put (person) in his place Tell (person) how to behave.

out of place Unsuitable; in the wrong surroundings.

take place Happen; occur.

- *The wedding will take place next week.*

take the place of Be used instead of.

plague

like the plague As much as possible. Usually *avoid person or thing like the plague.*

plain

plain dealing Honest and open business methods.

plain as a pikestaff Obvious; unmistakable.

plain sailing A course of action without any difficulties.

plain speaking Frank and honest speaking.

plate

on one's plate Occupying one's attention or time.

play

child's play Extremely easy to perform or solve.

- *This crossword is child's play.*

make great play with Place emphasis on.

play about or around with Fail to take seriously.

play along with Co-operate with.

play one's cards well or *badly, etc.* Make good (bad) use of one's opportunities.

play down Reduce the importance of.

play by ear 1. Perform on a musical instrument without having been taught or without using music.

2. Follow a course of action without any advance planning.

play false Betray; cheat.

play fair Act honestly.

play for time Act so as to gain time (to one's advantage).

play on (one's feelings, etc.) Use them to one's own advantage.

play to the gallery Try to achieve popularity; degrade one's abilities in order to obtain popularity.

play the game [LIT] Observe the rules. [MET] Behave honourably.

play into the hands of Behave so that one's actions are an advantage to someone else, usually an opponent or enemy.

play (merry) hell Create a great fuss.

play hell with Damage.

play off Use two opponents, one against the other, to one's own advantage.

play safe Act cautiously.

play up Be a nuisance.

play up to Flatter.

play truant Remain away from school.

play upon Take advantage of.

play upon words A pun; a verbal joke.

play with fire Act dangerously.

played out Exhausted; finished; out of date.

plead
plead the cause Speak favourably for; help by supporting.

please
please oneself Do as one desires.
- *I am going home—you can please yourself.*

pleased as Punch Extremely pleased.

pledge
pledge oneself Make a solemn and formal promise.

sign or take the pledge Formally undertake never to drink intoxicants—wine, spirits, beer, etc.

plentiful
plentiful as blackberries Extremely plentiful.

plight
plight one's troth Make a formal promise to marry. [Old f.]

plot
the plot thickens The affair becomes more complicated and exciting.

plough
plough back Reinvest (e.g. profits in a business) in order to increase further.

plough a lone furrow Act without help.

put one's hands to the plough Undertake a task.

pluck
pluck at one's heart strings Appeal to one's deepest feelings.
pluck up courage Acquire confidence and conquer fear.

plunge
take the plunge Decide to do something.

pocket
in one's pocket In one's control.
line one's pocket Make money (often dishonestly).
out of pocket Poorer financially.
  - *I am ten pounds out of pocket as a result of the arrangement.*
out-of-pocket expenses Expenses incurred and paid in transacting business.
put one's hand in one's pocket Spend or give money.
pocket an insult Submit to an insult without protest; ignore it.
pocket one's pride Become humble under compulsion or necessity.

point
at the point of On the verge of.
beside the point Irrelevant.
carry one's point See under **carry.**
a case in point An example.
  - *Many politicians make memorable speeches; Sir Winston Churchill was a case in point.*
come to the point Arrive at the crux, or what is really important.
culminating point Climax.
  - *The culminating point of the opera is the magnificent duet in the second act.*
I take your point I accept what you say (but).
in point of fact Actually.
make a point Contribute something to an argument.
  - *I was able to make my point before the discussion ended.*
make a point of Take special care and trouble about.
  - *She made a point of phoning her mother every week.*
make one's point Make one's opinion clear.
a moot point A point or detail which is unsettled and open to discussion or argument.
not to put too fine a point on it To speak bluntly.
off the point Irrelevant.
on the point of On the verge of.
the point The object.

- *The point of these discussions is that they enable the ministers concerned to get a clear idea of what is happening.*

point blank Direct; without any qualification.

- *He denied point-blank that he had ever entered the house.*

point a moral Emphasise some moral truth.

point of honour Matter affecting one's honour.

point of view Way of looking at something.

point out Indicate; remind a person.

- *May I point out that you have not yet paid your bill.*

possession is nine points of the law If one possesses something, one is almost entitled to it.

score points off Win in parts of argument, discussion, debate etc.

a sore point A subject upon which one is sensitive.

- *The fact that he is only five feet tall is a sore point with him.*

stretch a point Concede a certain amount.

strong point Distinctive characteristic; special skill.

- *Golf is not my strong point.*

take one's point Understand what one is saying.

to the point Directly relevant. Relevantly.

- *He spoke bluntly and to the point.*

point of view Personal opinion or aspect.

- *From the smokers' point of view the tobacco tax is too high.*

up to a point To some extent.

when it comes to the point At the appropriate moment.

poke
poke fun at Mock.
poke one's nose in Interfere.

poker
poker-face Expressionless face.
stiff as a poker Very stiff (e.g. in manner).

pole
pole to pole i.e. From the North to the South Pole. All over the world.

poles apart A very great distance apart.

- *The management and the trade union are poles apart on the matter of working conditions.*

up the pole 1. In difficulties.
  2. Insane.

polish
polish off Finish quickly.
 • *I can polish off the job in five minutes.*
polish up Improve. Smarten.

poor
take a poor view of Regard with disfavour.

port
any port in a storm When in difficulties, one must accept any solution.

possess
like a man possessed With furious energy.
what(ever) possessed you . . . ? How could you have been so rash as to . . . ?

possession
in possession of Possessing; having. See under **point.**

post
at one's post At one's appointed place, or official position.
beaten at the post Defeated at the last moment.
deaf as a post Completely deaf.
keep posted Keep informed.
left at the post Hopelessly beaten in competition.
post-haste Very quickly.

pot
go to pot Disintegrate. Become useless.
keep the pot boiling Enable any kind of enterprise, etc., to remain in an active condition.
pot-boiler Any literary or artistic work turned out merely to provide money for necessities.
the pot calling the kettle black One person accusing another of faults of which he or she is also guilty.
a pot-shot A deliberate shot at some stationary object.
take pot luck See under **luck.**

potato
hot potato Difficult matter to deal with.

pound
pound away [LIT] Strike heavily and repeatedly. [MET] Work vigorously.

pound of flesh Full and complete payment, regardless of circumstances. (Usually jocular.)

pour
it never rains but it pours Troubles never come singly.
pour oil on troubled waters Sooth a disturbed situation (usually with calming words).

power
do a power of Do a lot of.
more or all power to your elbow! Good luck to your efforts.
power behind the throne Person who is actually (if not apparently) in control.
the powers that be Those in command; the authorities.

practice
in practice In the sphere of action (as distinct from theory).
make a practice of Habitually do.
put into practice Put into action.

pray
past praying for Impossible to alter, to repair or to improve.
- *This old suit is past praying for.*

precious
precious few or little Very few or little.

premium
at a premium In short supply.
put a premium on Prize.

preparation
in course of preparation Being prepared.

present
at present At the present time; now.
present company excepted Excluding people who are here now.

press
be pressed for Have scarcely enough.
get a good or bad press Receive favourable (unfavourable) publicity.
press forward or on 1. [LIT] Push in a forward direction.
- *The crowd pressed forward to see his arrival.*
2. [MET] Hasten.
- *I want to press on with that work.*
pressgang Force to do.

pretty
pretty good, much, etc. 'Pretty' here is used in the sense of fairly, moderately, comparatively.
- *He is in pretty good health, considering his age.*
pretty penny Considerable amount of money.
pretty well or nearly Almost.
a pretty pass or mess See under **pass.**
sitting pretty In a fortunate position.

prevail
prevail upon Persuade.

prey
a prey to Suffering from.

price
at any price In any circumstances.

prick
prick up one's ears Become suddenly alert and attentive.

pride
pride of place Exalted position.
pride oneself on Feel satisfaction in.
put one's pride in one's pocket Same as *pocket one's pride.* See under **pocket.**
swallow one's pride Behave humbly.
take pride in Derive satisfaction from. Be proud or careful of.

prime
prime mover Person who first begins a process.

primrose
the primrose path The pleasant, easy-going, unthinking way of living.

prison
commit to prison Formally order to be sent to prison.

pro
pros and cons Arguments for and against.

probability
in all probability or likelihood Very probably; very likely.

profile
keep a low profile Remain inconspicuous.

progress
in progress Being done or undertaken.
- *Repairs to many of the houses were in progress.*

proof
child-proof Made so that children are unable to harm themselves by it.
foolproof See under **fool**.
proof against Able to resist.
- *This coat is proof against the coldest weather.*
proof positive Definite proof.
the proof of the pudding is in the eating The value or wisdom of any action can only be discovered by actual experience.
put or bring to the proof Test.
- *I think the plan will work, but let us put it to the proof.*

proportion
out of all proportion Far more than is deserved.
- *The cost is out of all proportion to the benefits we should get.*
sense of proportion Balanced and sensible view.

prospect
in prospect Being considered.
- *I have a much better job in prospect.*

proud
do one proud Treat one well.

prove
prove oneself Show oneself capable.

public
in the public eye Known to the general public.
public-spirited Doing or advocating things for the good of society.

puff
puffed up Proud.

pull
pull a (long) face Express disagreement, disgust, etc.
pull strings Use one's influence.
pull together Work together unitedly.
- *If we pull together, success is certain.*
pull off Succeed in doing.
pull one's punches [LIT] Fail to give the fullest force to one's

blows (in boxing). [MET] Speak (or act) gently. (Usually used in negative.)

pull one's socks up Become more efficient.

pull one's weight Use all one's efforts in support.

pull oneself together Make an effort to regain one's normal mental state.

pull out 1. Move away.

   2. Move to side.

   3. Withdraw.

pull rank Use one's superior position to achieve something.

pull (all) the stops out Make every effort.

pull strings Use influence (usually covertly).

pull through Survive.

pull up 1. (Noun) A stopping-place where drivers, etc., may stop for rest, food, etc.

   2. (Verb) Halt; stop.

   3. Reprimand.

pull up short Stop abruptly, and before one intended.

pulse

have or keep one's finger on the pulse Be well informed.

purple

purple patch Passage of obtrusively ornate writing.

purpose

on purpose; purposely Intentionally.

serve no purpose Be useless.

to the purpose Direct to the subject, practically and sensibly.

to no purpose Uselessly; without success. See under **serve.**

to some or little purpose With some (or little) result.

push

be pushed for Be short of.

give or get the push Dismiss or be dismissed.

push off Go away.

push-over Easy task.

put

not put it past someone Not be surprised if someone (does something).

put about 1. Worried; anxious. [Old f.]

   2. Nautical. Turn in the opposite direction.

   ● *The ship put about and returned to port.*

3. Circulate; make publicly known.

- *It was put about that the Cabinet was in disagreement.*

put across Successfully narrate, convince or influence.

- *He is a good teacher, who puts his subject across very well.*

put all one's eggs in one basket See under **basket**.

put it on Pretend. Feign or exaggerate an emotion, etc.

- *He says he's unwell, but I think he's putting it on.*

put one's back up See under **back**.

put by Save, usually for a special purpose.

put to death Execute; kill.

put down 1. Cease to hold.

- *Please put the shopping-bag down on the table.*

2. Suppress.

- *the General put down the rebellion in six weeks.*

3. Store for future use (wine, etc.).

- *We've put down two dozen bottles of port.*

4. Write; record.

- *Please put down the following facts.*

5. (Of animals.) Painlessly kill.

- *The dog was very old and we had him put down.*

6. Ascribe. Attribute.

- *I put his irritability down to his ill-health.*

put down to Attribute to.

put to flight Compel to run away.

be put in or *into force* Same as *come into force*, under **force**.

put one's nose out of joint See under **nose**.

put off 1. Delay. Postpone. Evade.

- *Never put off till tomorrow what you can do today.*

2. Repelled. Discouraged.

- *I meant to go, but was rather put off by the snow.*

put (something) on Feign (something).

put on airs; put on side Try to impress people by one's superiority.

put on the screw or *screws* Compel a person by pressure (as a screw increases pressure) to do what is desired.

put on steam Make a special effort to progress.

put out 1. Extinguish.

- *He put out the light.*

2. Remove from a house or other building; eject.

- *He put out the cat.*

3. Annoy; perturb. Inconvenience.

- *The old lady seemed put out.*

4. Dislocate. Strain.

- *I put my back out by moving the piano.*

put over Communicate.

put oneself out Take extra trouble.

put (person) right 1. Tell (person) what is correct.

2. Make (person) healthy again.

put (thing) right Repair.

put a stop or an end to Terminate; end.

- *The Government ought to put a stop to official waste.*

put to it, hard put to it Tested; confronted with difficulties. Pressed.

- *He was hard put to it to decide whether to stay in England or go abroad.*

put two and two together (and make four) Deduce from obvious facts.

- *Putting two and two together, he realised that the firm would soon be bankrupt.*

put up 1. Receive as a temporary guest; provide with a bed.

- *We can easily put you up for the night.*

2. Provide for a definite purpose, usually an investment.

put up at Reside; live at temporarily.

- *We put up at my brother's when we go to Oxford.*

put (someone) up to Cajole (someone) so that he agrees to

put up with Endure.

- *I can't put up with this toothache any longer.*

a put-up affair or job A previously arranged affair; a plot.

put upon Impose upon.

put in a (good) word Speak in favour of; recommend.

Pyrrhic

Pyrrhic victory Success at too great a cost.

Q

qualms
have no qualms about Have no doubts; not feel uneasy.

quantity
unknown quantity Thing or person having unpredictable influence or importance.

quarrel
pick a quarrel Take occasion to make complaint; provoke someone.

quart
fit or put a quart into a pint pot Make something fit into an inadequate space, time, etc.

quarter
at close quarters From a nearby position.
give no quarter Refuse to show mercy.
in every quarter; in all quarters Everywhere; in every direction.

queer
in queer street In an uncertain position; in difficulties.
queer card or customer or fish An eccentric and unusual type of person.
queer one's pitch Spoil one's chances beforehand, usually by secret dealings.
  • *I'd rather speak to him myself: if anyone else sees him first, it may queer my pitch.*

quest
in quest of In search of; to search for.

question

begging the question (Usually) Avoiding an argument or decision by bringing forward some immaterial point. But see **beg.**

beyond all question Without doubt; certain.

burning question A matter requiring an immediate examination and prompt action.

call in question Express doubt about; challenge.

come into question Be considered.

in question Mentioned; referred to.

- *The person in question has a very good reputation.*

is the question Is what is relevant.

it is a question of What is involved is.

open question Not certain; debatable.

out of the question Utterly impossible.

put a question mark against Query.

put the question Ask for an opinion or vote.

vexed question A problem or question very difficult to decide.

without question Without doubt.

quick

quick one Quick drink.

to the quick See *cut to the quick.*

quiet

keep quiet Say nothing.

on the quiet Unobtrusively.

quit

be quits (with) Be equal (with). Be revenged (on).

call it quits Regard it as equitable.

quite

quite a few A considerable number.

quite a different or another matter Not at all the same thing.

quite so I agree.

quite something A noteworthy matter.

R

r
the three R's Reading, (w)riting and (a)rithmetic—the first elements of education.

rack
on the rack In a condition of acute mental tension; intensely anxious.
rack one's brains Similar to *cudgel one's brains*
(go to) rack and ruin Complete decay; destruction.

rag
glad rags Best clothes. Formal dress.
rags to riches From poverty to success.
rag-tag and bobtail Disreputable people.

rage
all the rage Immensely popular or fashionable.

ragged
run ragged Exhaust(ed).

rails
off the rails Disorganised. Confused. (Usually applied to behaviour of people under strain.)

rain
it never rains but it pours Events, fortunate or unfortunate, rarely occur singly.
rain cats and dogs Rain violently.
(come) rain or shine [LIT] Whatever the weather. [MET] Whatever happens.

a rainy day Time of need, especially financial.

raise
raise a laugh Cause amusement.
raise one's eyebrows Express surprise.
raise one's glass to Toast the health of.
raise one's hat to Express admiration for.
raise one's voice 1. Speak.
- *No one raised his voice in opposition.*
2. Speak loudly, usually in anger.
- *Please don't raise your voice to me.*
raise the wind Obtain sufficient funds.

rake
rake's progress Progressive deterioration as a result of wickedness, over-indulgence, etc.
rake up Recall unnecessarily from the past.

ram
ram home Express or be felt very forcibly.

random
at random By chance; without deliberate selection.

range
within range Within an effective distance or area. Near enough to be heard, seen, controlled, etc.

rank
break ranks Depart from agreement with others.
close ranks Show solidarity with others.
rank and file The ordinary working members of an organisation.
rise from the ranks See under **rise.**

ransom
hold a person to ransom Threaten a person in order to gain concessions.
worth a king's ransom Extremely valuable.

rap
not worth a rap Worthless.
rap on or over the knuckles A sharp reproof.
rap out Speak sharply; snap.
take the rap Accept the blame or punishment.

rare
rare bird Very unusual (and valuable) person.

raring to go Eager to begin.

rat
like a drowned rat Very wet.
rat race Competition in society.
smell a rat Entertain suspicion.

rate
at any rate In any circumstances; whatever has happened or
    may happen.
    • *The Government, at any rate, is not to blame.*
at this or that rate If this (that) is true.

rave
raving mad Out of one's mind.

reach
out of reach Beyond the furthest distance to which one can
    stretch, or [MET] communicate.
within reach Accessible.

read
read between the lines Grasp the hidden significance of some-
    thing spoken or written.
read into Find implied or unintended meaning in.
take as read Assume to be accurate.

ready
at the ready Prepared to act.

reality
in reality Actually; in fact.

reap
see under **sow.**

rear
bring up the rear; be in the rear Travel behind; be at the back,
    as the last member of the party.
rear its ugly head Arise in all its unpleasantness.

reason
hear or listen to reason Allow oneself to be persuaded.
see reason Be persuaded.
stand to reason Be obviously reasonable or logical.
without reason Within the bounds of moderation.

reckon

reckon among Include among.

reckoning That which is due, or owing, financially or otherwise.

reckon on Rely upon. Similar to *count upon.*

reckon up Count. Summarise.

reckon with Include in one's plans (usually as a difficulty).

reconcile

reconcile oneself Subdue one's dislike or objections.

record

off the record Unofficial(ly) because not written down or openly acknowledged.

on record In a position of acknowledging openly and publicly.

put or set the record straight Correct a mistake or misunderstanding.

red

in the red In debt.

like a red rag to a bull An exasperation; an intense annoyance.

on red alert In a state of preparedness for danger.

red-handed In the act of doing something wrong.

red herring An attempt to divert attention from the chief facts by introducing some detail of no importance.

red-letter day Day of rejoicing.

red tape Official and frequently trivial formalities.

- *We have given up trying to build a house—there is too much red tape involved.*

to see red To become enraged.

to see the red light To have warning of difficulty or danger.

reel

reel off State quickly and fluently.

reference

in or with reference to Referring to; in connection with.

- *With reference to your letter of yesterday, we cannot accept the offer.*

without reference to Irrespective of. Without consulting or taking into account.

- *He acted without reference to his superior.*

reflection

due reflection Appropriate time for considering the matter.

- *After due reflection, we have decided to refuse.*

on reflection After reconsideration.
- *On reflection, I think I was wrong.*

refresh
refresh one's memory Put relevant facts in one's mind.

refresher
refresher course An additional course of studies, following an earlier one, taken to refresh one's memory.

refusal
the first refusal The first chance of buying an object before it is offered elsewhere.
- *I like the house, and the owner has given me first refusal.*

regard
as regards Concerning.
with regard to In respect of.

region
in the region of About. Approximately.

regular
keep regular hours Do the same thing at the same time every day.
regular as clockwork Regular as the movements of a clock.
- *He comes home at six every night, regular as clockwork.*

rein
give (free) rein to Allow to escape without restraint.
- *She is a child who likes to give rein to her imagination.*
keep a tight rein on Control strictly.

relish
no relish for No liking for.
- *I've no relish for long walks in wet weather.*

render
render an account Present a bill for payment.

repeat
does not bear repeating Is too disgraceful to repeat.
repeat oneself Say something again.

reproach
above or beyond reproach So good that criticism is impossible.

resistance
take the line of least resistance Take the action that is easiest.

resolution
form or *make a resolution* Determine; definitely decide.
- *I've made a resolution never to go to bed later than eleven.*

resort
in the last resort When everything else has failed.

respect
in all respects; in every respect In every way.
- *The new washing-machine is better in all respects than the old one.*

pay or *send one's respects* Present (or convey) one's polite greetings.
with respect If I may say so without giving offence.
with respect to Concerning.

rest
rest assured Be satisfied.
rest on one's laurels Having earned distinction or honours, to remain satisfied and do nothing further.
rest on one's oars Remain passive, after making progress.

retreat
beat a retreat Depart defeated; go away ignominiously.

return
by return (of post) Immediately.
in return for In exchange for.

rhyme
neither rhyme nor reason Nonsense; rubbish.
no rhyme or reason No reason whatever.
- *There's no rhyme or reason why I shouldn't go.*

rich
strike it rich Discover means of becoming wealthy or successful.

rid
get or *be rid of; rid oneself of* Dispose of; remove permanently.

ride
let something ride Ignore or accept it.
ride for a fall Behave rashly.
ride high Enjoy success.
ride one's hobby-horse See under **horse.**
ride out Survive (difficulty, etc.).

ride roughshod Proceed without consideration or regard for other people's views or feelings.

take for a ride Trick. Mislead.

riff-raff

Worthless members of society.

right

by rights Rightly; justly.

- *By rights, this house belongs to my father.*

get or keep on the right side of Obtain or retain favour of (person). Conform with (law).

get right Understand.

go right Happen as wanted or expected.

in the right Correct.

keep (person) right Keep (person) healthy or free from error.

put or set to rights Correct. Make good.

serves you right See under **serve.**

right as rain or a trivet In satisfactory condition.

come right See under **come.**

right and left or right, left and centre On all sides. In all ways.

- *The home team were beaten right, left and centre.*

right-hand man Chief assistant or supporter.

right of way Pathway, road, etc., established over private property by long-standing usage.

ring

ring back Make telephone call in answer to a prior one.

ring a bell Remind one of something.

ring the changes Change the order of a limited number of items, so as to produce variety, e.g. mutton, beef, lamb, etc., for dinner.

ring off End a telephone call.

ring true Sound true.

ring up Contact by telephone.

run or make rings round Do something very much better than.

- *He can run rings round me at tennis.*

riot

run riot Behave in disorderly way.

rip

let rip Throw off restraint.

rise

give rise to Cause.

rise from the ranks Be promoted from a private soldier to a commissioned officer. The phrase is also used in connection with anyone who has risen from a very inferior position to an important one in the same organisation.

rise in the world Become socially or financially more important.

rise to Succeed in acting in a manner appropriate to.

- *The hotel rose to the occasion by producing a magnificent wed ding-breakfast.*

rise with the lark Get up early—strictly speaking at sunrise, when the lark begins to sing.

take a rise out of Make (person) look ridiculous, generally by deceiving him or her.

risk

run or take risks Expose oneself to hurt.

risk one's neck Take a dangerous risk.

river

sell down the river Betray.

rob

rob Peter to pay Paul Take from one person (or thing) to pay another.

rock

(at) rock-bottom (At the) lowest possible (point).

- *Public confidence in the Government is at rock-bottom.*

on the rocks 1. On the verge of collapse.

2. (Of drink) With ice.

rod

make a rod for one's own back Prepare trouble for oneself.

rule with a rod of iron Govern or control with great severity.

- *Their father ruled the children with a rod of iron.*

roll

roll-call The list of names of those who should be present at some assembly.

rolling in money Very rich.

roll on . . . May . . . soon arrive.

roll up 1. [LIT]

2. [MET] Assemble; appear.

rolled into one Combined in one thing or person.

rolling
rolling stone One who never settles long in one place.

Rome
Rome was not built in a day Achievements take some time to bring about.

when in Rome Adapt yourself to the habits and customs of those among whom you are living.

romp
romp home Win easily.

roof
a roof over one's head A place to live or stay.

go through the roof 1. Become angry.

    2. (Of price) Increase sharply.

room
make room for Create space for thing or person by removing or compressing others.

not room to swing a cat in Very little space.

prefer a person's room to his company Prefer that person were absent, somewhere else.

room for improvement Less than satisfactory state of affairs, and capable of being better.

room and to spare Plenty of space.

roost
come home to roost Return to cause difficulty to whoever started the operation.

root
put down roots Settle happily (in a place).

root and branch Every part; the whole organisation.

take root Become established.

the root of the matter, trouble, etc. The base; the foundation of.

    ● *The root of the whole trouble is that teachers are underpaid.*

root out Remove completely; extract from its surroundings.

rope
give one enough rope Allow to continue in error until one brings the consequences upon oneself.

(know) the ropes (Be familiar with) the method and procedure.

rope in Persuade (person) to join.

rose

through rose-coloured spectacles Cheerfully, optimistically.

rot

stop the rot Halt deterioration.
the rot has set in Deterioration has begun.

rotten

rotten to the core Utterly bad.

rough

cut up rough Behave in angry way.
rough and ready Sufficient, but not elaborate.
rough and tumble 1. (Adjective) Disorderly.
    2. (Noun) Jostling behaviour.
rough diamond An uneducated or unsophisticated but worthy person.
rough edge of one's tongue Angry remark. Usually *make (person) feel the rough edge of one's tongue.*
rough edges Minor features (in thing or person) needing to be corrected.
rough house Disturbance, row.
rough it Live primitively.
   • *If you go camping, you must be prepared to rough it.*
roughly 1. In a rough manner.
   • *The police handled the prisoners roughly.*
   2. Approximately.
   • *There are roughly half a million people in the city.*
rough on Unfortunate for.
rough out Explain in outline.
sleep rough Sleep out of doors, on park-benches, etc.
take the rough with the smooth Be prepared to tolerate inconvenience, hardship, etc., as well as to accept the more agreeable aspects of life, etc.

round

all-rounder Person proficient at all aspects of an activity, e.g. a particular sport.
ask person round Invite person to visit one's home, usually for hospitality.
get round to Attend to after a time.
going the rounds Circulating; travelling around.
   • *There's a curious rumour going the rounds.*
roundabout way, route, etc. A straggling, indirect way.

- *We came into Liverpool by a roundabout way.*

round down Reduce to nearest or to a convenient whole number.

round numbers Strictly speaking, this idiom should refer to complete hundreds, thousands, etc. It is, however, constantly used in the sense of 'approximately'.

- *There are 2000 people in the village, in round numbers.*

round off Complete; add a final finish to.

- *He rounded off the performance with a song.*

round on Upbraid unexpectedly. Blame violently, and frequently undeservedly.

round robin A letter or other documents, usually of complaint, upon which all those concerned sign their names in a circle, so that everyone has the same responsibility and the leader remains anonymous. A petition passed from hand to hand for signature.

round-table conference A meeting at which representatives of all parties to a dispute meet on equal terms to discuss matters.

round trip Journey which ends at its starting-point.

round up 1. Gather together.

2. Increase to nearest whole number.

row

in a row One after the other.

rub

rub along Manage somehow.

rub down 1. Make (wood, plaster, etc.) smooth by friction.

2. Dry, clean or massage by rubbing.

rub in Remind, or keep reminding, person of something unpleasant.

rub off 1. Remove by rubbing.

2. Transfer or be transferred by contact or influence.

- *Some of the father's arrogance has rubbed off on the son.*

rub one's hands Express glee.

rub shoulders with Meet or associate with (people).

rub up 1. Polish.

2. Revive one's knowledge of a subject.

rub up the wrong way Irritate; annoy.

- *Her tactlessness always rubs people up the wrong way.*

rubber

rubber-stamp Officially approve without examination.

ruffle

ruffle person's feathers Irritate person. Disturb person's equanimity.

rug

pull the rug from under Act suddenly to leave person at a disadvantage.

rule

as a rule Usually. More often than not.

golden rule Basic, most important rule which ought never to be forgotten.
- *In golf, the golden rule is to keep one's eye on the ball.*

rule of the road The general rules governing traffic.

rule the roost or roast Be in the position of one who issues orders, and is in command.

rule of thumb [LIT] Measuring lengths by one's thumb. [MET] Measuring by guesswork based on experience.

rule out Exclude.

ruling passion the chief incentive in one's life.

work to rule Observe every rule and regulation in precise detail, thus making efficiency impossible. (Device used as alternative to open strike in industrial disputes, having the advantage of qualifying the employee for wages.)

run

also-ran Loser.

dry run Rehearsal. 1. (Verb) Manage.
- *They run a grocery business.*

2. (Noun) An extended number of performances or issues.
- *The play had a run of 500 nights.*

a good run A successful sequence.

on the run Being pursued from place to place.

run across Meet casually and unexpectedly.
- *I don't often run across such an interesting pub.*

run after Seek, pursue.
- *He runs after every pretty girl he meets.*

run against Similar to *run across.*

run along Go.

run amuck or amok Dash about wildly and senselessly.

run off or away with 1. Steal and depart with.
- *The assistant has run off with the week's takings.*

2. Win easily.

- *We expect to run away with the Cup.*

run away with the idea Assume hastily and incorrectly.

- *I don't want you to run away with the idea that I'm dissatisfied.*

run a chance of being May be.

run close Be very near in race, competition, merit, etc.

- *St Helens is probably the ugliest place in England, but Runcorn runs it close.*

run counter to Be in opposition to.

- *Your suggestions run counter to what we arranged yesterday.*

run down 1. Collide with and injure or kill. Similar to **run over**.

2. Overtake, and frequently capture as well.

3. Speak ill of.

4. Visit.

5. In poor health, through overwork, etc.

run dry Cease to flow.

run for 1. Run in an attempt to reach (bus, etc.)

2. Be candidate for (office, etc.).

run to earth Find after a search. [Or. Fox-hunting, from following a fox to its den, or 'earth'.]

- *I ran the quotation to earth in Shakespeare's Othello.*

run for it Run for some especially urgent reason.

a good run for one's money Time and opportunity in which to be free, or enjoy oneself.

run the gauntlet See under **gauntlet**.

run high Become heated; excited.

- *Feelings always run high during an election.*

run in Arrest.

run-in Quarrel.

runs in the family Is an inherited trait or characteristic.

- *Twins run in the family.*

run into See **run across,** also **run down** (1) and **run over** (2).

run into debt Incur debt.

run into the ground Exhaust.

run it fine Leave little room for error.

run like mad See under **mad**.

run low Become scanty.

- *Our oil-supplies are running low.*

run mad Become fantastically exaggerated and unreal.

- *The plans for rebuilding the City show capitalism run mad.*

run messages Carry messages.

run of the mill Ordinary. Unexciting. Average.

run on Hasten ahead. Also *a run on* A heavy (unexpected) demand for.

run out 1. Come to an end.
- *My patience has completely run out.*
- *We ran out of coal, and had to burn wood.*

2. Cricket. A batsman is 'run out' when the ball is thrown against the wicket before he has had time to complete a run.

run out on Abandon.

run over 1. Flow over.
- *The water run over the edge of the jug.*

2. Drive over; collide with.
- *The train ran over the man as he was crossing the line.*

3. Glance over; read through and check.
- *You'd better run (your eye) over these instructions before you go.*

run ragged Exhaust by ceaseless effort.

run rings round See under **ring**.

run a temperature Have temperature higher than usual, signifying illness.

run to Reach; have sufficient money or ability for.
- *This novel runs to over four hundred pages.*
- *I think I can run to another round of drinks.*

run to earth Find after search.

run or go to seed 1. [LIT] Grow rank and straggling. As a plant does after it has blossomed. 2. [MET] Deteriorate, with an effect of neglect and decay.
- *A house will soon run to seed if left unattended.*

run through 1. Exhaust; squander.
- *I ran through my pocket money very quickly.*

2. Read quickly.
- *I'll just run through these letters, and then we'll go out.*

3. Pierce completely.
- *The needle ran through her finger.*

run short of Be left without a sufficient supply.
- *I ran short of milk because the cat knocked over the jug.*

run up 1. Make rapidly.

2. Accumulate (money, debt, etc.).

run up a bill Incur debts, usually recklessly.

run up against Encounter as obstacle.

run wild Behave in undisciplined way.

runner-up The competitor immediately after the winner.

running

in the running With a chance of success.
- *He's in the running for promotion.*

make the running Take the leading part.

out of the running With no chance of winning.

running Consecutive.
- *We met several days running.*

(*Note*—This adjective invariably follows the noun.)

running fight A fight throughout which the defenders are running away and the attackers pursuing them.

take a running jump Go away.

rush

rush at 1. Move rapidly towards.

2. Deal with (task, etc.) impetuously.

rush off one's feet Exhaust with rapid sequence of tasks.

rush one's fences Be in too great a hurry for results.

rush headlong Rush recklessly, with all one's energy.

rush hour Period of maximum activity or traffic.

rustle

rustle up Find. Make quickly.

rut

in a rut In a fixed, dull, repetitive or unproductive way of life.

S

sabre
sabre-rattling Threat of retribution (by military force or by other means).

sack
give or get the sack Dismiss (or be dismissed) from employment.

sackcloth
in sackcloth and ashes Deeply penitent.

sacred
sacred cow Thing (especially idea or institution) that is (sometimes unreasonably) felt to be beyond criticism.

saddle
in the saddle [LIT] Riding a horse. [MET] In office; in control of an enterprise.
saddled with Burdened with.
  • *He was saddled with the responsibility of educating three small children.*

safe
better safe than sorry It is wise to take no risks.
it is safe to say One may say without fear of misleading.
on the safe side Leaving room for error.
safe and sound Unharmed.

safety
play for safety Show caution.
safety first Caution above all else.

safety in numbers No (or less) risk if there are sufficient amounts, quantities, etc.

said

easier said than done More easy to talk about than to actually do.

no sooner said than done Accomplished as soon as requested; finished very soon after being ordered, mentioned, etc.

when all is said and done After all.

sail

full sail [LIT] With all sails spread. [MET] Without hindrance.

sail near or close to the wind Go very near to something which is improper, illegal, dangerous, etc.

sail under false colours Pretend to be something that one is not. [Old f.]

set sail Start on a sea voyage.

sake

for God's or heaven's or goodness' sake Expression of exasperation.

for old times' sake In memory of former days.

salad

salad days Days of youthful inexperience.

sally

sally forth Go forth; come out (often in numbers, and suddenly or dramatically).

salt

rub salt into wound Exacerbate (trouble, etc.).

salt away Save (money, etc.).

salt of the earth Person(s) who are valuable members of society.

not worth one's salt or keep Worthless; not worth the cost of the salary one is paid.

take with a grain or pinch of salt Accept a statement, but with some doubt as to its complete truth.

- *We take most of what he says with a grain of salt.*

salvation

work out one's own salvation Discover, by experience, the solution to one's problems.

same

all or just the same; at the same time Nevertheless.

be all the same to Make no difference to.
not in the same street as Not as good as.

sand

happy as a sandboy Very happy.
have one's head in the sand Be unobservant or unaware.
the sands are running out There is not much time left.

sardines

like sardines Very close together.

satisfaction

give satisfaction Satisfy; be what is required.

sauce

sauce for the goose What is suitable for one person is equally suitable for another; the same rule applies to all people in similar circumstances.

save

save appearances or one's face Prevent or minimise embarrassment; deal tactfully with any embarrassing situation.
save one's breath (to cool one's porridge) Say nothing; keep one's advice to oneself.
  • *I warned her, but I might just as well have saved my breath.*
save one's skin Protect one from danger, damage, etc.
save oneself the trouble Refrain from doing something.
save the mark Expression used to emphasise a statement (usually one expressing surprise or irony) or to apologise for mentioning something unpleasant.
save the situation or day Find or provide a way out of difficulty.
  • *I ran out of petrol, but a passing motorist saved the situation.*
saved by the bell Rescued from an unpleasant situation by an occurrence.
saving grace Feature that redeems (person's or thing's) faults.

say

does not say much for Does not indicate quality in.
have one's say Say all that one wishes to say in one's own words. (Opposite: *have no say.*)
go without saying Be too obvious to deserve mention.
have (something) to say for oneself Be able to explain one's actions.
I say An introductory phrase to a remark conveying surprise or special interest.

- *I say, look at the view from over here.*

I wouldn't say no to I would like.

not to say And moreover.

there's no saying It is impossible to know.

to say nothing of Even disregarding.

that is to say In other words.

what do you say to? Would you like?

you can say that again! You are right!

saying

as the saying is; as they say A half-facetious, half-apologetic excuse for using a hackneyed phrase or cliché.

- *Well, hard work never hurt anyone, as the saying is.*

there is no saying It is not known.

scales

hold the scales Be an impartial judge.

tip or turn the scales 1. Weigh.

- *The boxer turned the scales at 14 stones.*

2. Bring about a decisive change in fortunes.

- *Rain on the second day of the Test match turned the scales in Australia's favour.*

scarce

make oneself scarce Absent oneself.

scatter

scatter-brained Careless; easily distracted; unable to concentrate on one thing.

scene

behind the scenes [LIT] Backstage in a theatre. [MET] Not in the public eye.

change of scene(ry) Move to different surroundings.

come onto the scene Become noticeable.

create or make a scene Cause any violent emotional disturbance.

not be one's scene Not be what one likes or is good at.

set the scene Describe the setting. Place in context. Prepare.

scent

false scent Course (of action, etc.) that will not lead to good result.

on the (right) scent Following course that will lead to good result.

put or throw off the scent Mislead.

scent (a mystery, scandal, etc.) Suspect.

school
of the old school Of a type characteristic of former times.
old school tie What influential people have in common.

score
know the score Know what the position is.
on that score As far as that matter is concerned.
pay off or wipe off or settle old scores Cancel an old injury or injustice by inflicting another adequate punishment.
score off Put at a disadvantage.

scorn
point the finger of scorn [Old f.] Sneer at; speak about with contempt.

scot
scot free See under **free.**

scrape
get into a scrape Get into trouble; commit some foolish action leading to trouble.
scrape acquaintance with Take special trouble to become acquainted with; deliberately set out to become friends with.
scrape through Succeed by a narrow margin.
scrape together Succeed, with difficulty, in accumulating something.
scrape up Same as *scrape together.*
See **barrel.**

scratch
bring to the scratch Reach a definite decision; decide to take definite action. [Old f.] (See *up to scratch.*)
come up to scratch Reach a required standard.
scratch the surface Not penetrate deeply into.
  ● *The Minister's speech only scratched the surface of the problem.*
scratch team, crew, etc. A number of people collected casually, not regular members.
  ● *Although we'd only a scratch team, we won all three matches.*
starting from scratch Starting from the beginning, without benefit of other people's or one's own previous work.
up to scratch Fit to deal with one's work; equal to what is required.
  ● *I've had influenza, and am still not up to scratch.*

you scratch my back and I'll scratch yours If you help me, I will help you.

screw
have a screw loose Be mad.
have one's head screwed on Have good sense.
put on the screw(s) See under **put**.
screw up one's courage Force oneself to be brave.

scrimp
scrimp and save Make economies.

scruple
make no scruple; have no scruples Have no hesitation. [Frequently applied to some action which might involve some 'scruple' or sense of what is right and wrong.]
- *The soldiers had no scruples about robbing their prisoners.*

sea
at sea Unaware; confused.
get one's sea-legs Learn to walk successfully on the moving deck of a ship; accommodate oneself to the rise and fall of the waves.
put to sea Leave the shore to start on a voyage.
sea of blood Scene of extensive bloodshed.

seal
one's lips are sealed One is completely silent.
sealed book A subject completely unknown.
- *Fifteenth-century art was a sealed book to him.*

set the seal on Conclude. Formally end. Give distinction to.
- *His fourth goal set the seal on the match.*
- *The presence of numerous international golfers set the seal on the tournament.*

seam
bursting at the seams Very full, crowded or packed.
come or *fall apart at the seams* Show signs of collapse.
seamy side More disagreeable or sordid feature (of life, etc.).

sear
the sear and yellow Old age.

season
for a season For a short time.

- *The play will run for a short season at Stratford before transferring to London.*

close season Period during which certain sports are not played.

compliments of the season Christmas greetings.

in season Ready for eating and in plentiful supply. (Used of foodstuffs.) See *a word in season.*

in season and out of season At all times, whether suitable or unsuitable.

out of season Unseasonable; at a wrong or inappropriate time

a word in season Advice given at an appropriate time.

second

(at) second hand 1. Not new,

2. By hearsay.

come off second-best Be beaten by superior force.

second childhood Childish behaviour at an age when it is not expected.

second to none Better than all others.

second nature Instinctive; an action which has already taken place so many times that it has become automatic.

second-rate Not of the best.

second thoughts Later, more mature consideration.

- *On second thoughts, I won't go to the theatre tonight.*

second wind In exercise, easy breathing after initial breathlessness. Also applied to other circumstances in which continued practice, experience, etc., makes them easier, more pleasant, etc.

- *After a year in this job, I'm just finding my second wind.*

secret

in the secret Among those permitted to know something that is kept from others.

keep a secret Not reveal a secret.

make no secret of State openly, without concealment.

open secret Supposed secret which everyone knows about.

security

hold as security Retain, in case of loss or failure to repay.

see

I'll see I'll consider the matter before deciding.

see about it Decide later.

see better days Enjoy greater prosperity.

see fair play Make sure that the rules are obeyed, that there is
no cheating.
see the last of Will not see or have to deal with again.
see life Experience many things.
see off 1. Accompany to the starting-place.
- *We saw him off at the station.*
2. Remove. Chase away. Defeat.
- *The revolution has seen off undemocratic government.*
see one's way Manage. Contrive. Also *see one's way clear.*
- *Can you see your way to repairing it immediately?*
see over Examine by walking round and looking.
see things Have hallucinations.
see through 1. [LIT] Perceive through something transparent.
- *I saw him through the window.*
2. [MET] Perceive the truth, in spite of attempts to deceive.
- *Any idiot can see through most television advertising.*
3. Ensure that a job is completed.
- *We are going to see the work through.*
(Note alteration in order of words.)
see to Give one's attention to.
see to it that Make sure that.
seeing is believing One's own observation is the best proof.

seed
run or go to seed See under **run.**
sow the seeds Bring into being, and thus be responsible for
future development.

seize
seize on Accept eagerly.
seize up Break down.

sell
sell off Sell.
sell out Sell whole of stock.
sell-out 1. Function for which all tickets have been sold.
2. Betrayal.
sell up 1. As *sell out.*
2. Sell everything prior to removal, going out of business, etc.

send
send down Suspend or expel from university.
send for Send message asking person to come or for thing to be
brought.

send off 1. Have (message, etc.) dispatched.

    2. Be present at (person's) departure. Also used as noun.

send on Dispatch onwards.

send packing Dismiss peremptorily. Also *send someone about his business.*

send up 1. Write, usually requesting information. (Also *send off*.).

    ● *I'll send up for the firm's catalogue.*

    2. Satirise. Parody. (Also noun *send-up*.)

    ● *The play sends up the advertising industry.*

send word Dispatch a message.

    ● *I'll send word that we'll be arriving late.*

sensation

create a sensation Produce a startling effect.

sense

sense of humour, etc. Ability to appreciate what is humorous, etc.

come to one's senses 1. Recover consciousness.

    2. Recover one's sense of proportion and of what is intelligent and just.

in a sense To a certain extent.

sixth sense Intuition.

take leave of one's senses Appear to have lost one's normal balance or sane state of mind.

sensible

sensible of Aware; conscious of.

separate

separate the sheep from the goats Separate worthy people, or (more loosely) those suited to a particular purpose, from those who are the reverse.

separate the wheat from the chaff Separate what is worth keeping from what is rubbish.

sepulchre

whited or painted sepulchre One whose virtuous appearance and manner conceals inward vice; a hypocrite.

serve

if my memory serves me right If I remember correctly.

serve someone right Punish justly and appropriately.

serve its turn Prove useful for a limited time.

serve its purpose Be suitable for what it is required to do. Opposite: *serve no purpose.*

- *The greenhouse is dilapidated, but it serves its purpose.*

serve two masters Observe two conflicting principles.

serves him right He has received what he deserves.

service

render or *do* or *perform a service* Be useful to; assist.

service flat One in which domestic help, meals, etc., are provided by the management.

set

set about 1. Begin; commence.

- *I'll set about preparing supper.*

2. Attack violently. Also *set on.*

- *The three thugs set about the barman.*

set one's affections on Concentrate one's liking upon; desire intensely.

set against 1. Opposed to.

- *His parents are very much set against the marriage.*

2. Balanced against.

- *The £5 you've paid now will be set against the £20 you borrowed last year.*

3. Put into conflict or opposition.

- *Civil war sets family against family.*

set apart Put on one side. Separate.

set aside Disregard; place on one side.

set-back A reversal or arrest of progress. A relapse.

- *The injury to the full-back was a great set-back to the team's chances.*

set back Impede or reverse the progress of.

- *the drought will set the country's progress back several years.*

set down 1. Write; place on record.

2. Deposit passengers.

set by Put on one side for future use.

set by the ears Exasperate; cause to quarrel.

set eyes on Emphatic form of 'see'.

- *I haven't set eyes on him for many years.*

set an example Exhibit oneself as an example or model to be followed.

set fair Likely to be satisfactory.

set a fashion Establish or begin a custom.

set foot in Enter.

set in Become established.

set on foot Start; initiate.

set forth, off, out Start; depart.

set free, at liberty Release.

set one's face against Oppose with determination.

set one's hand to Undertake.

set one's heart on Strongly desire to obtain.

set one's house in order Arrange one's own affairs properly; correct one's own faults.

set in Begin (applied to something which will continue for some time).
- *Winter has set in early this year.*

set off 1. Start on a journey.
- *He set off to Sheffield early next day.*

2. Make more effective; embellish.
- *The roses set off the dark beauty of her hair.*

set on See *set about* (2).

set out 1. State.

2. Begin journey.

3. Aim.

4. Show.

set over Place (person) in authority over.

set phrase Formal phrase.

set piece Prepared performance.

set purpose Determined purpose; one already decided.
- *It was his set purpose to discover his father's old home.*

set at rest Cause to subside; eliminate.

set right Make correct.

set sail See under **sail**.

set the seal on Complete; make final.

set store by See under **store**.

set or lay the table Prepare it for a meal.

set one's teeth on edge See under **teeth**.

set the Thames on fire Achieve sensational success.

set-to Contest; fight.
- *There was a set-to when the police asked the demonstrators to disperse.*

set to Become active; busy.
- *If we set to, we shall soon have the room tidy.*

set up 1. Formally establish; cause to exist.
- *The Minister will set up a committee to investigate the matter.*

2. Assume the right. Also *set up as.*

* *I don't set myself up as an authority on rare books.*

set upon Attack.

settle

settle down Become established; adopt regular habits; live a settled and normal life.

settle for Accept.

settle up Agree and pay (account etc.).

seven

in one's or the seventh heaven In a state of intense delight or ecstasy.

severe

leave severely alone Avoid.

sew

sewn up Arranged.

sex

weaker sex Women. (Jocular.)

shade

put in the shade Appear more prominent than. Outshine. Overshadow.

* *Their record of house building puts other towns in the shade.*

shades of That reminds one of.

shadow

cast a long shadow Exercise influence.

cast a shadow over Reduce success (fun etc.) of.

may your shadow never grow less May you always prosper.

shadow of one's former self Reduced in vigour or health.

worn to a shadow Exhausted.

shaggy

shaggy-dog story Long pointless joke.

shake

no great shakes Not very good or significant.

shake the dust from one's feet Depart from, usually in contempt or anger.

shake in one's shoes Tremble with fear and apprehension.

shake off Get rid of.

* *I wish I could shake off this cold.*

shake one's head Express refusal, disagreement or concern.

shake out Remove dust, etc., from garment, etc., by shaking.

shake up 1. Mix by agitating.

2. Rouse.

two shakes (of a lamb's tale) Very quickly.

shame

a burning or crying shame A great and terrible shame; one to make the cheeks burn with anger.

put to shame Cause to feel ashamed, or inferior.

- *The boy's playing would have put many a professional to shame.*

what a shame! How unfortunate!

shank

shanks' pony One's own legs.

- *We missed the last train and used shanks' pony.*

shape

in any shape or form At all.

in good or poor or bad shape In good (poor, bad) condition.

in the shape of In the form of.

shape up Develop.

take shape Begin to have recognisable form.

share

share and share alike Divide everything equally.

- *The three partners in the business agreed to share and share alike.*

sharp

as sharp as a needle or razor Very sharp. Very intelligent or alert.

sharp practice Behaviour which, while still technically legal, practically amounts to swindling.

sharp's the word; look sharp; be sharp Hurry up.

sharp tongue Capacity to be critical or sarcastic in speech.

sheep

black sheep A person with a bad record or reputation.

as well be hanged for a sheep as a lamb If one is in mild trouble, one might as well *go the whole hog* and incur serious trouble.

cast sheep's eyes Gaze in a foolish and amorous way at a person.

See also under **separate, wolf.**

sheer

sheer off Break off (usually applied to metal bolts, etc., coming apart under strain).

sheet

between the sheets In bed.

sheet anchor Chief support.

shelf

on the shelf No longer required to do active work; replaced by someone more effective. No longer capable of work. Too old or unattractive to marry.

shell

come out of one's shell Throw off one's reserve and become communicative.

shell out Pay.

shift

make shift Contrive to carry on. See also **makeshift**.

shift for oneself Take care of oneself.

- *Thanks for your help; I can shift for myself now.*

shift one's ground Adopt a new point of view or position in an argument, discussion, etc.

shilly-shally

Waste time trying to reach a decision.

shine

take a shine to Become fond of.

take the shine out of Make appear inferior and unimportant.

ship

shipshape (and Bristol fashion) Tidy and in good order.

when one's ship comes home or in When one becomes rich.

shoe

in a person's shoes In a similar position to him.

where the shoe pinches The real trouble or worry; the chief cause of financial anxiety. See also under **shake, dead.**

on a shoestring Cheaply.

shoot

shoot ahead Make extremely rapid progress.

- *The magazine was started only six months ago, but it has shot ahead rapidly.*

shoot one's bolt Make a final effort, having nothing left in reserve.

- *The team shot their bolt too early and were easily defeated.*

shoot up Rise or grow suddenly and rapidly.

shop

closed shop Factory, or part of one, in which employees have to be members of a trade union.

set up shop Begin to do something.

shop around Make comparisons before coming to a decision.

shut up shop Stop work.

talk shop Discuss one's profession, business, etc. (usually on informal or social occasions).

shorn

shorn of Stripped of.

short

bring or pull up short Check.

cut short Abbreviate. Interrupt.

fall short of Fail to reach.

for short As a shorter form.

go short Not have enough.

make short work of Dispose of quickly.

nothing or little short of Nearly as bad as.

run short Have only small quantities remaining.

sell short Disparage.

short and sweet Short.

short of Without sufficient.

- *I can't offer you tea, as we're short of milk.*

short change Give too little change from payment.

short-circuit Deal informally and quickly with (an official document, etc.), omitting the usual procedure.

- *Is there no way of short-circuiting these formalities?*

short cut A short way from one point to another, as distinct from the usual one.

- *The distance by the road is three miles, but there is a short cut through the park.*

short for An abbreviation of.

short-handed or short-staffed With an insufficient number of helpers; short of staff.

- *I'm sorry to keep you waiting, but we are short-handed this week through illness.*

in short Summarised; stated briefly.

- *The rumour, in short, is not to be trusted.*

in the short run or term Over a short period of time.

short-lived Not of long duration.

short of 1. Without going as far as.

- *We'll do anything to economise, short of selling the car.*

2. Not as much or as far as.

short of breath Panting (as result of illness, exertion, etc.).

short on Lacking.

short shrift very little time for explanation before inflicting punishment, or administering reproof, correction etc.

- *He tried to explain the mistake, but got very short shrift.*

in short supply Available in insufficient quantities to meet the demand.

short weight or measure Less than was ordered or paid for.

(make) short work of Dispose of quickly.

- *The children made short work of the chocolates.*

shot

a good shot An accurate or near accurate attempt. Opposite: *a bad shot.*

- *He made a good shot at repairing the toy.*

big shot Important person.

like a shot With extreme speed. Without hesitation.

a long or random shot A casual suggestion; a mere guess.

a shot in the arm Encouragement. Stimulus.

a shot in the dark A guess.

shoulder

have broad shoulders Be able to bear much responsibility.

have on one's shoulders Support; bear.

- *It is a terrible responsibility to have on one's shoulders.*

head and shoulders See under **head.**

old head on young shoulders See under **head.**

put one's shoulders to the wheel Work hard and steadily.

rub shoulders with Come into intimate contact with; become acquainted.

shoulder to cry on Person to comfort one.

shoulder to shoulder United in effort.

straight from the shoulder Directly and forcibly.

shout

all over bar the shouting Virtually finished.

shout at Speak loudly in rebuke.

shout down Silence (person) by shouting.

shout for Call for in loud voice.

show

for show As display only.

get the show on the road Begin an activity.

give the show away Betray one's secrets.

nothing to show for Nothing produced by. No profit from.

show cause Give good reason.

show-down A frank exposure; an open challenge.

show off Display one's cleverness with the intention of attracting attention and obtaining praise.

show of force Display of one's power.

show of hands Raising of hands to vote.

show of reason Apparent justice and logic.

- *The chef said, with a show of reason, that it was impossible to make an omelette without eggs.*

show up 1. Expose (usually to disadvantage).

- *The behaviour of those children shows up their parents.*

2. Escort someone upstairs.

- *The visitors have arrived; show them up.*

3. Be conspicuous, clearly visible (often to advantage).

- *The painting shows up well against that wall.*

shrug

shrug off Dismiss as unimportant.

shut

shut down Close. (Usually applied to business.)

shut one's eyes to Pretend not to notice.

shut out Exclude.

shut the door on or *to* Make impossible.

shut up Stop talking. Make person stop talking.

side

let the side down Fail to conform with colleagues' standards, efforts, etc.

on every side; on all sides From every direction, every source.

on the safe side See under **safe.**

on the side; as a side line In addition to one's normal work.

- *The garage mechanic earns quite a lot on the side.*

put on one side Leave for later attention.

side by side Standing close together.

side with Ally oneself with; openly sympathise with.

split one's sides Laugh very heartily.

sight

at first sight At the first (superficial) glance; immediately.

in sight of Near enough to see.

- *We shall soon be in sight of Southampton.*

in the sight of In the view of; as seen by.

- *In the sight of the world, they were a happily married couple.*

know by sight Be familiar with the appearance only.

- *I've never met him, but I know him by sight.*

lose sight of [LIT] Fail to see. Opposite: *catch sight of.*

- *At this distance you lose sight of the village.*

[MET] Fail to realise, or to remember.

- *You've lost sight of the fact that you are no longer young.*

lose one's sight Become blind.

not be able to stand the sight of Dislike intensely.

out of sight Beyond one's vision.

set one's sights on Aim at.

sight for sore eyes A very welcome, cheering thing to see.

out of sight, out of mind One forgets that which is not present.

sign

sign of the times Indication of present-day thought and feeling.

signal

give the signal or sign Indicate by sign or speech when some event should happen.

- *The captain gave the signal for the men to attack.*

silence

keep silent; keep or maintain silence Continue to remain silent.

pass over in silence Ignore.

silence is golden, but speech is silver to remain silent is better than to talk.

silent

silent majority Majority of people (usually of moderate views) who do not draw attention to themselves or make themselves heard (e.g. by militant action).

silk

make a silk purse out of a sow's ear Change the real character of a person; make a gentleman or lady of one who is not one; create something good out of poor materials.

take silk See under **take.**

sing

sing-song 1. (Noun) An impromptu concert, usually held by a community—soldiers, campers, etc.

2. (Adjective) Monotonous; flat and lifeless.

- *The sentry repeated his instructions in a sing-song voice.*

sing the praises of Praise highly and in general terms.

single

single-handed Unaided.

singleness of aim, purpose, heart Concentration; a single object in view.

sink

sink or swim Rely on one's own efforts; succeed or fail.

sit

sit back Relax.

sit on one's hands Fail to act.

sit tight Remain firmly in one's place.

sit up Be startled.

- *That dress of yours will make the neighbours sit up.*

sit up for Wait after the usual bedtime for somebody's return.

- *We shall probably be late coming home, so don't sit up for us.*

six

at sixes and sevens Muddled; in a state of confusion.

- *We have only just moved into the house, and everything is at sixes and sevens.*

six of one and half-a-dozen of the other An affair in which both sides deserve equal blame or merit.

- *The magistrates listened to the story of the quarrel between the two people, and decided that it was six of one and half-a-dozen of the other.*

skate

skate on thin ice Encroach on matter needing care.

skate over Deal with quickly or superficially. Avoid.

skeleton

skeleton at the feast Cause of worry or upset at enjoyable time.

skeleton in the cupboard A disgrace which the family, community, etc., does its best to conceal.

skeleton staff Small number of staff, just enough to keep things going.

skin

by the skin of one's teeth Very narrowly. Only just.

- *We caught the bus by the skin of our teeth.*

get under one's skin Annoy one.

skin and bone Very thin.

skin-deep Superficial; not lasting.
- *Beauty is only skin-deep.*

thick-skinned Insensitive (to criticism, other people, etc.).

sky

the sky's the limit There is no limit (to what can be achieved, done, spent, etc.).

slap

slap in the face A rebuff; an insult.

slap on the back Expression of congratulation.

slate

clean slate No record of misdemeanours.

wipe the slate clean Forget previous misdemeanours.

sleep

let sleeping dogs lie Refrain from stirring up trouble.

lose sleep over Worry about.

sleep off Recover from by taking a sleep.

sleep on a matter Allow a time to pass before finally deciding.
- *I'll sleep on the matter, and write to you tomorrow.*

sleep like a log or top Sleep peacefully and deeply.

sleeping partner One who is a partner (e.g. in a business) but plays no active part.

sleight

sleight-of-hand Extreme dexterity and quickness.

slide

let things slide or drift Do nothing; take no active steps; be negligent.

slightest

not in the slightest Not at all.

slip

give the slip Escape, and remain uncaptured.

let slip 1. Remark without thinking.

    2. Miss (a chance, etc.)

make a slip or slip up Make a slight (but frequently vital) error.
- *You've made a slip somewhere in these accounts.*

many a slip Many things may happen to prevent a desired or expected result.

slip away, out, off, across, etc. Move unobserved or quietly or quickly.

slip through one's fingers Escape; be lost.
slip of a girl Slim, young girl.
slip one's mind Be forgotten.
slip of the pen An error in writing.
slip of the tongue A verbal error.
slip up Make a mistake.

slot

slot in Fit in (between two others). Accommodate.
- *The dentist slotted me in at short notice.*

slow

slow(ly) but sure(ly) Not quickly, but making progress.
slow down Reduce speed.
slow up Same as *slow down.*

sly

on the sly Secretly and artfully.

small

feel (look) small Be humiliated. Feel humiliated.
no small Considerable.
small beer Trivial; unimportant.
- *The news is all very small beer.*

small-minded Petty.
small talk See under **talk.**

smoke

end or go up in smoke Have no result; end in nothing.
no smoke without fire All rumour has some truth in it, or some
   justification.

snake

snake in one's bosom Person ungrateful for kindness shown.
snake in the grass A hidden or hypocritical enemy.

snap

snap at 1. Try to bite (usually applied to animals).
   2. Speak irritably to.
   3. Accept eagerly.
snap one's fingers at Disregard; treat with contempt.
snap out of it Become more cheerful or active.
snap up Seize hastily.
- *It's a bargain I snapped up in the market.*

sneeze

not to be sneezed at Not to be treated as unimportant or insignificant. (Always used in the negative.)

- *The firm is offering a salary which isn't to be sneezed at.*

sniff

not to be sniffed at Not to be treated with contempt.

so

just so; quite so I agree; it is as you have stated.

and so forth Similar objects; in a similar way, etc.

- *He dealt in chairs, tables, and so forth.*

Similar to *and so on; et cetera.*

so far so good Good progress has been made up to now.

so-long Good-bye.

so long as Provided that.

so much for that That is the end of that.

so much so that To such an extent that.

so-so In inferior health; not too badly; moderately well.

- *His results in the exam were only so-so.*

so-and-so 1. Such and such a person. A general substitute for the specific name of a person or thing.

2. A mild term of abuse.

so to speak; in a manner of speaking Speaking generally, without being literally exact; speaking with a certain amount of metaphorical exaggeration.

so what? Does it matter?

sober

sober as a judge Not at all drunk.

sober down or up 1. Become more serious-minded and reliable.

- *The boy will sober down as he grows older.*

2. Recover from a temporary attack of hysteria or drunkenness.

- *We put him on the bed to sober up.*

sober-sides Person of sedate temperament and habits.

soft

a soft answer A well-mannered answer.

have a soft spot for Have room in one's affections for.

soft in the head Foolish.

soft-hearted Sympathetic and understanding (sometimes too much so).

soft job Very easy job (in view of the salary).

soft option An easy choice.
soft soap 1. Flattery; ingratiating behaviour.
   2. (Verb) Behave ingratiatingly.
soft-spoken Gently and politely speaking.
soft touch Gullible person.

sold
sold a pup Swindled; cheated.

soldier
come the old soldier (over) Claim greater experience (than), and
   consequently superior wisdom.
old soldier [LIT] A former soldier. [MET] Person of experience.
soldier on Continue, despite the difficulties.

something
have or be something to do with Be connected with.
see something of Meet occasionally.
something like 1. Approximately.
   2. (A thing) rather like.
something of To a certain extent.
- *He's something of a singer.*

song
for a song; a mere song Extremely cheap; at a merely nominal
   price
- *The painting was going for a song, so I bought it.*

make a song (and dance) about Create a fuss, disturbance, quarrel about (usually for trivial reasons).
- *The repair-bill is not worth making a song about.*

soon
sooner or later Eventually; in the end.

sore
like a bear with a sore head Grumpy.
sight for sore eyes Welcome sight.
stick out like a sore thumb Be prominent in an unpleasant or
   inappropriate way.

sort
a good sort a good fellow; a helpful person.
a sort of Something like.
of a sort; of sorts Not fully deserving the name.
- *He's a billiards player of sorts.*

out of sorts Not in good health; depressed and irritable. Similar to *off colour.*

sort out 1. Put in order by improving arrangement.

2. Punish. Reprimand.

soul

be unable to call one's soul one's own Be dominated by a person.

not a soul Absolutely no one.

● *When I reached the station, there was not a soul on the platform.*

the soul of A perfect example of.

soul-destroying Extremely dispiriting.

soul of discretion The essence of prudence.

sour

sour grapes Something referred to disparagingly, but only because it is out of reach.

sow

reap what one sows Be faced with the results of one's own actions.

sow the seeds of Originate; begin.

sow the wind and reap the whirlwind Perform ill-advised action and produce even worse consequences.

spade

call a spade a spade Speak quite plainly or bluntly.

spanner

throw a spanner in the works Interfere with, and check another person's plans

spare

go spare Become very angry.

not spare oneself Use all one's efforts.

spark

spark off Begin under stimulus.

speak

in a manner of speaking See *so to speak,* under **so.**

nothing to speak of Not worth comments.

on speaking terms Just acquainted. Opposite: *not on speaking terms,* which also means 'having quarrelled'.

speaks for itself Demonstrates without words; requires no explanation.

- *His record speaks for itself.*

speak too soon Make error by premature comment.

speak out Express (opinion) freely.

speak up 1. Speak more loudly.

2. Speak one's opinion (e.g. *for* or *against* something).
Also *speak out.*

speak volumes Convey much, while actually saying little or nothing.

speak well of Praise. Be to the credit of.

strictly speaking Speaking exactly, or according to a rule or promise.

- *Strictly speaking, I ought not to tell you this.*

to speak of Worth mentioning.

- *I have no savings to speak of.*

to speak to Well enough to have spoken to (person).

spell

spell out Explain very clearly.

- *The solicitor spelled out the consequences of taking legal action in the matter.*

under the spell of Fascinated by (person) or with (thing).

spick

spick and span Extremely neat and tidy.

spike

spike a person's guns Take some (sudden) action which ends opposition.

spin

spin out Draw out; prolong. Endure.

- *I don't think this gin will spin out for much longer.*

spin a yarn Tell a story.

spirit

in high spirits Cheerful. Opposite: *in low spirits.*

take in the right spirit Not be offended.

the spirit of the law The real meaning or intention of the law, as opposed to *the letter of the law,* the strict interpretation of its words.

spit

spit and polish Cleaning (of room, etc.). See **image.**

spite

in spite of Despite; notwithstanding.

in spite of oneself Though one would rather not have done it.
out of or *from* or *in spite* With malicious intention.

splash
make a splash Cause a sensation, excitement.
splash out on Spend money extravagantly on.

spleen
vent one's spleen Show ill temper.

splice
splice the mainbrace Take a stimulating drink to keep one's
  spirits up.

split
split hairs Quibble about trivial matters.
splitting headache Very severe one.
split second Very short moment of time.

spoil
spoiling for a fight Anxious and eager to quarrel or fight.
spoil the ship for a ha'porth of tar Ruin something by making
  a small economy.
spoil-sport One who impedes (by his words or behaviour) the
  enjoyment of others.

spoke
put spoke in one's wheel Frustrate one's purposes.

sponge
sponge on Systematically and constantly obtain money from
  one's friends.

spoon
wooden spoon Prize awarded to person coming last in race,
  competition, etc.

spot
in a spot In a difficulty.
knock spots off Easily surpass or beat.
spot Discover.
spot cash Immediate payment in cash.
spot check Random examination.
spot on Accurate.
spot the winner Bet successfully.
  ● *I was lucky enough to spot the winner in the two o'clock race.*
on the spot 1. At that particular place; there.

- *The police were on the spot within ten minutes.*

2. Immediately; without delay.

- *I'll attend to it on the spot.*

Similar to **there and then.**

put on the spot Place in a difficult position.

- *If it gets into the newspapers he'll be on the spot.*

spout

up the spout Ruined.

sprat

throw *or* **set a sprat to catch a mackerel** Risk a little to gain much. Make a small gift or concession in the hope of obtaining a large one.

spread

spread-eagled Having fallen to the ground with limbs spread out.

spread oneself Be lavish.

spring

spring a leak Begin to let in water.

spring something on one Surprise one with something.

where did you spring from? Where have you suddenly come from?

spur

on the spur of the moment Suddenly, without previous consideration.

square

all square Level; equal.

- *If I buy the next round, we shall be all square.*

back to square one Back to the beginning.

square deal Honest transaction.

square a man Bribe him.

square meal Satisfying meal.

square peg in a round hole Person not fitted for his position.

square up to Confront.

stab

have a stab at Make an attempt at.

stab in the back Cowardly attack. Betrayal.

stable

lock the stable door Take precautions when the accident they are to prevent has already happened.

staff

over-staffed With more employees than are needed.
under-staffed The reverse. Similar to *short-handed.*

stake

at stake Dependent upon what is about to happen.
have a stake in Be involved in (the welfare of).

* *All club members have a stake in the matter.*

stand

as matters or things stand In their present condition.
make a stand Refuse to budge.
stand aghast Be shocked, appalled.
stand alone Be without equal.
stand aloof Remain detached; refuse to share or cooperate with.
stand aside 1. [LIT] Stand where the progress of others will not be impeded. Also *stand back.*

    2. [MET] Give someone else an opportunity.

stand by 1. Wait in a state of readiness.

* *The troops have been ordered to stand by.*

    2. Support by word or deed.

* *He stood by his friend through all his troubles.*

    3. Be an observer.

* *I will not stand by and do nothing.*

stand on ceremony Behave stiffly and ceremoniously. (Usually used in the negative.)

* *Don't stand on ceremony—make yourself at home.*

stand a chance Have any possibility.

* *I don't think your horse stands a chance of winning.*

stand corrected Admit to being wrong.

* *I am sorry for the mistake—I stand corrected.*

stand down Retire.
stand on one's dignity Show—often absurdly—a sense of one's importance.
stand fast or firm Remain immovable.
stand for Represent.
stand one's ground Refuse to change one's statements or opinions.
Similar to *stand or stick to one's guns,*

stand in for Act as replacement for.

stand on one's own (two) feet *or legs* Accept full responsibility for one's own actions; accept no assistance.

stand in the way of Obstruct.

stand in a person's light Prevent his advancement; spoil his career. (Usually used in the negative.)

stand-offish Haughty; consciously superior; curt.

stand on Insist on.

stand out 1. Remain in opposition; refuse to cooperate.

- *The conspirators did their best to persuade all the men to join them, but three stood out.*

2. Be conspicuous.

- *The statue stands out against the trees.*

stand out for Insist upon.

- *The workers are standing out for higher wages.*

stand over 1. Stand near, usually to enforce an order.

- *She stood over the boy while he washed his face.*

2. Put aside for a time.

- *The accounts can stand over till next week.*

stand on one's rights Insist upon one's legal entitlements.

stand in good stead Prove useful to.

stand still Remain motionless.

standstill Stoppage. Usually *at a standstill* Not working. Not moving.

stand to Similar to *stand by* (1).

stand to win or lose Be in a position where one is capable of winning (or losing).

stand up 1. Stand on one's feet.

2. Be valid.

stand up for Support openly, by speech or action.

stand up to 1. Confront boldly; oppose.

2. Be capable of. Bear. Tolerate. Carry the weight of. Endure.

standard

standard of living Degree of material comfort achieved by a person, society, etc.

star

star-studded Having many 'stars' (famous people).

star turn A 'turn' or act by a famous performer. Frequently applied to any conspicuous or successful incident.

stare

stare one in the face Confront; be evident and obvious.

- *The troops saw defeat staring them in the face.*

stark
stark staring mad Extremely mad.

start
a fresh start A new beginning.
for a start or starters In the first place.
start life Begin one's career.
start off Begin to move.
start out Proceed (with an intention).
start up 1. Begin (business).
 2. Make (engine) work.
 3. Move suddenly (from seat, in surprise, etc.).
to start with In the first place.

stave
stave off Avert. Ward off.
- *A late goal staved off defeat.*

steal
steal a march on Gain an advantage for which one's adversary was not prepared.
steal the show Outshine others.
steal one's thunder Forestall him.
steal upon Creep softly upon.

steam
get up steam Summon energy for a special effort.
get steamed up Become angry or agitated.
let off steam Get rid of surplus energy.
run out of steam lose impetus.
under one's own steam Without assistance.

steer
steer clear of Avoid; evade.
steer a middle course Avoid extremes; act moderately; compromise.

step
in one's (foot-)steps Following one's example.
in step In conformity.
out of step Not in conformity.
step by step Slowly and methodically.
step down Give up position or post.
step in Intervene.

stepping-stone or stones [LIT] Stones in a stream used to enable one to cross with dry feet. [MET] Anything which may act as a means to an end (usually to an improvement).

● *She regards her present job purely as a stepping-stone.*

step up Increase.

take steps Start a course of action.

stew

stew in one's own juice Suffer the consequences of one's own (misguided) actions.

stick

give (person) stick Criticise or abuse (person). Also *get stick* Be criticised.

stick-in-the-mud An unenterprising, unambitious person.

stick one's neck out Take a risk.

stick at nothing Stop at nothing; be restrained by no scruple or impediment.

stick at something Continue to work at something.

stick out Same as *stand out* (2).

stick in one's throat [LIT] Choke one. [MET] Cause disgust or aversion.

stick to Remain faithful to.

stick to one's guns Not to be budged from one's position. Also *stick it out.*

stick up for Support.

stick up to Offer resistance to.

wrong end of the stick Misapprehension.

stiff

stiff as a poker or a ramrod Rigid; very formal.

stiff upper lip Firmness of character.

still

still life A phrase applied by artists to compositions in which there are only inanimate objects—flowers, fruit, furniture, etc.

still waters run deep Quiet, undemonstrative people are frequently those who have depths of emotion, etc., even though they are successfully concealed.

sting

sting in the tail Unpleasantness or disadvantage mentioned last.

take the sting out of Make less painful.

stir
cause a stir Create commotion.
stir the blood Inspire.

stitch
a stitch in time (saves nine) Timely action (avoids the need for more extensive action later).

stock
in stock Readily available, not needing to be specially obtained.
lay in a stock of Acquire supplies of.
on the stocks Being made, but not finished.
- *I have two novels on the stocks.*

stock rises Reputation increases.
stock still Absolutely motionless.
stock-in-trade [LIT] A tradesman's stock, or supply of goods for sale. [MET] Any possession, tangible or otherwise, which one employs in one's business or profession.
- *Her stock-in-trade consisted of plenty of confidence, a knowledge of French, and a charming smile.*

stock up on Gather together a supply of.
stockpile Store.
take stock Consider the total position.
take stock of Consider the value or possibilities of.
- *He took stock of his present position.*

stone
heart of stone Want of human feeling.
leave no stone unturned Use every possible effort to find out; investigate thoroughly.
people who live in glass houses should not throw stones Those who are vulnerable should not provoke attack.
stone blind or deaf Totally blind or deaf. Also, with the same effect, *stone cold* and *stone dead.*
stone's-throw A short distance.
- *The house was within a stone's-throw of the sea.*

stone-walling Persistent refusal to discuss, act, etc.
stony-broke Entirely without money.

stool
fall between two stools Fail as a result of not selecting one of necessary alternative courses of action.

stoop

stoop to conquer Humiliate oneself to achieve success in the end.

stop

come to a full stop Cease completely.

a dead stop A complete and sudden halt.

- *The car came to a dead stop in the middle of the road.*

stop-gap Temporary solution.

- *Stop-gap measures will not solve this crisis.*

stop at nothing Ignore all impediments.

stop off Make a halt.

stop over Stay for a night or for a short while.

stop short of Refrain from.

store

in store About to come.

- *I think you've a surprise in store.*

set store by or on Value; attach importance to.

storm

bow before the storm Yield to public indignation.

storm in a teacup Much excitement and trouble over a trivial matter.

take by storm Capture (hearts of people) by vigorous action.

story

cut a long story short Omit details of narrative.

the old, old or same old story The familiar pattern of events.

the story goes It is said.

stout

stout-hearted Brave.

straight

get something straight Understand something clearly.

keep a straight face See under **face**.

play a straight bat Behave or speak without equivocation.

put things or the record straight Express matters as they are, to remove muddle.

straight and narrow Virtuous way of life.

straight away; straight off Immediately. Without hesitation.

- *The doctor will see you straight away.*

straightforward 1. Without complications.
  2. Honest.

straight from the shoulder See under **shoulder**.

straight (out) Frankly.

straight tip A definite hint; also private and accurate information.

strain

strain at a gnat and swallow a camel Object to some trivial matter while condoning or permitting a far greater offence.

strain every nerve Use all efforts.

strain one's eyes 1. Make an extra effort to see.

- *If you strain your eyes, you can just see the church.*

2. Tire one's eyes.

- *Don't strain your eyes by reading such small print.*

strained relations Tension as result of disagreement etc.

stranger

be a stranger here Not live here.

be no stranger to Be accustomed to.

straw

clutch or grasp at a straw or straws Grasp at anything, however trivial, to escape disaster; gain hope from the slightest sign that may appear favourable.

the last straw Any final unendurable event; a culminating injury. Also *the straw that breaks the camel's back.*

make bricks without straw See under **brick**.

a man of straw See under **man**.

not care a straw or two straws Care nothing at all.

a straw or straws in the wind Hints which indicate what is likely to happen.

streak

(on) a winning streak (Having) one success after another.

stream

go or drift with the stream Follow the example of the majority.

street

streets ahead Much superior to.

right up one's street Very appropriate (for one's abilities, wishes, etc.).

strength

from strength to strength From one success to greater ones.

in strength In large numbers.

on the strength of Relying on.

stretch

at a stretch 1. With an effort; only by straining one's resources.
- *We can manage to entertain ten people to dinner at a stretch.*

2. Continuously.
- *Some lorry drivers are working ten hours at a stretch.*

at full stretch Using all one's resources.

by no stretch of the imagination In no way which it is possible for one to conceive.

strict

strictly speaking Using words with precise meaning.

stride

get into one's stride Become accustomed to and settle into one's job, etc.

make great or rapid strides Progress quickly.

take in one's stride Cope with easily.

strike

how does that strike you? What do you think of that?

it strikes me It seems to me.

on strike Refusing to work until some grievance is corrected.

strike at Aim a blow at.

strike at the root of Threaten destruction to.

strike back Return a blow.

strike fear into Frighten.

strike the happy medium Arrive at the best possible compromise.

strike home Strike a vital blow; strike directly at the heart or emotions.
- *It was only a short speech, but it certainly struck home.*

strike (it) lucky Have good luck.

strike while the iron is hot Take advantage of a suitable opportunity.

strike off Remove from an official list or record.
- *His name was struck off the register of doctors.*

strike on Luckily encounter.

strike out 1. Make violent movements with one's arms or legs.

2. Similar to *strike off*.

strike terror Create terror; terrify.

strike up Begin.

within striking distance (of) Near enough (to).

string

first or second string Principal *or* alternative person or thing one relies on.

have on a string Have (person) under one's influence.

no strings attached No conditions or restrictions.

string along Give (person) false expectations.

string together [Lit] Link, as by a string or cord. [MET] Arrange in sequence.
  - *I've strung together a few ideas for discussion.*

See **bow** and **pull.**

stroke

a stroke (of work) Any work. (Usually used in negative.)
  - *I haven't done a stroke all weekend.*

a stroke of genius Brilliant idea or act.

a stroke of luck Unexpected good fortune.

at a stroke By one action.

on the stroke (of) Punctually (at).

put one off one's stroke Cause one to falter in what one is doing.

stuck

get stuck in Start vigorously.

stuck up Vain; arrogant.

stuck with Forced to cope with or keep something unwanted.

study

in a brown study See under **brown.**

make a study of Pursue knowledge in.

stuff

knock the stuffing out of Overwhelm.

know one's stuff Be good at one's job, subject, etc.

that's the stuff That is what is needed!

stumble

stumble upon Discover by chance.

stumbling-block Obstacle.

stump

stumped for At a loss for.

stung

stung or wounded or cut to the quick See under **cut.**

subject

change the subject Talk of something else.

on the subject of Concerning.

a sore subject A subject about which one is particularly sensitive.

a subject for A matter for. A cause of.

success
nothing succeeds like success One success leads to another.

such
such-and-such a person See *so-and-so*.

such as it is If one can call it by that name.

such being the case Considering the present state of affairs.

suchlike Things, people, etc., of that kind.

• *I don't much care for night-clubs and suchlike.*

sudden
all of a sudden Without warning.

suit
suit the action to the word Do what one has promised, threatened, etc.

suit (one) down to the ground Be very convenient (to one).

suit yourself Do as you wish.

sum
sum total Complete total.

sum up Give a final résumé and analysis of what has occurred.

sun
a place in the sun Favourable situation.

catch the sun Be sunburnt.

under the sun In the whole world.

• *There's nothing new under the sun.*

Sunday
Sunday best Best clothes one has.

sure
make sure; make certain Render absolutely certain.

sure enough In accordance with something anticipated.

• *I said you'd come, and sure enough here you are.*

sure as fate Beyond a doubt, with absolute certainty.

surprise
taken by surprise Suddenly surprised; astonished.

to my surprise Contrary to what I expected.

suspense
in suspense In a condition of uncertainty.

swallow
one swallow does not make a summer One piece of good fortune (news, luck, etc.) does not mean that others will follow.
swallow an insult Submit to an insult without protest.
swallow up Engulf; cause to disappear.
- *An earthquake can swallow up an entire town.*
- *His wife's debts swallowed up all his savings.*

swan
swan-song Final performance of career.

swear
swear by Have great belief in. Recommend. Resort to frequently.
- *My wife swears by these indigestion tablets.*
swear like a trooper Use particularly bad language.

sweat
by the sweat of one's brow By hard (physical) work.
in a (cold) sweat [LIT] Perspiring. [MET] 1. In a state of anxiety. 2. In a hurry.
sweat blood Make an exceptional effort.
sweat it out Endure a difficult situation.
sweated labour People employed for long hours for low wages.

sweep
make a clean sweep (of) Get rid or dispose (of).
sweep off one's feet Captivate.
sweep the board Win everything that is to be won.

swell
swell the ranks of Add to an already large number of people or things.

swim
go swimmingly Proceed smoothly and well; become a complete success.
- *I am sure your party tomorrow will go swimmingly.*
in the swim Fully involved in what is going on.
- *We're new to the district, and not yet in the swim.*
swim with the tide Go with the majority.

swing

get into the swing Accustom oneself to the routine.

in full swing Making full progress.

- *The fête was in full swing when the storm came.*

go with a swing Proceed in a lively and enjoyable manner.

swing the lead Malinger.

swoop

at one fell swoop In one complete and sudden disaster.

sword

cross swords with Quarrel with. Engage in rivalry or controversy with.

- *He's not a man I'd like to cross swords with.*

sword of Damocles A disaster liable to occur at any moment; a threat to one's peace and happiness.

sworn

sworn enemies Irreconcilable ones.

syllable

in words of one syllable In the simplest and plainest words possible.

system

get something out of one's system Rid oneself of its influence on oneself.

T

t

cross the T's Be very accurate. Correct or finish something in
detail.

to a T Exactly.
- *This measurement is correct to a T.*

tab

keep tabs on Keep a check on.

pick up the tab Pay.

table

turn the tables on someone Convert relatively weak position to
strong one.

tack

Course of action. Thus *change tack, on the right, wrong, tack,*
etc.

tail

have one's tail between one's legs Be cowed and humiliated,
like a frightened dog.

tail off Become weaker.

tail wind Following wind.

turn tail Turn one's back and run away.

with one's tail up In good spirits.

take

taken aback Disconcerted; surprised.
- *The man was utterly taken aback when they recognised him.*

take after Resemble, physically or otherwise.
- *Mary takes after her father, and is very musical.*

take against Begin to dislike.

take back Withdraw.

- *I take back everything I said.*

taken by Attracted by.

take down 1. [LIT]

- *Take down that book* (or *take that book down*) *from the shelf.*

2. [MET] Record; write.

- *Take down this letter, please.*

take down a peg See under **peg**.

take for Assume to be. Treat like.

- *He seems to take me for an idiot.*

take for granted Assume as a fact.

take in good or *bad part* Accept good-naturedly or angrily.

- *I hope you'll take my advice in good part.*

take to heart Be seriously affected.

- *He has taken your words to heart, and will try to be more careful in future.*

take heed of or *to* Attend, be warned by.

- *Take heed of what I've told you.*

take hold of Seize; grasp.

- *The boy took hold of the ladder, and began to climb.*

take in 1. Mislead; deceive.

- *We were completely taken in by his story.*

2. Receive, as a means of livelihood.

- *Miss Brown takes in lodgers.*

3. Escort to a dining-room, etc. [Old f.]

- *Our host took in the principal guest.*

take ill Become unwell.

take it Endure difficulty.

take it from there Deal with matters as they arise.

- *Let's make him an offer and take it from there.*

take it or leave it Do what you wish.

take it badly Respond (to news) with distress.

take it from me Accept what I say as true. Also *take my word for it*.

take leave of one's senses Cease to behave wisely. Do something rash.

take a liking, dislike, fancy, etc., to The same as 'like', etc., except that the effect is rather more emphatic and spontaneous.

take off 1. Mimic.

- *He took off the headmaster perfectly.*

2. Rise from the ground.

● *The aeroplane will take off at three o'clock.*

take-off Piece of mimicry or caricature.

take a lot of doing Be difficult to do.

take oneself off Depart, generally abruptly or indignantly.

● *They took themselves off without saying good-bye.*

take offence or *umbrage* Be annoyed; angry.

● *He always takes offence at any kind of criticism.*

take on Accept responsibility for.

● *I've taken on the organisation of our Hospital Fête.*

See *take upon oneself.*

take out 1. Obtain the issue of (in a legal sense).

● *I am taking out a patent for the invention.*

2. Extract.

● *The dentist took out five of Mary's teeth.*

3. Accompany (for a walk, etc.); in charge of.

● *Father isn't at home; he's taken out the dog.*

take it out of one 1. Exhaust; weaken.

● *So much hill-climbing takes it out of me.*

2. Have revenge. (More usually, *take it out on.*)

● *Just because you're in a bad temper, don't take it out on the dog.*

take over Take the place of someone else.

● *You stay with the children until ten o'clock, and then I'll take over.*

take-over bid Attempt by a company to purchase another.

take pains or *trouble* Make a considerable effort.

● *I took pains to explain the facts clearly.*

take part in Share; co-operate; act with others.

● *Her sister takes part in all local events.*

take sides Support one adversary against another.

● *A judge should remain impartial, and not take sides.*

take silk Become a Queen's Counsel, an honour which entitles a barrister to wear a silk gown in Court, instead of the cloth one previously worn.

take one's stand Decide upon a mental attitude; base one's argument.

take stock of Examine thoroughly and in detail.

● *He decided to take stock of the present condition of affairs.*

take one's time Take as much time as one needs (to do something).

take to Form a liking for.

● *The baby took to the kitten at once.*

Similar to *take a liking to.*

take to one's bed Go to bed, usually for some time, as the result of illness, etc.

- *My husband feels so ill that he has taken to his bed.*

take to task Blame; reprove.

- *His wife took him to task for his forgetfulness.*

take too much Become intoxicated.

- *Though Bill enjoys a drink he never takes too much.*

take in tow [LIT] Attach a cable, etc., to a vehicle, ship, etc., to pull it along. [MET] Take charge of; be responsible for

take up 1. Absorb; occupy.

- *Most of their time is taken up in decorating the house.*
2. Life.

- *We will take up the carpet and send it to be cleaned tomorrow.*

take up the threads Resume after an interruption.

take up with Become friendly or intimate with.

take (matter) up with (person) Ask (person) about (matter).

take upon oneself Assume or accept responsibility without being asked.

take the will for the deed Accept the desire to be kind and helpful, even if nothing practical results.

taken with Captivated by.

tale

live to tell the tale Come through ordeal.

old wives' tale Superstitious tradition, often foolish but believed to be true by some people at the moment and many in the past. Also, an unconvincing story.

tale-bearer One who spreads rumours, and who tells malicious stories of other people.

tell its own tale Need no explanation.

tell tales out of school Reveal another person's private affairs; discuss them with inappropriate people, or at inappropriate times.

thereby hangs a tale There is an interesting story or explanation concerned with that event.

talk

do the talking Act as spokesman.

idle talk Foolish, useless talk; gossip.

know what one is talking about 1. Understand what one says.
2. One is an expert.

money talks Having money gives one power.

small talk Talk concerning trivialities; formal and polite conversation.

table-talk Conversation of the friendly and entertaining type which takes place among intimates at a meal. Applied especially to the talk of famous people.

talk about . . . On the subject of . . .

talk back Reply (defiantly).

talk down to Speak to (one) as if one were inferior in some way.

talk the back or hind legs off a donkey or horse Be very talkative.

talk (person) into or out of Persuade (person) to do or not to do.

talk out Discuss until conclusion is reached.

talk over Discuss.

talk round Convince; bring to one's own way of thinking.
- *He wouldn't come at first, but we talked him round.*

talking of As we are discussing.
- *Talking of money, have you paid the gas bill yet?*

talk through one's hat or the back of one's neck Talk nonsense.

tangent

go off at a tangent Diverge from main topic of conversation.

tape

have taped Understand. Have under control.

tar

tarred with the same brush Having the same defects as someone else.
- *She is rather conceited, and her son is tarred with the same brush.*

task

take person to task Upbraid him.

hard task-master Person (or thing) imposing heavy burden.

taste

leave a nasty taste in the mouth Cause unpleasant memories or feelings (at end of matter).

there's no accounting for taste Everyone has different tastes, some of them difficult to understand.

a taste for A natural appreciation of, or liking for.
- *I have no taste whatever for Japanese art.*

teach

that will teach him (to do) That will punish him (for doing).

tear

tear to tatters, ribbons, etc. [LIT] Tear roughly into small pieces.
[MET] Destroy (e.g. someone's argument).

tear oneself away Make oneself leave (usually used in negative).
 ● *It was such a good exhibition that I could hardly tear myself away.*

tear one's hair Be angry, very anxious, perplexed.
 ● *I was tearing my hair with impatience at the delay.*

tear a strip off Reprimand severely.

tears

bathed, drowned or dissolved in tears Weeping excessively.

crocodile tears Hypocritical grief; tears shed by one who is not,
 in fact, grieving at all.

reduce to tears Compel to weep by pity or distress (or, occasionally, by excessive laughter).

tease

tease out Separate (parts of problem, discussion, etc.) into
 components.

teens

in one's teens; teenage At any age from thirteen to nineteen
 inclusive.

teeth

armed to the teeth Having many weapons

draw the teeth of Weaken.

get one's teeth into Start work seriously on.

grit one's teeth Suppress one's feelings. Show determination.

in the teeth of In spite of; without regard to.
 ● *They married in the teeth of her parents' opposition.*

lie in one's teeth Tell serious and blatant untruths. (Emphatic
 form of 'lie'.)

make someone's teeth chatter Cause one to tremble or shiver so
 much that the upper and lower teeth click together.

put teeth into Give effectiveness (to law, rules, etc.)

set one's teeth on edge [LIT] Cause a grating or tingling sensation around one's teeth, through their contact with acid,
 etc. [MET] Cause a general discomfort at some particularly
 harsh sound, or by embarrassing action or speech.
 ● *For heaven's sake oil that wheel—it sets my teeth on edge.*

show one's teeth Threaten. Show one's power.

skin of one's teeth See under **skin.**

teething troubles Initial difficulties.

tell

as far as one can tell As far as one knows.

I told you so I did warn or tell you in advance.

tell off 1. Select a number of persons by name for a special purpose.

- *The captain told off six men to act as escort to the prisoners.*

2. Reprove. Express one's views frankly and unfavourably.

- *I told him off for keeping me waiting.*

tell on Have an adverse effect on.

tell that to the Marines (or, more correctly, *the Horse Marines.* such a corps being non-existent, as Marines are a sea-going force) Tell that story to someone who doesn't exist, since no one who does exist is likely to believe it.

there's no telling It is impossible to know or guess.

you never can tell Appearances are misleading.

you're telling me! That is true!

temper

lose one's temper; be out of temper Exchange one's good temper for a bad temper; be angry, irritable, annoyed, in an unpleasant mood. Opposite: *keep one's temper.*

tempers the wind to the shorn lamb Arrange matters to suit the weakest element.

ten

ten to one It is ten chances to one that it will happen; very probably. (Similarly other numbers.)

- *Tell him you've broken the vase; ten to one he won't be angry.*

tenterhooks

on tenterhooks In a state of acute anxiety or suspense.

terms

come to terms Reach a formal and businesslike arrangement.

- *If you're willing to sell your house, we can soon come to terms.*

in terms of In the language of.

on good or *bad terms with* Having friendly *or* unfriendly relationship with (normally applied to relationships between people). Similarly *on speaking terms* = in a relationship which is such that both parties speak to one another.

- *We have always been on bad terms (we are not on speaking terms) with our neighbours.*

on one's terms With the conditions (e.g. price, rules) laid down by one.

test

put to the test Make (person or thing) undergo examination or trial.

stand the test of time Continue to be effective despite normal effects of passage of time.

thank

have only oneself to thank for Be the cause of (something disagreeable).

thank goodness, heaven, etc. A general ejaculation of gratitude.

thank one's (lucky) stars Be grateful.

> ● *You may thank your lucky stars that you weren't in the house when the party was on.*

thanks to Owing to; because of

no thanks to No credit or gratitude is due to.

that

and all that And other matters of that kind.

at that Thereupon. Then.

> ● *At that, the meeting broke up.*

in that Since. In so far as.

just like that Quickly and easily, without thinking.

> ● *I could understand his point of view, in that I'd been in a similar position myself.*

that will do No more, or nothing else is required. That is sufficient.

that's more like it You (or thing, progress etc.) are becoming more satisfactory.

that's that A concluding emphasis to a statement.

> ● *I refuse, and that's that.*

that is to say To express differently, or more fully.

> ● *He's a cutler—that is to say, he sells knives and sharp tools.*

then

then and there Immediately. On the spot. Also *there and then*.

there

there you are This is what you need.

thick

a bit thick Rather hard to tolerate.

in the thick of In the densest, most congested part [LIT and MET].

> ● *We were in the thick of the crowd.*

- *Don't disturb me—I'm in the thick of a job.*

thick and fast In large numbers, very quickly.

thick as thieves Very friendly.

thick end of the stick Worst aspect of the bargain.

thick-skinned Not sensitive to reproach, criticism, etc.

- *He's too thick-skinned to see the impression he makes.*

through thick and thin Through every trouble or difficulty, good fortune or bad fortune.

thin

into thin air So as to be invisible.

thin end of the wedge Small but dangerous precedent.

thin on the ground In short supply.

thin on top Balding.

thing

all things being equal Unless other matters in the situation happen to change.

and another thing Moreover.

just one of those things Something unavoidable.

make a thing of Create fuss over.

just the thing; the very thing Exactly what is needed or appropriate.

- *This carpet is just the thing for the bedroom.*

know a thing or two Be experienced, shrewd.

not know the first thing about Know nothing of.

of all things From among all the things which might have happened.

- *And now—of all things!—we shall have to move house.*

on to a good thing Engaged in a profitable or beneficial activity.

- *As the only vet in the town, he's on to a good thing.*

taking one thing with another Weighing the advantages against the disadvantages; considering all the circumstances.

the thing (to do) *or* **the done thing** The correct procedure. The custom. The fashion.

the thing is The important point is.

think

have another think coming Be mistaken in what person thinks.

think a lot of Esteem highly.

think back to Recall to mind.

think better See **better**.

think big Have ambitious thoughts, plans, etc.

think fit or *proper* Decide; consider suitable or appropriate.
think for oneself Be capable of independent thought.
think highly or *much of* Admire.
think little or *nothing of* Treat casually; regard as normal. Have
   low opinion of. Also *not think much of.*
think no end of Have a very high opinion of.
think no more of Forget.
think out Meditate upon; consider.
   • *We must think out some other way of repairing it.*
think over Consider at some length.
   • *I'll need a few days to think it over.*
think through Consider until problem is solved or conclusion
   reached.
think twice Consider very carefully.
think up Devise.
way of thinking Point of view; personal aspect.

this
this, that and the other Various unspecified things.

thorn
a thorn in the flesh or *in one's side* An infliction; an annoyance
   which one has to endure.

thought
food for thought Something worth serious thought.
take no thought for Do not worry or concern yourself about.
take thought Consider thoroughly.
train of thought Direction in which one's thinking is moving.

thrash
thrash out Discuss in order to reach a conclusion.

thread
hang by a thread Be in precarious position or state.
lose the thread (of an argument, etc.) Stop understanding.
pick up the thread(s) Resume after an interruption.
   • *It's difficult to pick up the thread of this book after a week.*
thread or *edge one's way* Move to one's destination through
   narrow or crowded streets.
   • *We threaded our way through the crowds at the station.*

threshold
on the threshold [LIT] The 'sill' (horizontal piece of wood or

stone) that forms the bottom of the door-frame at the entrance of a building. [MET] The beginning of anything.

- *The scientist felt he was on the threshold of solving a tremendous mystery.*

throat

at each other's throats Disagreeing or quarrelling.

cut one's own throat Damage oneself.

cut one another's throats Damage one another (in competition, etc.).

ram down one's throat Bring forcibly to one's attention.

through

By means of.

- *He obtained the information through his own efforts.*

through and through Thoroughly.

through with Finished with.

throw

throw away Lose by neglect or recklessness.

- *He threw away his chances of winning.*

throw dust in the eyes of Obscure the facts; mislead.

- *The Prime Minister was accused of throwing dust in the public's eye.*

throw good money after bad Risk further loss in attempt to make good a previous one.

throw in Give in addition.

- *The herrings were ten for £1 and the fishmonger threw in an extra one.*

throw in the towel Surrender.

throw off Discard. Get rid of.

- *He appears to have thrown off his cold.*

throw oneself into Engage energetically in.

throw one's hand in Abandon (project, etc.).

throw one's lot in with Join.

throw open Make accessible.

- *They intend to throw open the house to the public.*

throw out Reject. Distract.

throw out a suggestion Make a suggestion, usually tentatively.

throw over Abandon; discard; have no further association with.

throw to the lions Put (person) in dangerous position.

throw up the sponge Surrender; abandon abruptly; admit complete defeat.

throw one's weight about Be domineering.

thumb
thumb-nail sketch 1. Small, quickly done picture.
2. Brief description in words.
thumbs up (or down) Permission (or refusal).
under one's thumb Under one's control or influence.

thunder
like a thunderclap or thunderbolt Causing great astonishment.
● *The news of his resignation was like a thunderclap.*
thunders of applause Applause so noisy and continuous that it
suggests thunder.
thunderstruck Overcome with astonishment.

tick
tick off Check (by placing a small mark, e.g. against items in a
list).

tide
tide over Continue until changed and usually improved conditions take place.
● *I need £10 to tide me over till I can get to the bank.*

tie
black tie A black tie worn with a dinner-jacket. (The idiom is
used as indicating the whole outfit.)
tie in with Relate to.
white tie A white tie worn with white waistcoat, coat with
'tails', and black trousers—the more formal evening dress.

tiger
paper tiger Fierce-looking but ineffectual person.

tight
on a tight-rope Precariously balanced.
run a tight ship Administer an organisation efficiently.
tight-fisted Mean.
tight-lipped Uncommunicative.
tight spot or corner Difficulty.

time
against time With all speed.
all in good time Let us wait until the time is right.
all the time Continuously.
at one time Formerly.

at times At intervals; occasionally.

- *He seems at times to know more than he says.*

Similar to *now and then; now and again.*

beat time The action of a conductor indicating the 'beats' in the music with his baton.

before one's time Before one was born. Compare *born before one's time.*

behind the times Not modern.

bide one's time Wait patiently.

- *If we bide our time it will all come right.*

for the time being Temporarily; during the time that is immediately coming.

- *We are going to Rome as soon as we can, but are staying in London for the time being.*

from time to time Occasionally.

- *I only go to the cinema from time to time.*

a good time 1. A highly pleasurable time.

- *Jane and Joan are at Brighton, having a thoroughly good time.*

2. A considerable period.

- *I am going into the town, and shall not be back for a good time.*

have no time for Be unable or willing to spend time dealing with.

high time Fully time.

- *It is high time that we went home.*

in (the) course of time Eventually; after some time had passed.

in time 1. Before it is too late.

- *The doctor came in time to save her life.*

2. After some considerable time had passed.

- *In time he forgot all about her.*

in good time Early; with time to spare.

- *Be at the station in good time.*

in one's time At some time in or during one's past life.

- *I've seen many changes in my time.*

in one's own good time At a time convenient to oneself.

in one's own time Outside working hours.

in no or less than no time Very soon; almost immediately.

- *We shall be ready in less than no time.*

Similar to *in half a tick; two-twos; half a jiffy.*

keep good (bad time) (of clock, etc.) Be accurate (inaccurate).

kill time Use up spare time by finding something to do.

lose no time Act at once.

make good time Travel more quickly than expected.

no time at all Very short time.

not before time Late.

once upon a time Some time ago; in the past. (The traditional beginning to children's stories.)

- *Once upon a time there lived a king with three sons.*

part-time Time which does not occupy all the usual working day.

- *Marjory has a part-time job taking care of young children.*

pass the time of day (with) Exchange greeting (with a person).

pressed for time Short of time; very busy.

- *I can't stay more than ten minutes, as I am pressed for time.*

stated time A time already fixed.

take time by the forelock Act promptly and without delay.

there's no time like the present If something needs to be done, it is best to do it at once.

time after time Repeatedly.

- *The fence has had to be rebuilt time after time.*

time and again Frequently.

- *The children have been warned about the danger time and again.*

time flies Time passes quickly.

time immemorial see *time out of mind.*

time's up The stated time has come to an end, is finished.

- *Time's up—you must say good-bye.*

time of day The time, the hour.

- *What's the time of day?*

time of life Age.

- *At my time of life I can't be expected to dance.*

time of one's life A most enjoyable period.

- *I had the time of my life at the party.*

time off Time spent away from work.

time on one's hands Time to waste, to spare; superfluous time.

- *As I had a good deal of time on my hands, I decided to explore the City.*

time out of mind; from time immemorial Longer than can be remembered.

time was There was a time.

time will tell All will become known with the passage of time.

times out of or *without number* Many times; times beyond counting.

work against time Use special efforts to finish a piece of work within a stated time.

- *We are working against time to complete the house by Christmas.*

tip

on the tip of one's tongue (Word) known to speaker but forgotten. On the verge of being spoken.

tip off Warn. Also **tip-off** Warning.

tip the balance or scales Exert influence in favour of one of two sides.

tip the wink Give (person) warning or information, usually privately.

tiptoe

on tiptoe [LIT] Standing on the tips of one's toes. [MET] A state of excitement and tension.

- *The children were on tiptoe when the day of the party arrived.*

tip-top Excellent; the best of its kind.

- *We had a tip-top breakfast at the hotel.*

tit for tat An equivalent; something, frequently unpleasant, given in return for something else.

tittle-tattle Idle, chattering gossip.

to

to and fro (= to and from.) From one spot to another and back again.

- *The sentry paced to and fro.*

toing and froing Aimless movement.

toe

be on one's toes Be alert or ready.

toe the line Conform, usually under pressure, to rules, etc.

- *The Party expects MPs to toe the line.*

tread on one's toes Offend one's feelings, prejudices, etc.

toffee

cannot do something for toffee Cannot do it at all.

toffee-nosed Snobbish.

token

by the same token Further; moreover. Similarly.

Tom

(any) Tom, Dick, or (and) Harry Persons taken at random. Any unspecified people.

- *It's not the sort of club that admits any Tom, Dick or Harry.*

ton

like a ton of bricks Very heavily or severely.

weigh half a ton Be very heavy.

tone
tone down Reduce severity (of remarks, statement, etc.).

tongue
hold one's tongue Become silent; cease to speak.
keep a civil tongue in one's head Avoid impoliteness.
lose one's tongue Be too bashful to speak. Opposite: *find one's tongue.*
tongue-tied Silent through embarrassment or fear.
wag one's tongue Talk indiscreetly, or too much.
  • *Too many tongues have been wagging for the matter to remain confidential any longer.*
with one's tongue hanging out Very thirsty.
with one's tongue in one's cheek Without meaning what one says; insincerely.

too
none too Less than.

tooth
a sweet tooth A liking for sweet things—jam etc.
tooth and nail With extreme fierceness.

top
at the top of one's voice Very loudly.
from top to toe [LIT] From one's head to one's feet. [MET] From beginning to end.
  • *She was impeccably dressed from top to toe.*
on top of 1. In addition to.
  2. In control of.
on top of the world In excellent spirits.
over the top (Behaving) in an exaggerated or too extreme a manner.
top gear The highest gear of a car engine.
top speed; full speed As fast as possible.
top of the tree or ladder The highest point in one's business or profession.
  • *He has reached the top of the tree as a surgeon.*
top up Fill up something partly empty. Finish; conclude.
  • *Please top up the oil and water.*
  See under *sleep.*

topsy-turvy
In a state of confusion or disarray. Inverted, the normal position reversed.
- *After the party, the whole room was topsy-turvy.*

Similar to *upside down.*

torn
be torn between Have difficulty in choosing between.
that's torn it! That has ruined everything!

toss
toss up Decide by spinning a coin. See **heads or tails.**
Hence *win the toss, lose the toss.* See **argue.**
a toss-up A complete uncertainty; as likely as unlikely.
- *It's a toss-up whether I will be able to come.*

touch
finishing touches Final details.
in touch with In communication, or contact, with.
- *I haven't been in touch with him for some years.*

lose touch Cease to have any communication with.
Opposite: *keep in touch (with).*
- *I used to see him a lot, but I've lost touch with him lately.*

out of touch 1. Not in communication.
2. Lacking up-to-date knowledge. Not understanding.

personal touch Detail(s) showing individual influence or concern.

touch and go Extremely doubtful or precarious.
- *It was touch and go whether we should arrive in time.*

touch down Land. (Of aircraft).

touch (person) for (something) Persuade (person) to give (something).

touch off Trigger.

touch on Same as *touch upon.*

touch up Restore or improve by a number of small details (especially with a brush or pen).

touch upon Refer to briefly.

touch wood Expression meaning 'I hope my luck continues'.

tower
tower of strength A great support and help.
in a towering passion or *rage* Dominated by tremendous danger.

town

go to town (on) Be extravagant (in doing).

on the town Enjoying oneself in places of entertainment.

talk of the town Subject of general conversation or gossip.

track

be on the track of Be pursuing or searching for.

cover one's tracks Conceal what one has done.

keep track of Follow course or progress of. Opposite: *lose track of.*

make tracks Depart.

right or wrong track Right or wrong course, argument, investigation, etc.

track down Find.

track record History of performance.

trade

trade in Use as part payment.

trade on Take advantage of.

trick of the trade Device known only to those in particular profession, job, etc.

trail

blaze a trail Set a new trend. Do something new.

trail one's coat Attempt to start a quarrel or argument.

trail off Become weaker and feebler.

● *He began by shouting, but his voice trailed off into a mere whisper.*

tread

tread on the heels of Follow immediately after.

tread under foot Treat with contempt. Usually *trodden under foot.*

treasure

treasure (up) Retain, as something precious and valuable.

● *We should treasure every moment of such a day as this.*

tree

grow on trees Be plentiful.

● *Money doesn't grow on trees.*

trial

give a trial Test.

trial and error Repeated attempts until success is achieved.

trial of strength Contest to discover who is stronger or strongest.

trial run Test.

tribute
pay tribute [LIT] To pay a fixed amount to a ruler or other governor. [MET] Admit one's indebtedness to some helper or benefactor.
tribute to Sign of merit in.

trice
in a trice [LIT] A period of time equal to one-third of a second. [MET] Very quickly.

trick
do the trick Do what is necessary (to put something right, etc.).
up to one's tricks Aware of one's characteristic behaviour, devices, etc.
up to one's (old) tricks (again) Behaving in characteristic manner (deviously, mischievously, etc.).

trivet
right as a trivet In sound health or condition.

trivial
the trivial round The routine of everyday life; the succession of small regular duties.

trot
on the trot One after the other.
trot out Quote, often glibly or predictably; exhibit; produce in support.
  ● *He trotted out the old proverb that there's no time like the present.*

trouble
go to the trouble of doing Concern oneself to do. Also *take the trouble to.*
look or ask for trouble 1. Wish to cause dissension, conflict, etc. 2. Take risks.
no trouble No inconvenience.
trouble brewing or trouble in store Trouble likely to occur at some later time.

trousers
be caught with one's trousers down Be found at a disadvantage.
wear the trousers Be dominant. (Usually of women).

truck
have no truck with Refuse to deal with.

true

(run) true to form (Happen) predictably, in accordance with expectation or past experience.

trump

trump-card Piece of valuable information, knowledge, etc., or an unexpected idea, produced surprisingly to outwit or defeat an opponent.

- *The Prime Minister played his trump-card by saying that negotiations had in fact already begun.*

trump up Falsely state, tell maliciously and untruthfully.

turn up trumps Act helpfully.

trumpet

blow one's own trumpet Boast of one's own work or actions.

trumpet call [LIT] Tune played by a trumpet or trumpets alone, usually in manner of a summons. [MET] An urgent summons to action.

- *His speech was a trumpet call for public protest.*

trust

take on trust Accept without proof.

trust with Consign to without serious misgivings.

truth

arrive at the truth Discover what really occurred.

the naked (plain, simple, sober, or stark) truth The truth, and nothing but the truth.

to tell the truth Actually.

truth is stranger than fiction Things which actually happen are sometimes more unexpected than the things which are invented in literature.

truth will out The truth will always be revealed eventually.

try

try conclusions Start a struggle that must have a definite ending.

try it on Do something in order to see whether or not it is allowed.

try one's hand at Attempt.

- *I'm going to try my hand at Chinese cookery.*

try on Put on a garment to see if it fits.

try out Put to the test.

tub
tub-thumper Ranting orator.

tuck
tuck in(to) Eat heartily.
tuck up Wrap closely in bedclothes, etc.

tug
tug-of-war Conflict in which each side seeks to retain own position rather than occupy other's.

tumble
tumble to Understand.

tune
in tune In agreement. In harmony. Opposite: *out of tune.*
to the tune of At a cost of.
  ● *The town is building a new hall to the tune of thirty million pounds.*

tunnel
tunnel vision Inability to understand more than one view.

turn
as it turned out As it resulted; happened; as the sequel.
  ● *Everyone thought farmers would be ruined, but as it turned out they were more prosperous than before.*
at every turn Continually.
by turns In rotation. Alternatively.
do a good or bad turn Help (or the reverse).
done to a turn Cooked perfectly.
in turn In succession.
not know which way to turn Not know what course of action to follow or where to find help.
not turn a hair Remain calm, in control, unperturbed.
on the turn Changing.
out of turn Before or after the proper time.
take a turn for the better Pass from one state to a better one.
take turns; take it in turns Act in rotation or regular order.
  ● *We took turns in mowing the lawn.*
to a turn Exactly.
turn-about Change (of opinion, policy, etc.).
turn to (good) account Use; make use of successfully.
turn adrift Cast out to wander.
turn against Change from like to dislike; regard with aversion.

turn-around Change from decline to improvement.

turn around Face in opposite direction.

turn-about Change (of opinion, policy, etc.).

turn aside Alter the direction in which one is going. Temporarily leave one occupation for another.

turn one's back on Deliberately ignore.

turn the corner Pass a crisis successfully.

- *The patient has turned the corner, and will recover.*

turn down 1. [LIT] Fold over and flatten down.

- *He turned down the collar of his coat.*

2. [MET] Refuse or decline definitely.

- *He turned down every offer of help.*

turn of events Change in the course of events, or happenings.

- *A year later, owing to a strange turn of events, I found myself in Paris again.*

turn of phrase Manner of expressing things.

turn one's hand to Undertake a variety of work, or work that is not one's normal occupation.

- *I'm a carpenter by trade, but I can turn my hand to bricklaying or painting.*

See under **head.**

turn an honest penny See under **penny.**

turn in 1. Deliver.

2. Go to bed.

turn inside out [LIT] Turn so that the inner is outside, and vice versa. [MET] Examine or explore with extreme thoroughness.

- *I've turned my desk inside out, but cannot find the missing paper.*

turn off or on 1. Stop (or start) something by turning (a tap, knob, switch, etc.).

2. Turn (car, oneself) in different direction.

turn on 1. Become aggressive towards.

2. Excite.

turn out 1. Manufacture.

- *We can turn out three thousand cups a week.*

2. Compel to leave; evict.

- *The family were turned out of their cottage because they could not pay their rent.*

3. Empty (usually to tidy).

- *She turned out her desk.*

4. Transpire. Be the final outcome.

- *It turned out that he was George's father.*

5. Similar to *turn off* (1).

turn-out 1. Display.
- *The Lord Mayor's show was a magnificent turn-out.*

2. Number of people coming (to attend, vote, etc.).

turn over 1. Cause to fall over.

2. Hand over.

turn-over The money taken in a business, shop, etc.

turn out well Succeed in life.
- *He's a sensible and clever boy, and ought to turn out well.*

turn of speed Capacity for speed.
- *This car has a fine turn of speed.*

turn the tables Reverse the position.

turn the tide Reverse the course of events.

turn of the tide [LIT] The point at which the sea ceases to flow out and begins to flow back, or vice versa. [MET] The point at which success is followed by failure, or vice versa.

turn to Begin work.

turn and turn about First one, then the other, for equal periods.

turn turtle Turn upside down in the sea.

turn up 1. Arrive; appear.
- *Our guests did not turn up until nearly midnight.*

2. Find.

turn up one's nose Sneer.
- *Now he has become well known he turns up his nose at plain food.*

turn up for the books Something unexpected (and usually welcome).

turn upon Blame or attack.

tweedle

Tweedledum and Tweedledee People whose opinions (or appearance) are alike.

twiddle

twiddle one's thumbs Waste one's time. Be forced to be kept idle. Similar to ***kick one's heels.***

twinkle

in the twinkling of an eye Very quickly.

twist

round the twist Mad.

twist one's arm [LIT] Hurt one's arm by twisting it. [MET] Bring pressure to bear to persuade someone.
- *I think he'll come if you twist his arm.*

See **finger**.

twister
One who 'twists', or systematically cheats.

two
for two pins I would I am strongly tempted to.
in two-twos or *two ticks* In a moment; almost instantly.
two-faced Hypocritical.
two penny-halfpenny Cheap. Insignificant.
two-time Deceive.

U

u-turn
Reversal of one's direction.

ugly
ugly duckling Something or someone originally despised but ultimately successful, admirable, etc.

under
come under Be classified with.
- *Cups and saucers come under crockery.*

fall under [MET] Similar to *come under.*
underdog Person in an inferior position.
- *The English are reputed to have a special sympathy for the underdog.*

under one's wing Under one's protection, guidance.
under way See under **way.**

understanding
come to an understanding Agree and co-operate, after discussions and explanations.
on or with the understanding According to an agreement, instruction, etc.
- *You may go to the disco, on the distinct (clear) (precise) understanding that you are back before midnight.*

up
all up with Hopeless for.
be up (with person) Be wrong.
- *What's up with him? Something must be up.*

be or come up against Encounter (usually obstacle).

be up to 1. Be occupied with.
- *What's the baby up to now?*

2. Capable of.
- *I don't feel up to driving all that way.*

3. Up to the standard of.
- *The work isn't up to what she expects.*

on the up and up Improving.

something is up Something is wrong. Something unusual is happening.

up against Close to.

up and about Well enough to leave one's bed after an illness.

up and coming Promising well.

up and doing Active.

up and down 1. [LIT].

2. To and fro.

ups and downs Good times and bad times.

up in arms Indignant; resentful.

up to The responsibility of.
- *It's up to you to decide.*

up to date See under **date.**

up and doing Active; busy.
- *We must be up and doing if we are going to catch the train.*

up-end Place so that the small or narrow end is uppermost.
- *We shall have to up-end it to get it out of the room.*

up to the eyes Immersed; completely occupied with.
- *I am up to the eyes in work.*

up to the hilt To the limit, the greatest possible extent.
- *The property is mortgaged up to the hilt.*

up to now Until the present time.

come up to the scratch See under **scratch.**

up to a thing or two Alert; shrewd.

up to something Privately planning; plotting some scheme.
- *I guess by the look on her face that she is up to something.*

upstage [LIT] The front of the stage, the position of most prominence. [MET] Put (person) at a disadvantage.

up to it Capable of doing anything.
- *The hill is steep: are you up to it?*

up-to-the-minute Most recent or fashionable.

(not) up to much (Not) good.

- *I didn't think the party was up to much.*

up to you The responsibility is yours.

up a gum-tree In a difficulty.

well up in Knowledgeable about.

what's up? What is happening?

upon

upon which When this occurred.

- *The boy admitted that he stole, upon which his father thrashed him.*

uppers

on one's uppers Very poor; completely destitute.

upper crust Aristocracy.

upper hand Mastery. Usually *have the upper hand.*

upside

turn upside-down Throw into confusion.

uptake

slow (or quick) on the uptake Slow (or quick) to understand.

upward

upward of More than.

use

make (good) use of or *put to (good) use* Utilise, employ.

no use Useless.

- *It's no use grumbling. I'm no use at singing.*

used to Accustomed to.

use up Finish. Consume the remainder of.

useful

make oneself useful Give assistance.

V

v

v-sign Gesture of hand with first and second finger extended, the others clenched, as sign of contempt (when back of hands faces outward) or victory (when palm faces outward).

vain

in vain Ineffectively; without any result.
take in vain Treat lightly.

valour

the better part of valour Discretion. Carefulness. Wise action.
 • *The general decided on the better part of valour, and surrendered.*

value

set a value on Estimate the value of.

van

in the van In the front.

variance

at variance In a state of quarrelling or disagreement.

veer

veer round Change one's opinions, language, behaviour, mood, etc.
 • *At first Simon agreed with me; then he veered round and agreed with Brian.*

veil

draw a veil over Remain silent about; conceal.
take the veil Become a fully initiated nun.

velvet
velvet glove Gentleness. See under **fist**.

vengeance
with a vengeance To an excessive degree.
- *There will be trouble with a vengeance when the boss hears what happened.*

vent
give vent to Give expression to; allow (one's emotions) to escape. See **spleen**.

ventilate
ventilate a grievance Same as *air a grievance.*

venture
nothing venture (nothing win or gain) One must be bold (if one wishes to win something).
venture on Take the risk of making.

verdict
bring in or return a verdict The legal phrase for a jury recording a decision.

verge
verge on Come close to.

very
the very thing See *just the thing,* under **thing**.
very well See under **well**.

vested
vested interest [LIT] Permanent rights. [MET] Personal involvement; keen commitment.

vet
Abbrev. for 'veterinary surgeon', one who examines and cures sick animals. Now frequently used as a verb in the sense of examining and, where necessary, correcting any form of work.
- *I shall be glad if you'll vet what I've written.*

vex
vexed question Difficult, often-debated problem.

view
bird's-eye view A comprehensive view from above, such as a bird would obtain.

- *You get a bird's-eye view of Paris from the Eiffel Tower.*

bring into view Reveal to one's sight.

extreme views Opinions which do not find favour with the majority.

in full view (of) Plainly visible (to).

to have in view To be contemplating, planning.

in view of After consideration of. Taking into consideration.

- *In view of what you tell me, I shall not go.*

in my view In my opinion.

one-sided view A prejudiced and limited outlook.

on view Available for inspection.

take a serious (etc.) view of Adopt a serious (etc.) attitude to. See also *dim*.

taking a long view Planning over a long period.

with a view to With the purpose of. In the hope of.

villain

villain of the piece Person responsible for mistake, wrong-doing, etc.

violet

shrinking violet Shy person.

viper

viper in one's bosom Person who betrays one who has befriended him or her.

virtue

by or *in virtue of* As a result or consequence of.

- *By virtue of his position, the Lord Mayor is the chief magistrate of the city.*

make a virtue of necessity Gain an advantage, or pretend to be acting virtuously (e.g. out of a sense of duty or goodwill, etc.), when one is in fact under compulsion.

have the virtue of Have the good quality of.

- *This sofa has the virtue of being convertible into a bed.*

visit

visit the sins on Punish a person for the sins someone else has committed.

voice

give voice to Express; state publicly.

in good voice Having voice in good condition (for singing, etc.)

a voice in the matter A share in the control; a right to express one's views.

with one voice Unanimously.

vote

vote down Reject by voting.

vote in Elect by voting.

vote of confidence Expression of trust.

vote of thanks Expression of gratitude.

vote on Judge by voting.

W

wade
wade in(to) Make vigorous attack (on).

wag
tongues are wagging There is gossip.

wagon
hitch one's wagon to a star 1. Entrust oneself to luck or belief in good fortune.
   2. Support person in hope of sharing their success.
on the wagon Abstaining from alcoholic drink.

wait
wait and see Await outcome of events.
wait (up)on 1. Pay a formal visit. (Now almost obsolete.)
   2. Attend to the wants (of).
   • *The dinner was good, but there weren't enough people waiting on the guests.*
wait up Not go to bed (expecting someone's arrival).
you wait Abbreviation for 'You wait and find out what will happen'.

waiting
play a waiting game Delay so as to gain later advantage.

wake
in the wake of In the footsteps or path of. Immediately after.
   • *Refugees follow in the wake of war.*
Also *in one's wake* Close behind one.

walk

walk away with Win with ease.

walk into Encounter through unwariness.

walk it Succeed or win easily.

walk of life Occupation; profession.

walk off one's feet Exhaust one by walking.

walk-out Departure, usually as mark of protest.

- *The orchestra staged a walk-out when the conductor prolonged the rehearsal.*

walk out on Leave, unexpectedly and usually in pique (so that difficulties are caused).

- *You can't really blame his wife for walking out on him.*

walk over 1. Treat with contempt. Also *walk all over (person)*.

2. Win because of lack of competition.

a walk-over An extremely easy victory.

walk the streets 1. [LIT] e.g. Because of loneliness.

2. Be a prostitute.

wall

go to the wall Fail as result of competition.

send or drive up the wall Cause (person) to become angry, frustrated, etc.

walls have ears Beware of eavesdroppers.

with one's back to the wall Desperately, as a final defence.

See **weak** and **writing.**

wane

on the wane Diminishing; decreasing in power.

want

for want of Because of lack of.

- *It is rotting for want of paint.*

found wanting Discovered to be unsatisfactory.

in want of In need of.

want for Lack.

war

be in the wars Show signs of physical damage.

cold war Unfriendly relations between nations shown by propaganda, lack of diplomatic or economic co-operation, etc., but not by fighting.

on the warpath Angry. In a mood for angry action.

wage war Conduct war.

war to the knife or the death A bitter and ruthless struggle.

war of nerves Unfriendly relationships between nations, with attempts to undermine confidence, morale, etc., or to make threats, but not to fight.

warm

make it (things) warm for someone Create difficulties for person.

wart

warts and all Including blemishes.

wash

come out in the wash Reach satisfactory conclusion.

wash one's dirty linen in public Discuss or reveal one's own shortcomings, scandals, etc., publicly.

wash one's hands of Refuse any responsibility for.

- *Do as you like; I wash my hands of the whole business.*

wash out [LIT] Remove by washing.

- *I've washed out the stain on your coat.*

Postpone or cancel because of rain.

- *Sports day was washed out.*

[MET] Obliterate.

- *He tried to wash out the memories of the past.*

wash-out Useless person.

washed-out Tired, incapable of effort, as result of energetic activity (or over-indulgence).

washed-up At the end of one's resources.

waste

go or run to waste Be wasted.

waste one's breath Talk in vain.

- *You'll simply be wasting your breath if you talk to him.*

watch

on the watch In a state of watchfulness. Similar to *on the alert*.

set a watch Arrange for systematic watching.

a watched pot never boils Time seems long when one is waiting for something to happen.

watch like a hawk Watch (person) vigilantly.

watch it or out or yourself or your step Take care.

water

hold water 1. [LIT] Contain without leaking.

- *That bucket won't hold enough water.*

2. [MET] Be true, and capable of being tested.

- *His account of the robbery won't hold water.*

in deep water(s) In great difficulties.

in hot water In trouble.

of the first water Of the finest possible quality; to the greatest degree.

like water off a duck's back Without effect.

make one's mouth water Be intensely attractive, delightful to eat or see.

water down Weaken.

water under the bridge What has happened and cannot be changed.

See also **cold** and **still**. For Waterloo see **meet.**

wave

wave aside Dismiss as irrelevant.

wave down Halt by signalling with wave of hand.

wavelength

on the same wavelength Understanding another person's train of thought, attitudes etc.

wax

be wax in one's hands Be subservient to one.

wax and wane Increase and decrease.

way

across the way or *street* or *road, etc.* On the opposite side.

all manner or *sorts* or *kinds of ways* A large variety of ways.

all the way The whole distance.

by the way Incidentally. (The phrase is used when a speaker wishes to pass abruptly from one subject to another which has little or no connection with it.)

by way of 1. By passing through.

- *We came by way of Banbury.*

2. As substitute for. With the intention of making.

- *He sent her flowers by way of an apology.*

clear the way Remove obstacles.

come one's way Become available.

find a way Discover a method.

find its way Reach destination.

get in (or out of) the way Obstruct (or the reverse).

- *Please get out of my way.*
- *Is this ladder getting in the way?*

get into the way of Acquire the habit of doing.

get or *have one's own way* Get what one wants.

give way 1. [LIT] Break.
- *The railings gave way, and three people fell in the river.*
2. [MET] Yield.

go one's way 1. Depart.
2. Be favourable to one.

go one's own way Follow one's personal desires, without accepting guidance or advice.

Similar to *have one's own way; follow one's own devices.*

go out of one's way Make special effort.

go the way of all flesh Die.

have a way with Be skilful in dealing with.

have everything one's own way Always get what one wants.

have it both ways Enjoy two benefits simultaneously.

have one's own way Do as one wishes.

in a bad way In an unsatisfactory condition.

in a big way Lavishly. Enthusiastically.

in a fair way Likely to.

in a small way In modest circumstances.
- *He's a builder, but only in a small way.*

in a way In certain respects; to a certain extent.

in many ways In many respects. Also *in more ways than one.*

in no way Not at all.

in the way Obstructing; forming an obstruction.
- *I can't empty the bottle—there's a piece of cork in the way.*

in the way of In a position to obtain.
- *She put me in the way of several good bargains.*

lead the way 1. Act as leader.
2. Show by example what ought to be done.

a long way off Very distant.

look the other way Pretend not to notice.

lose one's way Go astray.

make one's way 1. Progress; travel on one's journey.
2. Succeed in one's profession.

make way [LIT] Step aside. [MET] Retire from office.

nothing out of the way Nothing unusual.

on the way Coming.

once in a way Occasionally.

one way and another Taking everything together.

one way or another By some means.

over the way Same as *across the way.*

parting of the ways Time for important decision.

there are no two ways about it It is certain. It is impossible to argue.

under way Beginning; moving.

way of life Style in which one leads life.

way of thinking Opinion.

way of the world What normally happens in life.

ways and means Methods of overcoming difficulties.

wing one's way Travel swiftly, as a bird flies.

wayside
fall by the wayside Fail. Cease to persevere.

weak
have a weakness for Be fond of.

in a weak moment or moment of weakness At a time when one was not fully in control of oneself.

the weakest goes or go to the wall Those least able to help themselves are pushed aside or ignored.

weak in the head Idiotic.

weak-kneed Easily intimidated.

wear
fair wear and tear The normal lessening in value due to constant use.

wear away Cause to disappear by friction.

wear down Exhaust. Tire.

wear one's heart on one's sleeve See under **heart**.

wear one's years well Not show signs of age.

wear off Diminish and finally disappear.

 • *The effects of the shock will soon wear off.*

wear on Pass or diminish slowly.

 • *The hours wore on; night came.*

wear out 1. [LIT] Render useless by wear.

 • *My boots are worn out.*

 2. [MET] Exhaust.

 • *She had not slept all night and was completely worn out.*

wear thin Approach its end.

wear well or badly Last a long (or short) time. Remain in working order, or presentable, for a long (short) time. (Also, jocularly, of people: retain (or lose) one's strength of youthfulness.)

worse for wear Damaged.

weather

make heavy weather of Treat as though it were a very serious matter. Find difficult.

under the weather Not in full health.

weather the storm Survive. ('Storm' is frequently used for financial and other troubles.)

weed

weed out Remove unwanted person or thing, often from a group.

weigh

weigh down Overburden.

weigh heavy on Depress.

weigh in 1. Enter a race or contest, having been weighed.
2. Enter (argument, quarrel, etc.) forcefully.

weigh one's words Choose what one says very carefully.

weigh up Estimate. Come to a judgement about.

welcome

be welcome to Have permission to.

outstay one's welcome Outstay as visitor for longer than is expected or convenient.

well

as well Also. In addition.
- *Come early, and bring your sister as well.*

as well as In addition to.

be as well to Be sensible.

let well alone Do not interfere.

very well A general expression of agreement and assent.

(all) well and good Unemotional or neutral acceptance of decision, etc.
- *If you decide not to believe me, well and good.*

well and truly Thoroughly.

well built or well set-up Physically well constructed; fit.

come off well Have good success or luck.

well disposed (to) Inclined to favour.
- *The Council is well disposed to the idea.*

do oneself well Live in comfort. Enjoy oneself.

do well out of Profit from.

well done! Exclamation of approval.

well founded Justifiable.

well, I never! Abbrev. of 'Well, I never heard anything so extraordinary!' A common expression of astonishment.

just as well Fortunate.

well-lined purse Plenty of money.

well off See under **off.**

well out of something Fortunate not to be involved in something any longer.

- *I never enjoyed the job and am well out of it.*

well-rounded or *-turned* **phrases, sentences,** *etc.* Elegant and graceful speech.

well-to-do Fairly rich.

well up on Very knowledgeable about.

wish person well Hope person prospers.

whale

have a whale of a time Have a very enjoyable time.

what

give (person) what for Reprimand (person).

I tell you what I make this suggestion.

- *I tell you what—let's go to a cinema.*

know what's what Be able to discriminate between what is of value and use, and what is not.

what for? Why?

what have you Anything else similar.

what's-his-name; what do you call him? A substitution for a name one has forgotten.

- *This morning I met that tall man with red hair—old what's-his-name.*

Similar to *so-and-so.*

what of it? What does that matter?

what with Because of.

wheat

sort (separate) the wheat from the chaff Distinguish between the useful and the useless.

wheel

wheel and deal Scheme (usually in politics).

wheels within wheels Small, often unknown motives and influences, which contribute to the general result. Secret procedures.

wherewithal
the wherewithal That which is necessary to accomplish something. Money.

whether
whether or no Whether or not.

while
a good while A long time.
a little while A short time. Opposite: *a long while.*
  • *I'll telephone you in a little while.*
for a while For some time.
once in a while At long intervals. Occasionally. Similar to *from time to time.* See under **worth.**

whip
have the whip hand Be in a position to control.
whipping-boy Scapegoat.

whistle
clean as a whistle Very clean(ly).
whistle for Have no hope of getting.

whit
not a whit Not at all.

white
bleed white Extract (from person or business, etc.) all possible wealth.
white or pure as driven snow Absolutely white.
white as a sheet Extremely pale; colourless.
white at the lips Extremely angry. Very afraid
white hope Person expected to succeed. See also under **feather, lie, tie, elephant.**

whole
on the whole Having considered all sides of the matter.
  • *I think, on the whole, we had better stay at home.*
whole-hearted Enthusiastic. Without doubts.

why
the whys and wherefores The reasons for any action or the existence of any condition. The explanation.

wide
wide awake 1. [LIT] Entirely awake.
  2. [MET] Alert, aware.

wild

wild and woolly Incoherent. Idiotic.

wild-goose chase A practically hopeless search or other enterprise.

wild guess Utterly haphazard guess.

out in the wilds Far from civilisation. Not in a town. (Usually jocular.)

wildfire

like wildfire With extreme rapidity.

wile

wile away (the time, etc.) Pass, occupy (the time).

will

against my will Contrary to my wishes.

at (one's own sweet) will Exactly as one pleases.

free will Right, or power, to decide one's own course of action. Hence *of my own free will:* without any compulsion being exercised on me.

where there's a will there's a way If there is determination to do something, a means of doing it will be found.

a will of one's own Spirit, determination, of one's own.
- *Our baby is only a month old, but he's already shown that he has a will of his own.*

willy-nilly Just as one pleases. Whether one likes it or not.

with a will Energetically.

with the best will in the world However well disposed one may be.

win

win hands down Succeed very easily.

win over Convert to one's own point of view; persuade to become one's ally.

win the day Be victorious.

win through Succeed by perseverance.

wind

close to the wind See under **sail.**

get wind of Obtain early information about something that is likely to happen.

get or have the wind up Become *or* be fearful, anxious or nervous.

in the wind Likely to happen.

like the wind Extremely quickly.

sail near (close to) the wind See under **sail**.

sound in wind and limb Healthy.

see how the wind blows Test opinion.

straw in the wind See under **straw**.

take the wind out of one's sails Disconcert, usually by gaining an advantage over one, e.g. by anticipating one's arguments or suddenly revealing a secret.

which way the wind blows What developments are likely to happen. What opinions are being held. What the position is, or is likely to become.

windbag Person who talks too much.

wind of change Tendency to reform

wind up Conclude; bring to an end.

See under **second**.

wing

clip the wings See under **clip**.

stretch (spread) one's wings Exert one's (new-found) power, influence, etc.

take under one's wing Protect.

   ● *Please take the new typist under your wing until she settles in.*

take wing Start flying.

waiting in the wings Ready to become prominent

wink

as easy as winking Very easy.

forty winks A short sleep.

not a wink No sleep at all.

wink at Tactfully ignore.

wipe

wipe out Remove. Destroy.

wire

get one's wires crossed Be or talk at cross purposes. Be confused.

wise

none the wiser No more informed than previously.

put person wise Give person information. Correct person's misapprehension or lack of knowledge.

wise after the event Knowledgeable when it is too late. Failing to foresee.

wise to Aware of.

wish

wish to goodness Wish intensely, emphatically. (Polite version of 'Wish to God'. 'Goodness' is similarly used in 'Hope to goodness' and 'Trust to goodness'.)

wish a person joy Wish him, or her, luck; congratulate.

wish a person joy of Hope he may find some pleasure or satisfaction in.

wishful thinking Thinking, or belief, based on wishes rather than facts.

wishy-washy

Feeble. Unsystematic.

wit

addle one's wits Make one's mind hopelessly confused.

at one's wits' end See under **end.**

frighten (etc.) out of one's wits or witless Terrify greatly.

have or keep one's wits about one Be alert, observant and intelligent.

live by one's wits Make one's living by ingenuity.

witch

witch-hunt Persecution. Ruthless hounding of people alleged (sometimes wrongly or unfairly) to be at fault.

withers

wring one's withers [Old f.] Cause acute distress.

within

within call or hail Near enough to hear the sound of a voice.

within oneself Not using one's whole energies.

wives

old wives' tale Superstition.

wolf

cry wolf See under **cry.**

keep the wolf from the door Live without suffering acute poverty.

lone wolf Person who prefers to act alone.

throw to the wolves Sacrifice.

wolf in sheep's clothing A plausible deceiver; one whose apparent harmlessness conceals his true character.

wonder

do wonders Have remarkable success.

nine days' wonder An event which causes great excitement for a short time and is then forgotten.

no wonder Not surprising. (The phrase is often used on its own, meaning 'I am not in the least surprised'.)

● *It is no wonder that she is always tired.*

small wonder Same as *no wonder.*

the wonder is What is surprising is.

wonders never cease How surprising! (Ironical or jocular.)

work wonders Have excellent results.

wood

cannot see the wood for the trees Is prevented from seeing the main issue because of details.

out of the wood Free from difficulties.

wool

be wool-gathering Allow one's thoughts to wander. Similar to *day-dreaming.*

pull the wool over one's eyes Deceive one.

word

as good as one's word Faithful in keeping a promise.

fine words butter no parsnips Words are less adequate than deeds.

from the word go See *word go* at *go.*

give one's word Make a promise.

hard words Harsh and unpleasant statements, not necessarily true.

have the last word Make the final (and supposedly decisive) contribution in a discussion, quarrel, etc.

have a word with Talk briefly to.

have words Quarrel.

in a word In brief. To sum up.

in other words Expressed in different words.

in so many words Verbally and explicitly.

keep one's word Do as one promised.

mum's the word Keep silent.

put in a (good) word for Express confidence in or support for (person or thing).

put into words Express in words that which one thinks.

put words into someone's mouth Suggest that someone has said something he has not in fact said.

say the word Give permission or instruction.

say a good word for; put in a good word for Speak in favour of.

say a few words Make a brief speech.

take at one's word Accept a statement literally, and as the truth. Also *take one's word for it.*

take the words out of someone's mouth Say something just before someone else had the chance to say the same thing.

upon my word! Exclamation, expressing astonishment. [Old f.]

waste words Talk in vain. Talk with no result.

word for word Exactly as spoken or written; verbatim.

- *This is, word for word, the message he gave me.*

word of honour Solemn promise.

a word in the ear A private statement, or hint.

word in edgeways Any entry into a conversation.

- *He talks so much that one can't get a word in edgeways.*

(by) word of mouth Verbally; spoken, as contrasted with written, speech.

word-perfect Exact, absolutely accurate.

words fail me I am too surprised (shocked, etc.) to speak.

work

all in a day's work Nothing exceptional or specially troublesome.

at work on Engaged or employed on.

donkey-work Rough or hard work, necessary for the completion of a task.

have one's work cut out Have a difficult task.

make short work of Finish quickly.

- *The new machine makes short work of the washing.*

set to work Begin work.

work off Get rid of by working.

work one's passage Earn a privilege or advantage by doing work in return.

work out 1. Solve.

- *Have you worked out the sum yet?*

2. Be calculated.

- *The cost works out at £40 a square metre.*

3. Plan.

- *I'll work out the details of our holiday over the weekend.*

4. Come to a satisfactory conclusion. Enjoy success.

- *Their marriage just didn't work out.*

work up 1. Create by degrees.

- *From one small shop, she worked up to a very fine business.*

2. Rouse or excite.

- *It was a thrilling game, and the spectators became very worked up.*

work upon Exert influence upon.

worked-up Angry. Excited. Nervous. Apprehensive.

world

all the world and his wife Everyone; all the people there are.

for all the world 1. Precisely.

- *She looks for all the world like her sister.*

2. Under any circumstances.

- *I wouldn't like his job for all the world.*

have the best of both worlds Enjoy two different sets of circumstances. Compromise.

out of this world Exceptionally wonderful.

the best of both worlds Benefit from two quarters.

the (whole) world over Everywhere.

think the world of Be devoted to.

what in the world Whatever. (Used for special emphasis.)

- *I can't understand what in the world he's bought it for.*

worm

even a worm will turn Even the weakest person may be goaded into defiance or rebellion.

worm (one's way) in Insinuate.

worm out Discover by persistent questioning.

worn

worn-out Tired. Made ineffectual by too much use.

worse

change for the worse Deterioration.

the worse for wear [LIT] Damaged by use. [MET] Not at one's best; tired out; unwell.

worst

at the worst In the worst possible circumstances; even if the worst happens.

do one's worst Do one's utmost in evil, mischief, etc.

get the worst of it Be defeated in a contest.

if the worst comes to the worst If matters become as bad as they can possibly be.

worth

for all one's worth With all one's efforts.

for what it is worth If it has any value.
worth one's salt; worth one's keep See under **salt**.
worth its or *one's weight in gold* Very valuable or useful.
worth while; worth one's while; worth it Worth spending time
 or trouble over.
 - *I would try to sell the business, but it isn't worth while.*

wrap
take the wraps off Reveal.
under wraps Secret. Usually *keep under wraps.*
wrap up Conclude.
wrapped up in Entirely devoted to; absorbed in.
 - *He is wrapped up in his family.*

write
write off Treat as no longer of any value.

writing
the writing on the wall Clear warning of disaster.

wrong
get person wrong Misunderstand him.
get on the wrong side of Arouse dislike of.
go wrong Make an error.
in the wrong Having made error.
the wrong way round Opposite to what it should be.
wrong-headed Perverse and obstinate.

wrought
wrought up Worked up. Tense and excited.

Y

year
all the year round Throughout the year.
getting on in years Becoming old.
year in, year out Continuously.
years of discretion An age at which one is supposed to have acquired a certain amount of wisdom and discretion.

yellow
yellow-livered Cowardly.
yellow press Sensational newspapers, usually with chauvinistic tendencies.
yellow streak Capacity for cowardice.

yeoman
yeoman service Sound and excellent work.

yet
as yet Until now.
  • *As yet, I have seen no signs of deterioration.*

yours
you and yours You and your family.

yourself
pull yourself together Take control of your feelings.

CORRECT ENGLISH

B. A. PHYTHIAN

This practical guide and reference handbook will help you improve your own use of English in everyday life and enhance your appreciation of good English writing.

The book first provides handy summaries of the main rules of grammar and punctuation. It then examines some of the more common errors in spoken and written English, before giving practical advice on spelling and helpful definitions of words which are frequently confused and misused.

The second half of the book focuses on the correct and effective use of English in a wide variety of contexts, and illustrates the different types of language and style which contribute to the subtlety and variety of English expression. A particularly useful feature of the book is an extensive guide to the conventions of written English in everyday life, including business and commercial English, letters, reports, summaries and précis, and English for examinations.

TEACH YOURSELF BOOKS

ENGLISH GRAMMAR

B.A.PHYTHIAN

This book will give you a sound grasp of English grammar, and an appreciation of the subtlety and variety of English expression.

Separate chapters deal with the nature and function of all the principal parts of speech, and detailed consideration is given to sentence structure through a study of clauses and phrases. A particularly feature of the book is that exercises to test and reinforce comprehension are built in after each section, with further revision exercises at the end of each chapter.

TEACH YOURSELF BOOKS

A CONCISE DICTIONARY OF PHRASE & FABLE

B.A.PHYTHIAN

Why are people at sixes and sevens, dressed to the nines, talking sixteen to the dozen or having forty winks? Where do fleas in the ear, dogs in the manger, bats in the belfry or flies in the ointment come from? The origins and development of these and another 1500 everyday words and expressions can be found in this fascinating and wide-ranging dictionary. Other books by the author in the series include: A Concise Dictionary of English Slang; A Concise Dictionary of Correct English; A Concise Dictionary of Foreign Expressions; A Concise Dictionary of Confusables.

TEACH YOURSELF BOOKS

A CONCISE DICTIONARY OF CORRECT ENGLISH

B.A.PHYTHIAN

This lively guide to the correct use of modern English grammar will be welcomed by all speakers of English interested in correct current usage. While still firmly based on authoritative sources (Fowler, Gowers, Partridge and the Oxford dictionaries), the revised second edition includes many updated and completely new entries reflecting the ever-changing face of accepted language. Wherever appropriate, explanations are accompanied by examples given in context and reference made to further sections in the book. Other books by the author in the series include: A Concise Dictionary of English Slang and Colloquialisms; A Concise Dictionary of Phrase and Fable; A Concise Dictionary of Foreign Expressions; A Concise Dictionary of Confusables.

TEACH YOURSELF BOOKS

A CONCISE DICTIONARY OF ENGLISH SLANG

B.A.PHYTHIAN

Slang is spicy, often humorous, sometimes vulgar, and occasionally novel and therefore obscure. It is one of the most volatile components of language, and is in a constant state of change. It is part of the tendency towards less formal English that has developed throughout the twentieth century. This dictionary provides a valuable and easy-to-use insight into current English for both students and general readers. Other books by the author in the series include: a Concise Dictionary of Phrase and Fable; A Concise Dictionary of Foreign Expressions; A Concise Dictionary of Confusables and A Concise Dictionary of Correct English.

TEACH YOURSELF BOOKS

CREATIVE WRITING

DIANNE DOUBTFIRE

A lively and comprehensive handbook packed with practical advice for everyone with the urge to write.

This book looks at every form of writing — articles, short stories, poetry, plays, novels and non-fiction — and the different techniques of writing for adults or children, radio or TV. It offers clear guidelines for developing your talent and acquiring the basic craftsmanship which is the key to success. Dianne Doubtfire — established author, tutor and lecturer in creative writing — shares her experience and expertise to show how, given dedication and determination, you can not only improve your writing, but have the added satisfaction of seeing it in print.

TEACH YOURSELF BOOKS

OTHER TITLES AVAILABLE
IN TEACH YOURSELF

☐	0 340 42996 8	**Correct English**		£4.99
		B. A. Phythian		
☐	0 340 35873 4	**English Grammar**		£4.99
		B. A. Phythian		
☐	0 340 55633 1	**Concise Dictionary of Phrase and Fable**	£6.99
		B. A. Phythian		
☐	0 340 57496 8	**Concise Dictionary of Correct English**	£6.99
		B. A. Phythian		
☐	0 340 58743 1	**Concise Dictionary of English Slang**	£6.99
		B. A. Phythian		
☐	0 340 28765 9	**Creative Writing**		£4.99
		Dianne Doubtfire		

All these books are available at your local bookshop or newsagent, or can be ordered direct from the publisher. Just tick the titles you want and fill in the form below.

Prices and availability subject to change without notice.

HODDER AND STOUGHTON PAPERBACKS, P.O. Box 11, Falmouth, Cornwall.

Please send cheque or postal order for the value of the book, and add the following for postage and packing:

UK including BFPO – £1.00 for one book, plus 50p for the second book, and 30p for each additional book ordered up to a £3.00 maximum.

OVERSEAS, INCLUDING EIRE – £2.00 for the first book, plus £1.00 for the second book, and 50p for each additional book ordered.

OR Please debit this amount from my Access/Visa Card (delete as appropriate).

CARD NUMBER ☐☐☐☐☐☐☐☐☐☐☐☐☐☐☐☐

AMOUNT £ . . . .

EXPIRY DATE . . . .

SIGNED . . . .

NAME . . . .

ADDRESS . . . .

. . . .